JONATHAN EDWARDS
THE HOLY SPIRIT IN REVIVAL

JONATHAN EDWARDS

THE HOLY SPIRIT IN REVIVAL

THE LASTING INFLUENCE OF THE HOLY SPIRIT IN THE HEART OF MAN

MICHAEL A. G. HAYKIN

SERIES EDITORS
DR JOHN D. CURRID AND ROBERT STRIVENS

EVANGELICAL PRESS

EP   EVANGELICAL PRESS

Evangelical Press
Faverdale North, Darlington, DL3 0PH England
email: sales@evangelicalpress.org

Evangelical Press USA
P. O. Box 825, Webster NY 14580 USA
email: usa.sales@evangelicalpress.org

www.evangelicalpress.org

© Evangelical Press, 2005. All rights reserved. No part of this publication may be reproduced, stored in a retrieval system or transmitted, in any form, or by any means, electronic, mechanical, photocopying, recording or otherwise, without the prior permission of the publishers.

First published 2005

> The EMMAUS series has been created to speak directly to pastors, teachers and students of the Word of God on those issues that impact on their everyday ministry and life.

British Library Cataloguing in Publication Data available

ISBN-13 978 0 85234 599 3   ISBN 0 85234 599 2

*To John and Jennifer van Leeuwen,
for the joy of their friendship and to whom
I personally owe a tremendous debt
— 'tis small payment*

Let your heart be lifted up to God for me among others, that God would bestow much of that blessed Spirit on me that he has bestowed on you, and make me also an instrument of his glory.

– Jonathan Edwards to George Whitefield, 12 February 1740

Contents

Abbreviations	ix
Acknowledgements	xiii
Chronology	xvii
Introduction	1

1. Jonathan Edwards: His life and legacy — 7
2. The threefold work of the Holy Ghost:
   The cross and the work of the Spirit — 31
3. A very extraordinary dispensation of providence:
   The work of the Holy Spirit in the *Faithful Narrative* — 43
4. The most glorious of God's works:
   Saving grace, not the extraordinary gifts of the Spirit — 59
5. The transatlantic evangelical revival — 75
6. The authentic Spirit — 91
7. The Comforter is come:
   Sarah Edwards and the vision of God — 109
8. True piety ... reaches the heart:
   The advocacy of heart religion in
   the *Religious Affections* — 121
9. The *Humble Attempt* and praying for revival — 137

Concluding thoughts — 149
APPENDIX 1: Jonathan Edwards,
   Directions for judging of persons' experiences — 153
APPENDIX 2: Beauty as a divine attribute:
   The western tradition and Jonathan Edwards — 159
APPENDIX 3: Esther Edwards Burr (1732-1758)
   and Edwardsean piety — 171
A concluding prayer — 179
Notes — 183
Select bibliography — 219

I have many times had a sense of the glory of the third person in the Trinity, in his office of Sanctifier; in his holy operations communicating divine light and life to the soul. God in the communications of his Holy Spirit, has appeared as an infinite fountain of divine glory and sweetness; being full and sufficient to fill and satisfy the soul: pouring forth itself in sweet communications, like the sun in its glory, sweetly and pleasantly diffusing light and life.

– Jonathan Edwards, Personal Narrative *(c.1740)*

ABBREVIATIONS

CITATIONS FROM JONATHAN EDWARDS' works are normally from the Yale University Press edition of *The Works of Jonathan Edwards* (1957-). The following abbreviations are employed in both the notes (after the initial reference) and the text.

Distinguishing Marks   *The Distinguishing Marks Of a Work of the Spirit of God* (1741)

Faithful Narrative   *A Faithful Narrative of the Surprising Work of God in the Conversion of Many Hundred Souls in Northampton, and the Neighbouring Towns*

	and Villages of New [sic] Hampshire in New-England (1737)
Humble Attempt	An Humble Attempt to Promote Explicit Agreement and Visible Union of God's People in Extraordinary Prayer, For the Revival of Religion and the Advancement of Christ's Kingdom on Earth, pursuant to Scripture-Promises and Prophecies concerning the Last Time (1748)
Religious Affections	A Treatise Concerning Religious Affections (1746)
Some Thoughts	Some Thoughts Concerning the present Revival of Religion in New-England (1742)

Love is a sweet affection and will always be attended with pleasure provided it has returns of love and can be sure of the enjoyment of its object which is always the case of divine love. This holy love has a peculiar sweetness in it that surpasses all other love as that which is heavenly surpasses that which is earthly. It is the inward spring of happiness. He who has divine love in him he has a wellspring of true happiness that he carries about in his own breast, a fountain of sweetness, a spring of the water of life.

– Jonathan Edwards, The Spirit of the True Saints is a Spirit of Divine Love *(c.1735-1739)*

ACKNOWLEDGEMENTS

IN A REVIEW of George Marsden's definitive biography of Jonathan Edwards, Benjamin Schwarz describes Edwards as 'America's most penetrating, rigorous, and subtle theologian, as well as its most literarily accomplished and influential', in short, a 'towering figure'.[1] It is not surprising therefore that any church historian, including the present writer, who is responsible for teaching the history of the church since the Reformation, must spend time reading Edwards and seeking to communicate something of the riches of his theology and spiritual vision to students.

My initial reading of Edwards in the 1980s began in this way. But Edwards, like other great theologians in the history of the church, has a way of absorbing more and more of one's attention.

So it was that in the late 1980s, while I was teaching at Central Baptist Seminary in Toronto, Ontario, I ventured to teach a whole course on Edwards' *Religious Affections*. Since that first course on Edwards, I have taught courses on his theology a number of times, most recently at Heritage Seminary in Cambridge, Ontario, at Puritan Reformed Theological Seminary, Grand Rapids, Michigan, and at Toronto Baptist Seminary, where I am currently the principal. I am very grateful to Heritage Seminary and Toronto Baptist Seminary and to Dr Joel Beeke of Puritan Reformed Theological Seminary for these opportunities to immerse myself in the Edwardsean corpus. I would also like to thank the students who have taken these courses over the years and who have helped sharpen my thinking.

In teaching these courses I found that while much was written on Edwards and on his view of revival,[2] there was not a compact book-length study of Edwards as a theologian of revival. It was out of this perceived lacuna that this book has grown. In an earlier work, *Jonathan Edwards: The Man, his Experience and his Theology*, which was published in 1995, I did attempt to enunciate something of Edwards' theology of revival as a response to the use being made of him by advocates of the so-called Toronto Blessing.[3] Ultimately, though, I was not very happy with the book, for I felt it was far too rushed to serve as a scholarly study of Edwards on the subject of revival. Nevertheless, I have utilized some of the material from that work, as well as other studies done on Edwards over the years for various conferences, magazines and journals. In particular, I am grateful to Dr Edgar Andrews and Roger Fay for the opportunity to write a series of articles on Edwards for the *Evangelical Times*.

I am also grateful to what was Ligonier Ministries of Canada for the opportunity to give seminars on Edwards at various points in the 1990s, and then to Heinz Dschankilic and Sola Scriptura Ministries – the successor of Ligonier Ministries of Canada – to speak on Edwards at a number of conferences in more recent years. I would also like to record my gratitude for the opportunity to speak on Edwards, and then on his wife and family, at two Canadian Carey Family Conferences – in 1990 and 2003, respectively. Chapter 2 of the present work evolved from an informal tutorial I gave in the late 1990s to Denis Capatos, then of Waterloo, Ontario. Denis contributed much to the shape of the chapter. He has since moved to the United States and more recently to western Canada. I have lost touch with him, but wish to record my deep gratitude to him.

Typists are the unsung heroes of academic work. I am thankful to Marina Coldwell and Ruth Engler for some of the typing of this book. I am also grateful for the help given by my tutorial assistant, Scott Bowman, and my research assistant, Ian H. Clary, at various points. Ian also coordinates the work of The Jonathan Edwards Centre for Reformed Spirituality, which operates under the auspices of Toronto Baptist Seminary, and my involvement with such a centre has also played a part in the writing of this book. For help with the Edwards text of Appendix 1, I wish to thank Sandy Finlayson, director of library services at Westminster Theological Seminary, Philadelphia, Pennsylvania, and Caleb J. D. Maskell of The Jonathan Edwards Center at Yale University.[4] I also wish to thank Dr Kenneth P. Minkema of Yale Divinity School for helpful advice given in the course of my writing this book. Finally, I wish to thank David Clark and the staff of Evangelical Press for their patience and skill in seeing this book into print.

I have dedicated this book to two dear friends, John and Jennifer van Leeuwen. I owe them an enormous debt that I can never repay. Inscribing this book to them is a small way of saying thank you. *Deo, optimo et maximo, gloria.*

Michael A. G. Haykin
Dundas, Ontario
September 2005

CHRONOLOGY[1]

1703
OCTOBER 5: born at East Windsor, Connecticut

1710
JANUARY 9: Sarah Pierpont born at New Haven, Connecticut

1721
LATE SPRING: conversion

1726
OCTOBER: begins preaching in Northampton, Massachusetts

1727
FEBRUARY 15: ordained at Northampton as assistant minister to Solomon Stoddard

JULY 28: marries Sarah Pierpont in New Haven

1729
FEBRUARY 11: Solomon Stoddard dies; Edwards becomes senior pastor

1734-1735
Northampton revival

1737
Faithful Narrative published in London, England

1738
APRIL-OCTOBER: preaches the sermon series *Charity and Its Fruits* (not published until 1852)

1740
Great Awakening in New England begins
OCTOBER 17-19: George Whitefield preaches in Northampton
DECEMBER: writes *Personal Narrative*

1741
JULY 8: preaches *Sinners in the Hands of an Angry God* at Enfield, Connecticut
SEPTEMBER 10: delivers *Distinguishing Marks* at Yale commencement; it is published soon after

1742
JANUARY 19-FEBRUARY 4: Sarah Pierpont Edwards has extraordinary experiences
FALL-WINTER: writes *Some Thoughts*

1743
MARCH: *Some Thoughts* published

1746
Publishes *Religious Affections*

1747
OCTOBER 9: David Brainerd dies in Edwards' home
OCTOBER: *Humble Attempt* published
AUTUMN: begins work on *An Account of the Life of the Late Reverend Mr. David Brainerd*

1748
FEBRUARY 14: daughter Jerusha dies
DECEMBER: completes *An Account of the Life of the Late Reverend Mr. David Brainerd*

1750
Controversy between Edwards and his church comes to a head
JUNE 22: dismissed as pastor of Northampton
JULY 2: preaches *Farewell Sermon*, which is published in 1751

1751
AUGUST 8: installed as pastor at Stockbridge, Massachusetts

1754
DECEMBER: *Freedom of the Will* published

1755
FEBRUARY 11-13: reads recently finished *End for Which God Created the World* to Joseph Bellamy and Samuel Hopkins; *The Nature of True Virtue* probably completed soon afterwards (both published 1765)

1757
MAY: *The Great Christian Doctrine of Original Sin defended* finished
SEPTEMBER 29: offered the presidency of the College of New Jersey

1758
FEBRUARY 16: assumes the presidency of the College of New Jersey
FEBRUARY 23: inoculated for smallpox
MARCH 22: dies of complications from the inoculation
APRIL 7: daughter Esther Edwards Burr dies
OCTOBER 2: Sarah Pierpont Edwards dies of dysentery in Philadelphia
Original Sin published

INTRODUCTION

THE WRITINGS OF THE New England divine Jonathan Edwards (1703-1758) are of special importance when it comes to the subject of revival, because he is, as Martyn Lloyd-Jones once described him, 'pre-eminently the theologian of Revival'.[1] His writings on revival possess ongoing value, because, first of all, they are rooted in a personal and intimate acquaintance with revival. The earliest letter that we possess from his hand, written to his elder sister Mary, when he was but twelve years of age, tells of a revival in his hometown of East Windsor, Connecticut, under the preaching of his father, Timothy Edwards (1669-1758). He describes it as 'a very remarkable stirring and pouring out of the Spirit of God', in which it was common on Mondays, after the Word had been preached the day before, for 'above thirty persons to speak with Father about the condition of their souls'.[2] More significantly, a revival that made a profound impact on the Connecticut Valley during the winter of 1734/1735 first began in his church in Northampton, Massachusetts, and was subsequently described and analyzed in his *A Faithful Narrative of the Surprising Work of God in the Conversion of Many Hundred Souls in Northampton, and the Neighbouring Towns and Villages of New Hampshire in New-England* (1737). Over 100 years later this powerful book was still being consulted as a handbook on the nature of revival.[3]

Five years after this regional revival there occurred what is known as the Great Awakening, a revival that swept the entirety of the American colonies from 1740 to 1742. Although the English itinerant evangelist George Whitefield (1714-1770) was the main human instrument in this revival, Edwards also played a very prominent role in it. He, too, travelled and preached extensively beyond the borders of his own parish.[4] Even more significantly, in print Edwards was this revival's most theologically astute champion – as well as its most perceptive critic. This dual role with regard to the revival called forth some of Edwards' finest books. Among these works are ones that are still regarded as Christian classics, of which the most notable is *A Treatise Concerning Religious Affections* (1746).[5]

Edwards' reflections on revival are still of immense value, because Edwards possessed a wonderful facility for meticulous and minute observation. This facility can be seen in the intriguing and detailed investigation that he conducted during the early 1720s into the way that spiders made their webs.[6] Later in his life, this gift, now exercised in the realm of pastoral ministry and theology, yielded a profound understanding of the human heart and its workings. Sereno E. Dwight, Edwards' great-grandson and one of his early biographers, stated that Edwards' 'knowledge of the human heart, and its operations, has scarcely been equalled by that of any uninspired preacher'. Dwight goes on to mention three probable sources for this insightful understanding of the human heart: Edwards' perceptive reading of the Scriptures; 'his thorough acquaintance with his own heart'; and his grasp of philosophy.[7]

Thus, it should not be surprising that the combination of personal experience and empirical insight – insight that is thoroughly rooted in Scripture – produced some of the most significant literature on revival in the history of the church. To quote Lloyd-Jones again: 'If you want to know anything about the psychology of religion, conversion, revivals, read Jonathan Edwards.'[8]

One further reason for the classic nature of Edwards' corpus of work on revival is the fact that Jonathan Edwards was blessed with a heart devoted to the pursuit of the glory of God. 'The great and last end of God's works', Edwards could write, 'is most properly and comprehensively called, "the glory of God".'[9] According to Joseph G. Haroutunian, even 'a superficial perusal of the essays and sermons of Edwards reveals a mind passionately devoted to God, permeated with the beauty and excellence of God'.[10] Haroutunian cites as an example in this regard a passage from the sermon *Ruth's Resolution*, which Edwards preached during the revival in Northampton in 1735 and which was published three years later. Reflecting on Ruth's determination to cleave to her mother-in-law, Naomi, and to embrace her God, the God of Israel, as her own (Ruth 1:16), Edwards stated that this God is:

> ... a glorious God. There is none like him, who is infinite in glory and excellency: he is the most high God, glorious in holiness, fearful in praises, doing wonders: his name is excellent in all the earth, and his glory is above the earth and the heavens: among the gods there is none like unto him; there is none in heaven to be compared to him, nor are there any among the sons of the mighty, that can be likened unto him... God is the fountain of all good, and an inexhaustible fountain; he is an all-sufficient God; a God that is able to protect and defend ... and do all things... He is the king of glory, the Lord strong and mighty, the Lord mighty in battle: a strong rock, and an high tower... He is a God who hath all things in his hands, and does whatsoever he pleases: he killeth and maketh alive; he bringeth down to the grave, and bringeth up; he maketh poor and maketh rich: the pillars of the earth are the Lord's... God is an infinitely holy God: there is none

holy as the Lord. And he is infinitely good and merciful. Many that others worship and serve as gods, are cruel beings, spirits that seek the ruin of souls; but this is a God that delighteth in mercy; his grace is infinite, and endures for ever: he is love itself, an infinite fountain and ocean of it.[11]

As Haroutunian notes, this passage is characteristic of Edwards' view of God, especially the focus on God's unique excellency and the fact that the God whom the believer seeks to glorify and serve is 'the Creator of the universe and the Fountain of all beauty and excellence'.[12] Indeed, here we are at what Mark Noll has called the 'unifying centre' of Edwards' theology, namely, 'the glory of God … as an active, harmonious, ever unfolding source of absolutely perfect Being marked by supernal beauty and love'.[13] It was this God-centred perspective that led Edwards to support and promote the revivals of his day, because he saw God at work in them, bringing glory to himself.[14] Written from this perspective, it was these works on revival that have been recognized by later evangelical authors as providing something of a benchmark for reflection on the nature of spiritual awakening.[15]

Ours is a day in which the Christian world is deeply interested in revival and spirituality. It is a day in which all kinds of things are being claimed as 'spiritual' and the description of 'revival' is being affixed to all sorts of movements. How to discern what is indeed the real thing is a pressing issue. Obviously, first and foremost, Scripture must guide us. And this is the first place that Edwards would direct us. His theology was 'constructed out of a lifelong and intimate study of the Scriptures',[16] and he was rightly convinced of their utter sufficiency for the church in every age and clime. Edwards' writings, though, under the Scriptures, can show us the way an earnest Christian of another era discerned the marks of an authentic biblical spirituality and can help us to do the same for ourselves today.

Here, we need to take our cue from some eighteenth-century English Baptists who, when their churches were spiritually stagnant and lethargic, avidly read Edwards' writings on revival. Among them was John Sutcliff (1752-1814), pastor of Olney Baptist Church in Buckinghamshire. His reading of Edwards, in 1784, led him to propose to his fellow pastors in the Northamptonshire Association, an association that was comprised of a number of churches in the Midlands, that they set apart one hour on the first Monday evening of every month to pray for revival. On the basis of Sutcliff's proposal, the churches of the association were urged to specifically pray that the 'Holy Spirit may be poured down on our ministers and churches, that sinners may be converted, the saints edified, the interest of religion revived, and the name of God glorified'.[17] Behind this call to prayer lay the conviction, derived from both the Scriptures and Edwards, that a radical change in their denomination's spiritual state could only be achieved by an outpouring of the Spirit of God, the true agent of revival.

Indeed, so great was Edwards' influence on Sutcliff and his circle of friends, which included Andrew Fuller (1754-1815) and William Carey (1761-1834), that after Sutcliff's death in 1814 Fuller noted there were 'some, who have been giving out of late, that "If Sutcliff and some others had preached more of Christ, and less of Jonathan Edwards, they would have been more useful"'. To which Fuller rightly replied: 'If those who talk thus, preached Christ half as much as Jonathan Edwards did, and were half as useful as he was, their usefulness would be double what it is.'[18] Fuller, like Sutcliff, understood the utterly pivotal role that Edwards' writings had played in the revival that had come to the English Calvinistic Baptist denomination during their lifetime.[19]

It is my prayer that this study of Edwards' key works on revival and the role of the Holy Spirit in revival might encourage a re-reading of Edwards' books on revival, and that we who describe ourselves as evangelicals might come to view him as a reliable mentor in this area of vital importance and a skillful navigator among the shoals and shallows of spiritual experience. As a result, it might well be that we would experience God the Holy Spirit moving among us as he once moved among the English Calvinistic Baptists of the late eighteenth century, when they learned about revival from the pen of 'America's theologian'.[20]

Oh what a legacy my husband, and your father, has left us![1]
— Sarah Edwards, letter to Esther Edwards Burr upon hearing of the death of Jonathan Edwards, 3 April 1758

Chapter 1

JONATHAN EDWARDS: HIS LIFE AND LEGACY[2]

JONATHAN EDWARDS WAS BORN on 5 October 1703, at East Windsor, Connecticut. Timothy Edwards, his father, was the pastor of the town's Congregational church for more than sixty-three years. His mother, Esther (1672-1770), was the daughter of Solomon Stoddard (1643-1729), the powerful pastor of the Congregational church in Northampton, Massachusetts, from 1669 till his death in 1729, who was sometimes described by his theological opponents as a 'congregational Pope'.[3]

Edwards received his elementary education from his father – an education that included Latin, which he began to study at seven. His father and mother also gave him a thorough nurturing in Puritan piety. In Edwards' *Personal Narrative*, he notes of this time in his life:

> I had a variety of concerns and exercises about my soul from my childhood; but had two more remarkable seasons of awakening... The first time was when I was a boy, some years before I went to college, at a time of a remarkable awakening in my father's congregation ... I used to pray five times a day in secret, and to spend much time in religious talk with other boys; and used to meet with them to pray together... I, with some of my schoolmates joined together, and built a booth in a swamp, in a very retired spot, for a place of prayer... My affections seemed to be lively and easily moved, and I seemed to be in my element, when engaged in religious duties.[4]

But this childhood spirituality – albeit a prognostication of his future interests – soon disappeared and, in his words, he 'returned like a dog to his vomit, and went on in ways of sin'.[5]

Meanwhile, Edwards entered the Collegiate School of Connecticut in New Haven (later to become Yale University) in 1716. Although he went on to graduate from the Collegiate School in 1720 at the head of his class academically, Edwards had neither inner peace nor saving faith. Writing later of his life at this time, Edwards said that it was characterized 'by great and violent inward struggles' regarding wicked inclinations and objections against God's sovereignty in salvation.[6]

Conversion and the Resolutions

It was probably in the spring of 1721 that Edwards was converted[7] as he was reading 1 Timothy 1:17.[8] Edwards later said:

> There came into my soul, and was as it were diffused through it, a sense of the glory of the Divine Being; a new sense, quite different from any thing I ever experienced before. Never any words of scripture seemed to me as these words did. I thought with myself, how excellent a Being that was; and how happy I should be, if I might enjoy that God, and be rapt up to him in Heaven, and be as it were swallowed up in him for ever... From about that time, I began to have a new kind of apprehensions and ideas of Christ, and the work of

redemption, and the glorious way of salvation by him. An inward, sweet sense of these things, at times, came into my heart; and my soul was led away in pleasant views and contemplations of them. And my mind was greatly engaged to spend my time in reading and meditating on Christ, on the beauty and excellency of his person, and the lovely way of salvation, by free grace in him.[9]

In this text about his conversion, Edwards highlights the 'inward, sweet sense' that gripped his soul as he read the Scriptures and meditated upon what they say about God and Christ and the salvation that has been accomplished by divine grace. Such biblical meditation was central to his piety. Samuel Hopkins (1721-1803), one of his close friends and his first biographer, noted that Edwards was, 'as far as it can be known … much on his knees in secret, and in devoutly reading of God's word, and meditation upon it'.[10]

Not long after his conversion, Edwards drew up what are known as the *Resolutions* (1722-1723), in which, at the outset of his ministry, he committed himself to keeping a list of seventy guidelines to help him stay passionate in his pursuit of God and his glory.[11] Samuel Hopkins commented that these *Resolutions* 'may be justly considered the basis of his conduct, or the plan according to which his whole life was governed'.[12] Though young when he wrote them, they bespeak a mature understanding of genuine piety and the way such piety should be evident in all of one's life and pursued with ardour and zeal. In the first resolution, for example, he '[r]esolved, that I will do whatsoever I think to be most to God's glory, and my own good, profit, and pleasure, in the whole of my duration'. Resolution five subjected his use of time to scrutiny: 'Resolved, never to lose one moment of time; but improve it the most profitable way I possibly can.' The final resolution, the seventieth, recognizes the importance of being circumspect in all of his speech: 'Let there be something of benevolence, in all that I speak.' And in resolution fifty-six, Edwards admits to times of spiritual failure but is resolved 'never to give over, nor in the least to slacken my fight with my corruptions, however unsuccessful I may be'.[13]

Call to Ministry, Marriage and Children

After two relatively brief stints of pastoring – first, to a small Presbyterian congregation in New York (August 1722 – April 1723) and then at a Congregationalist church in Bolton, Connecticut (November 1723 – May 1724) – Edwards moved back to his hometown of East Windsor. He finished his M.A. thesis in the summer between these pastorates and subsequently received his degree that fall. From 1724 to 1726, Edwards was a tutor at his Alma Mater in New Haven, though it was a situation in which he was not entirely happy. He finally found his niche in August 1726, when he was invited to become assistant to his grandfather Solomon Stoddard in Northampton, Massachusetts. Three years later, in 1729, when Stoddard died, Edwards became the sole pastor of the church.

Edwards married within a year of his arrival at Northampton. He had known his bride, Sarah Pierpont (1710-1758), since 1719 and his days at Yale.[14] Her father, James Pierpont (d.1714), had been the minister of the First Congregationalist Church, New Haven, Connecticut, from 1685 until his death and had played a leading role in the founding of Yale College. Her mother, Mary Hooker, was the granddaughter of Thomas Hooker (1586-1647), one of the key founders of Puritan New England. Sarah herself was converted around 1715, when she was but five.[15]

Jonathan's first recorded words about his future wife were penned in the front page of a Greek grammar.

> They say there is a young lady in [New Haven] who is beloved of that almighty Being, who made and rules the world, and that there are certain seasons in which this Great Being, in some way or other invisible, comes to her and fills her mind with exceeding sweet delight, and that she hardly cares for any thing, except to meditate on him – that she expects after a while to be received up where he is, to be raised out of the world and caught up into heaven; being assured that he loves her too well to let her remain at a distance from him always. There she is to dwell with him, and to be ravished with his love, favor and delight forever. Therefore, if you

Jonathan Edwards

Reprinted from Albert D. Belden, George Whitefield: The Awakener *(London: Sampson Low, Marston & Co. Ltd., 1930), III.*

present all the world before her, with the richest of its treasures, she disregards it and cares not for it, and is unmindful of any pain or affliction. She has a strange sweetness in her mind, and sweetness of temper, uncommon purity in her affections; is most just and praiseworthy in all her actions; and you could not persuade her to do anything thought wrong or sinful, if you would give her all the world, lest she should offend this great Being. She is of a wonderful sweetness, calmness and universal benevolence of mind; especially after those times in which this great God has manifested himself to her mind. She will sometimes go about, singing sweetly, from place to [place]; and she seems to be always full of joy and pleasure; and no one know for what. She loves to be alone, and to wander in the fields and on the mountains, and seems to have someone invisible always conversing with her.[16]

At the time that this text was written, Jonathan was probably twenty and Sarah but thirteen. Though too young to court – New England women at this period of time were generally married in their mid-twenties, though the average marrying age for the seven of Jonathan's sisters who married was thirty[17] – Jonathan was clearly taken with Sarah's piety, spiritual maturity, and the fact that her outward deportment matched her inner spirituality. It is not surprising that Jonathan does not mention in this paragraph what others frequently remarked on; namely, Sarah's physical beauty. Samuel Hopkins recalled that Sarah was 'comely and beautiful'.[18] For Jonathan, though, it was evidently Sarah's inner beauty that attracted him.[19]

Four years after this initial encounter, Jonathan and Sarah were married. Their marriage was celebrated on Friday, 28 July 1727, just over five months after Jonathan had been ordained as an assistant pastor to his grandfather Solomon Stoddard in the Congregationalist church in Northampton. Jonathan rode over from Northampton to New Haven, where Sarah was living. Elisabeth Dodds, author of a study of the marriage of Jonathan and Sarah, states that Sarah was married in a 'pea-green satin brocade' dress.[20] She gives no primary evidence for this remark, though if Sarah did wear a green dress at her wedding it would have delighted Jonathan. The young Massachusetts pastor would later stoutly maintain that green was God's favourite colour, since green 'fitly denotes Life, flourishing prosperity and happiness'.[21]

More importantly, Samuel Miller, one of the nineteenth-century founders of Princeton Theological Seminary, would remark that 'perhaps no event of Mr Edwards' life had a more close connexion with his subsequent comfort and usefulness than this marriage'.[22] Sarah was so adept at managing the household affairs of the family that Jonathan was able to give himself unreservedly to all of the aspects of his ministry. Samuel Hopkins would remember Sarah as 'a good economist', who 'took almost the whole care of the temporal affairs of the family, without doors and within'.[23] This appears to have well suited her husband, who once remarked, 'I am fitted for no other business but study!'[24] Throughout their married lives Sarah and Jonathan were deeply devoted to one another, and her godliness, evident in Edwards' description of Sarah cited above and more fully explored later in this book, fully matched his.[25]

Sarah and Jonathan had eleven children, all of whom survived infancy. In a day when infant mortality was extremely high, this is truly amazing. Cotton Mather (1663-1728), the influential New England Puritan, for instance, had fifteen children, only two of whom lived beyond infancy. And in the previous century, John Owen (1616-1683), 'the Calvin of England',[26] and his wife Mary Rooke had eleven children, of whom only one survived into adulthood. Leonard Sweet, in a marvellous reflective essay comparing Edwards with Benjamin Franklin (1706-1790), notes the irony in the fact that six of the Edwards children were born on a Sunday – a seventh, Eunice, missed it by a half-hour – when eighteenth-century folk wisdom asserted that the day on which one was born was the same day as when one was conceived.[27] With regard to Edwards' interaction with his family, it should be noted that the frequent portrayal of him as stern and implacable is belied by his tenderness as both a husband and a father, and 'whose children seemed genuinely fond of him'.[28] Hopkins clearly states that his children 'reverenced, esteemed, and loved him'.[29]

Revival in Northampton, 1734-1735

The Northampton church had enjoyed a number of small revivals during Stoddard's long pastorate, the last one having been in 1718. After that time, though, Edwards judged there had been little spiritual advance. In his words:

> Just after my grandfather's death, it seemed to be a time of extraordinary dullness in religion: licentiousness for some years prevailed among the youth of the town; they were many of them very much addicted to night-walking, and frequenting the tavern, and lewd practices, wherein some, by their example, exceedingly corrupted others. It was their manner very frequently to get together in conventions of both sexes, for mirth and jollity, which they called frolics; and they would often spend the greater part of the night in them, without regard to any order in the families they belonged to: and indeed family government did too much fail in the town. It was become very customary with many of our young people, to be indecent in their carriage at meeting, which doubtless would not have prevailed to such a degree, had it not been that my grandfather, through his great age (though he retained his powers surprisingly to the last), was not so able to observe them. There had also long prevailed in the town a spirit of contention between two parties, into which they had for many years been divided, by which was maintained a jealousy one of the other, and they were prepared to oppose one another in all public affairs.[30]

As Edwards notes in this text, the adults in the town were split into two factions. They were the 'haves' and the 'have-nots', those who were wealthy and had property and those who were jealous of them and who sought to diminish their power and influence.[31] Most of these adults were taken up, not with the things of God and his kingdom, but with other cares and pursuits, especially the pursuit of material wealth. Outwardly they were orthodox, but they had no inward religion. Their orthodoxy was dry and lifeless.

Not surprisingly their children were, in Edwards' own words, 'very much addicted to night-walking, and frequenting the tavern, and lewd practices'. As American historian Richard Lovelace has noted, if these teens had had drugs, they would have used them.[32]

In the early 1730s, however, there began to be a growing sensitivity to sin and a willingness to listen to religious counsel.[33] A series of sermons on justification by faith alone – the doctrine that had been so central in the Reformation – were particularly used of God to awaken the lost and the spiritually indifferent. The series was preached by Edwards in November and December 1734 and especially stressed that God, in justifying sinners, does so on the basis of his mercy alone. Those whom God saves are not saved because God sees anything in them that would merit his favour and blessing. To quote Edwards: When God justifies a person, he 'has no regard to anything in the person justified, as godliness, or any goodness'. In fact, Edwards went on to say, 'Before this act [of justification], God beholds him only as an ungodly or wicked creature.' Justification entails God choosing to reckon Christ's perfect righteousness to the sinner and in this way the sinner can be declared righteous.[34]

It was the exposition of this central feature of the New Testament that Edwards saw as the major catalyst that the Holy Spirit used to begin an extraordinary revival in Northampton.

> There were then some things said publicly ... concerning justification by faith alone... It proved a word spoken in season here; and was most evidently attended with a very remarkable blessing of heaven to the souls of the people in this town... And then it was, in the latter part of December [of 1734], that the Spirit of God began extraordinarily to set in, and wonderfully to work amongst us; and there were, very suddenly, one after another, five or six persons, who were to all appearance savingly converted, and some of them wrought upon in a very remarkable manner.[35]

Edwards here makes a direct connection between the preaching of biblical truth and the onset of revival by his use of the connective 'then'. It was *after* the preaching of justification by faith alone – which Edwards also denotes as 'the way of the Gospel ... the true and only way'[36] – that the Spirit began to work so 'wonderfully' and 'suddenly'.

Soon, Edwards narrated, an intense concern to be right with God and to walk with him gripped the town:

> Although people did not ordinarily neglect their worldly business; yet there then was the reverse of what commonly is: religion was with all sorts the great concern, and the world was a thing only by the bye. The only thing in their view was to get the kingdom of heaven, and everyone appeared pressing into it. The engagedness of their hearts in this great concern could not be hid; it appeared in their very countenances. It then was a dreadful thing amongst us to lie out of Christ, in danger every day of dropping into hell; and what persons' minds were intent upon was to escape for their lives, and to fly from the wrath to come. All would eagerly lay hold of opportunities for their souls; and were wont very often to meet together in private houses for religious purposes: and such meetings when appointed were wont greatly to be thronged.[37]

Out of a town of about 1,200 people, Edwards initially reckoned that some 300 were saved in about six months.[38] At the revival's height, in March and April 1735, there would be about thirty people a week professing conversion.[39] Edwards would later judge that there were not as many converts as he had thought during the actual time of the revival.[40] Nevertheless, he never doubted that what took place during 1734 and 1735 was a tremendous, God-wrought awakening in the town.

At the time, the impact on the town and church meetings was nothing less than dramatic: 'This work of God, as it was carried on, and the number of true saints multiplied, soon made a glorious alternation in the town: so that ... the town seemed to be full of the presence of God.'[41] Nor was the revival limited to the town of Northampton. It spread swiftly to thirty-two other towns throughout the Connecticut Valley.

Edwards' account of this revival, the *Faithful Narrative*, was first published in London in 1737. Among those who read it at that time and were deeply impressed by it was Howel Harris (1714-1773), the Welsh Calvinistic Methodist evangelist, who came to possess a copy of the book in February 1738. After reading it, he was led to pray, 'O go on with Thy work there [i.e. in New England] and here.'[42] Harris' prayer received an answer in 1740 to 1742, when God again visited New England with revival, but this time on a much more extensive scale.

THE GREAT AWAKENING, 1740-1742

This revival has come to be known as the Great Awakening, and it made a profound impact not only on New England but also on American colonies to the south. Estimates of those converted in New England alone, where the population was around 250,000 at the time, range from 25,000 to 50,000. These figures, it should be noted, do not include conversions of those who were already church members.[43] In the middle of the revival William Cooper (1694-1743), the Congregationalist minister of Brattle Street Congregationalist Church in Boston, gave his perspective on what God was doing in his day:

> The dispensation of grace we are now under is certainly such as neither we nor our fathers have seen; and in some circumstances so wonderful, that I believe there has not been the like since the extraordinary pouring out of the Spirit immediately after our Lord's ascension. The apostolical times seem to have returned upon us: such a display has there been of the power and grace of the divine Spirit in the assemblies of his people, and such testimonies has he given to the word of the gospel... A number of preachers have appeared among us, to whom God has given such a large measure of his Spirit, that we are ready sometimes to apply to them the character given of Barnabas, that 'he was a good man, and full of the Holy Ghost, and of faith' (Acts 11:24). They preach the gospel of the grace of God from place to place with uncommon zeal and assiduity. The doctrines they

insist on, are the doctrines of the Reformation, under the influence whereof the power of godliness so flourished in the last century. The points on which their preaching mainly turns are those important ones of man's guilt, corruption, and impotence; supernatural regeneration by the Spirit of God, and free justification by faith in the righteousness of Christ; and the marks of the new birth. The manner of their preaching is not with the enticing words of man's wisdom: howbeit, they 'speak wisdom among them that are perfect' [1 Cor. 2:4,6]. An ardent love to Christ and souls warms their breasts and animates their labours. God has made those his ministers active spirits, a flame of fire in his service; and his word in their mouths has been as a fire; and as a hammer that breaketh the rock in pieces [Ps. 104:4 and Heb. 1:7; Jer. 23:29].[44]

Here, Cooper places the revival in New England within the broad sweep of church history. He is utterly convinced that no other revival, in either his lifetime or that of his Puritan forebears, is comparable to what God was doing in the early 1740s. In some respects only at the time of Pentecost could one find something genuinely comparable. The preaching through which God had brought about this revival, though, did not contain anything new. Essentially it was the same doctrine of salvation that was trumpeted forth at the time of the Reformation. And the preaching style fit the doctrine: It was plain and ardent.

Cooper goes on to specify what he considers so extraordinary about the revival. First, there is the incredible way that it has swept through 'some of the most populous towns, the chief places of concourse and business'. Then, there are the numbers that have professed conversion: 'Sinners have been awakened by hundreds.' During the winter of 1740/1741 in Boston alone, Cooper states, there were 'some thousands under such religious impressions as they never felt before'. People of all ages, from the very elderly to the very young, have been saved; the elderly 'snatched as brands out of the burning, made monuments of divine mercy' and 'sprightly youth ... made to bow like willows to the Redeemer's sceptre'. Moreover, God has drawn to himself some of the grossest sinners in New England: drunkards, fornicators, and adulterers, people addicted to profanity and 'carnal worldlings have been made to seek first the kingdom of God and his righteousness'. On the other hand, many of those who deemed themselves upright and moral have become convinced that 'morality is not to be relied on for life; and so excited to seek after the new birth, and a vital union to Jesus Christ by faith'.[45]

Now, among the preachers whom Cooper is clearly likening to Barnabas were Edwards and the English Methodist George Whitefield. The latter had landed in America at Lewes, Delaware, on 30 October 1739, and did not return to England until early 1741. He met Edwards for the first time nearly a year later, on Friday, 17 October 1740. Whitefield's memorable visit at the Edwards home lasted until the Sunday evening, October 19. In his journal entry for that day, Whitefield wrote:

> Felt great satisfaction in being at the house of Mr. Edwards. A sweeter couple I have not yet seen. Their children were not dressed in silks and satins, but plain, as become the children of those who, in all things, ought to be examples of Christian simplicity. Mrs. Edwards is adorned with a meek and quiet spirit; she talked solidly of the things of God, and seemed to be such a helpmeet for her husband, that she caused me to renew those prayers which, for some months, I have put up to God, that He would be pleased to send me a daughter of Abraham to be my wife.[46]

There were, however, other leaders in the revival of quite a different stamp than either Edwards or Whitefield.

James Davenport (1716-1757), for instance, was a minister from Southold, Long Island, whose preaching in the early stages of the revival could not be faulted. But as the revival progressed, his words and deeds became increasingly tinged with fanaticism. Although Davenport eventually came to his senses, admitted his errors and sought to make restitution, he had helped to unleash a 'wildfire' spirit that in many places made havoc of the revival. Moreover, Davenport's antics provided anti-revival forces, known as the Old Lights, with a highly visible target for their attacks. To them he came to epitomize the anarchy and destruction of church harmony that the revival inevitably brought in its wake. The captain of these forces was Charles Chauncy (1705-1787), the co-pastor of Boston's prestigious First Church. As the religious situation in New England began to polarize between those who took Chauncy's position and those who defended the revival, excesses and all, a Presbyterian named John Moorehead, who was sympathetic to the revival, prayed: 'God direct us what to do, particularly with pious zealots and cold, diabolical opposers!'[47]

Edwards' reflections on the revival

The answer to Moorhead's prayer came by way of a book, Jonathan Edwards' *A Treatise Concerning the Religious Affections*. Prior to the appearance of this book in 1746, Edwards had produced a couple of works that sought to find a middle ground between 'pious zealots', such as Davenport, and 'cold, diabolical opposers', such as Chauncy: *The Distinguishing Marks of a Work of the Spirit of God* (1741) and *Some Thoughts concerning the present Revival of Religion in New-England* (1742). It is, however, the *Religious Affections*, which is his consummate work on revival. Iain Murray has rightly described it as 'one of the most important books possessed by the Christian church on the nature of true religion'.[48] The first two of these works receive extensive examination in the chapters to follow.

One final work of Edwards' related to the subject of revival that should be taken note of is his *An Humble Attempt to Promote Explicit Agreement and Visible Union of God's People in Extraordinary Prayer, For the Revival of Religion and the Advancement of Christ's Kingdom on Earth*, which appeared in January 1748. In this work, Edwards made a stirring appeal for 'many people, in different parts of the world, by express agreement to come into a visible union in extraordinary, speedy, fervent, and constant prayer, for those great effusions of the Holy Spirit, which shall bring on that advancement of Christ's church and kingdom, that God has so often promised shall be in the latter ages of the world'.[49] Edwards was thoroughly convinced, and rightly so, on the basis of Scripture and the history of the church, that 'when God has something very great to accomplish for his church, it is his will that there should precede it the extraordinary prayers of his people'.[50] Unlike some of his other works, this book did not have a great impact in Edwards' own lifetime. Towards the end of the eighteenth century, though, it exercised a profound influence. As was noted in the introduction, a circle of Calvinistic Baptists in the English Midlands, of whom the names of Andrew Fuller and William Carey are today the best known, were deeply impacted by this work and knew God-given revival as a result of their following its practical admonitions.

THE COMMUNION CONTROVERSY AND DISMISSAL FROM NORTHAMPTON

The year 1748, which saw the publication of Edwards' *Humble Attempt*, is also significant in that it witnessed the beginning of a controversy that engulfed his congregation in Northampton.[51] The heart of the controversy involved a practice that Edwards' grandfather Solomon Stoddard had instituted during the previous century. Around the time that Stoddard assumed the pastorate of the Northampton congregation in 1672, what was known as the Half-Way Covenant had been adopted by the church. This measure, which had been promulgated by a 1662 synod in Boston, allowed the unregenerate children of believing parents to have their infants baptized, provided that these unregenerate children embraced the Christian world-view and sought to lead a moral life. Participation in the Lord's Supper and voting remained the privilege of those who could profess conversion and thus were full members of the church.

By 1677, it appears that Stoddard was questioning the efficacy of the Half-Way Covenant, which was designed to encourage those who were 'halfway' members to go the whole distance and be converted. The influential Boston theologian Increase Mather (1639-1723), Stoddard's brother-in-law by marriage, noted in a sermon that he preached 3 May 1677, that there were some in New England (and Stoddard is most likely in view) who were determined 'to bring all Persons to the Lords Supper, who have an Historical Faith, and are not scandalous in life, although they never had

Experience of a work of Regeneration on their Souls'.[52] Stoddard was coming to the conviction that the Half-Way Covenant actually hindered the progression of 'halfway' members toward conversion.

Two years later, at the Reforming Synod of 1679, Stoddard and Increase Mather debated the issue, though there is no clear evidence that Stoddard had yet reached the view Mather would later describe as Stoddard's 'strangest notion', namely that the Lord's Table is 'a converting ordinance'. But a sermon Stoddard preached in 1690 on Galatians 3:11 clearly indicates that the Northampton pastor had come to the firm belief that the 'Lord's Supper is appointed … for the begetting of grace as well as for the strengthening of grace'.

This innovation, known today as Stoddardeanism, was fiercely attacked by Increase Mather and others, including the Puritan poet Edward Taylor (c.1645-1729), pastor in Westfield, Massachusetts. Stoddard's able defence of his views, though, convinced many in western Massachusetts, and Stoddardeanism became the official position of the Northampton congregation.

Now, the conviction that this practice was thoroughly unscriptural had been deepening in Edwards' mind for quite some time before he openly declared in December 1748 that a person must profess to be regenerate before he or she would be allowed to come to the Lord's Table. In taking this position, Edwards found himself opposed by most of his congregation, as he details in a letter he wrote in May 1749 to the Scottish Presbyterian minister John Erskine (1721-1803):

> I have nothing very comfortable to inform of concerning the present state of religion in this place. A very great difficulty has arisen between me and my people, relating to qualifications for communion at the Lord's table. My honored grandfather [Solomon] Stoddard, my predecessor in the ministry over this church, strenuously maintained the Lord's Supper to be a converting ordinance; and urged all to come who were not of scandalous life, though they knew themselves to be unconverted. I formerly conformed to his practice, but I have had difficulties with respect to it, which have been long

increasing; till I dared no longer to proceed in the former way: which has occasioned great uneasiness among my people, and has filled all the country with noise; which has obliged me to write something on the subject, which is now in the press.

I know not but this affair will issue in a separation between me and my people. I desire your prayers that God would guide me in every step in this affair.[53]

The atmosphere that the controversy created in Northampton is well displayed in another letter that Edwards wrote to his good friend Joseph Bellamy (1719-1790) at the close of that year:

You may easily be sensible, dear Sir, that 'tis a time of great trial with me, and that I stand in continual need of the divine presence and merciful conduct in such a state of things as this. I need God's counsel in every step I take and every word I speak; for all that I do and say is watched by the multitude around me with the utmost strictness and with eyes of the greatest uncharitableness and severity, and let me do or say what I will, my words and actions are represented in dark colors.[54]

While there were other issues that were raised in this controversy – Edwards' failure to regularly visit his congregants, for example[55] – the central issue had to do with what Edwards described as 'the qualifications necessary for admission to the privileges of members'.[56]

In late June, the male members of the Northampton congregation voted on whether or not they wished Edwards to continue as their pastor. Of the 230 male members who could vote, a mere twenty-three voted in Edwards' favour, though it should be noted that there were some who refrained from voting.[57] During the controversy, and especially in the week of his dismissal, Edwards displayed remarkable calmness. David Hall, a fellow minister, who was involved in trying to resolve the controversy, wrote in his diary that Edwards 'appeared like a man of God, whose happiness was out of reach of his enemies, and whose treasure was not only a future but a present good, overbalancing all imaginable ills of life, even to the astonishment of many, who could not be at rest without his dismission'.[58]

The reasons for such calmness were at least twofold. The God whom Edwards loved and adored was a sovereign ruler in all human affairs, and what had taken place between him and his congregation ultimately came from the hand of a sovereign and omni-benevolent God. As he mentioned in a letter written to John Erskine but four days after he preached his *Farewell Sermon*:

> We are in the hands of God, and I bless him. I am not anxious concerning his disposal of us. I hope I shall not distrust him, nor be unwilling to submit to his will. And I have cause of thankfulness, that there seems also to be such a disposition in my family.[59]

Second, Edwards genuinely loved his people, and despite what had happened, he was determined not to be embittered towards them. In fact, in the course of his *Farewell Sermon*, he urged those who had supported him to:

> ...avoid all bitterness towards others... [and] however wrong you may think others have done, maintain, with great diligence and watchfulness, a Christian meekness and sedateness of spirit... Indulge no revengeful spirit in any wise, but watch and pray against it: and by all means in your power, seek the prosperity of this town: and never think you behave yourselves as becomes Christians, but when you sincerely, sensibly and fervently love all men of whatever party or opinion, and whether friendly or unkind, just or injurious, to you, or your friends, or to the cause and kingdom of Christ.[60]

MISSIONS AND WRITING AT STOCKBRIDGE

After his dismissal from Northampton, Edwards became the pastor of a church in what was then the frontier village of Stockbridge, in the heart of the Berkshire Mountains in western Massachusetts, and a missionary to some 250 Mohican and sixty Mohawk

Indians.[61] The usual account of his time at Stockbridge from 1751 to early 1758 concentrates on Edwards' literary achievements. And this is not surprising, for it was during these years that Edwards wrote those books that established him as the 'greatest Christian theologian of the eighteenth century'.[62] Among these works was his notable defence of Calvinism, *A Careful and Strict Enquiry into the Modern Prevailing Notions of that Freedom of Will, Which is Supposed to be Essential to Moral Agency* (1754). As a result of this focus, though, Edwards' commitment to missions at Stockbridge has not really been appreciated.[63] Clear evidence of this fact is that until 1999 not one of the sermons he preached to the Stockbridge Indians had been published.[64] Yet, as Edwards' most recent biographer George Marsden has noted, Edwards' pre-eminent goal during his time at Stockbridge was to reach these Indians with the life-giving gospel.[65]

Historically, there have been some who have argued that Edwards' deep commitment to a Calvinist world-view effectively hindered the formulation of a rich missionary vision and any missionary praxis. In an article published in the late 1970s, for instance, James Manor states that 'Edwards himself was too close to traditional calvinism [*sic*] and too concerned with the defense of the sovereignty of against the arminians [*sic*] to be termed a mission activist'. How mistaken Manor's views are is clear from Edwards' focus at Stockbridge. Manor does acknowledge that Edwards' writings were a catalyst for the thinking of missionaries such as William Carey.[66] Moreover, as Ron Davies has more than adequately shown, Edwards' theological vision was a global one, in which, as he looked to the future, he saw ever-increasing victories in the missionary advance of the kingdom of Christ.[67]

Edwards' vision of the missionary growth of the kingdom of Christ had been with him since his earliest pastorate in New York (1722-1723). For example, in the *Personal Narrative*, a text that he drew up probably in 1740, but which reflects on experiences at least twenty years prior, Edwards notes of his early days as a believer:

> I had great longings for the advancement of Christ's kingdom in the world. My secret prayer used to be in great part

taken up in praying for it. If I heard the least hint of anything that happened in any part of the world, that appeared to me, in some respect or other, to have a favorable aspect on the interest of Christ's kingdom, my soul eagerly catched at it; and it would much animate and refresh me... I very frequently used to retire into a solitary place, on the banks of Hudson's River, at some distance from the city, for contemplation on divine things, and secret converse with God; and had many sweet hours there. Sometimes Mr. Smith and I walked there together, to converse of the things of God; and our conversation used much to turn on the advancement of Christ's kingdom in the world, and the glorious things that God would accomplish for his church in the latter days.[68]

As this text details, private prayer and 'sweet hours' of personal conversation were vehicles for Edwards' missionary longings. Reading and Scripture meditation were also focused in this direction, as another extract from the *Personal Narrative* reveals:

My heart has been much on the advancement of Christ's kingdom in the world. The histories of the past advancement of Christ's kingdom, have been sweet to me. When I have read histories of past ages, the pleasentest thing in all my reading has been, to read of the kingdom of Christ being promoted ... and my mind has been much entertained and delighted, with the Scripture promises and prophecies, of the future glorious advancement of Christ's kingdom on earth.[69]

What is also noteworthy about both of these texts is the Christ-centredness of Edwards' global vision. It was the 'advancement of *Christ's* kingdom' that he ardently longed for.[70]

Another very significant text that needs to be briefly considered with regard to Edwards' missionary thought is his biography of David Brainerd (1718-1747). Brainerd was a young missionary to native North American Indians in New York, Pennsylvania and New Jersey, who died of tuberculosis in Edwards' own home. Edwards inherited all of Brainerd's literary remains and soon after

Brainerd's death he began shaping them into the biographical narrative that successive generations have known as *An Account of the Life of the Late Reverend Mr. David Brainerd*. This work first appeared in 1749 and has never been out of print. It is undoubtedly one of Edwards' most important books.[71]

In it, Edwards sought to accomplish two ends: display a model of authentic spirituality – a concern had arisen during the Great Awakening about the nature of true piety – and recommend 'a self-denying missionary sensibility'.[72] In the latter aim, Edwards succeeded far better than he knew, for, as Joseph Conforti has observed, the book 'had its greatest impact on [nineteenth-century] American missionaries'.[73] For Edwards, Brainerd was a constant reminder of the sort of missionary that the church needs. He was a man, in Edwards' words, 'who had indeed sold all for Christ and had entirely devoted himself to God, and made his glory his highest end'.[74]

Final days

In late 1757, though, Edwards reluctantly accepted an invitation to become president of the College of New Jersey, now Princeton University, arriving in late January of the following year to take up his role. Accompanying him was one of his daughters, Lucy (1736-1786). Esther Edwards Burr (1732-1758), another of his daughters, was already residing in Princeton, since her recently deceased husband, Aaron Burr Sr (1715-1757), had been Edwards' predecessor.

Edwards had been at the college only a few weeks when he was inoculated against smallpox, which was raging in Princeton and the vicinity. The vaccine initially appeared to be successful, but complications set in and Edwards, never a strong man physically, died on 22 March 1758. Among his last words there was a message for his wife, who was still at Stockbridge with most of their children. To Esther and Lucy, the two daughters present at his bedside, he said a little before his death:

> It seems to me to be the will of God that I must shortly leave you; therefore give my kindest love to my dear wife, and tell her, that the uncommon union, which has so long subsisted

between us, has been of such a nature, as I trust is spiritual, and therefore will continue forever: and I hope she shall be supported under so great a trial, and submit cheerfully to the will of God. And as to my children, you are now like to be left fatherless, which I hope will be an inducement to you all to seek a Father who will never fail you.[75]

Just before his death, those at his bedside, supposing he was unconscious, were lamenting what his death would mean to the college and to the church, when they were surprised by what proved to be his last words: 'Trust in God, and ye need not fear.'[76] To the end Edwards maintained a God-centred focus: The living God was all-sufficient and would ever care for his family.[77]

When Sarah heard of the death of her husband, she wrote to their daughter Esther, 'O what a legacy my husband, and your father, has left us!'[78] As the following chapters will hopefully show, it was a legacy not only for members of his immediate family, but also for the entire church.

If one were to ask, what exactly was his legacy, a number of answers can easily be given. Throughout an extensive corpus of treatises, sermons, notes and letters, Edwards repeatedly lays before his readers the true purpose of their existence: the glory and triumph of the triune God in history and eternity. Contemporary evangelicals, largely indifferent to the glory and beauty of God, would profit much from this emphasis. Or one could note that at the beginning of Edwards' life Calvinism was in serious decline. In the providence of God and by his grace, Edwards played a key role in its restoration to a place of spiritual vigour and influence. Additionally, although Edwards is not regularly thought of in terms of missions, there is no doubt that Edwards' writings provided a major stimulus for the birth of the modern missionary movement.

What we want to focus on with regard to Edwards' legacy is his pneumatology of revival and renewal. During the revivals that came to New England during his lifetime, there was much blessing – yet also much confusion about what was truly the work of the Spirit. Edwards turned to Scripture as the pre-eminent authority in determining what was genuine spirituality and actually the work of the Spirit. In doing so, he has given us a rich body of material on the lineaments of true revival.

Let us pray for the Spirit.

– Jonathan Edwards

Chapter 2

THE THREEFOLD WORK OF THE HOLY GHOST: THE CROSS AND THE WORK OF THE HOLY SPIRIT

DURING THE 1740S, Jonathan Edwards was engrossed in the subject of revival, both real and anticipated; defending the revival that was then sweeping New England, yet also critiquing its excesses, subjecting it to theological analysis and seeking to kindle a steady passion for further displays of such sovereign moves by the Spirit. Among his final writings on this subject is a fascinating treatise published in 1748 and entitled *An Humble Attempt to Promote Explicit Agreement and Visible Union of God's People in Extraordinary Prayer, for the Revival of Religion and the Advancement of Christ's Kingdom on Earth.*[1] This treatise had been inspired by information Edwards received during the course of 1745 about a prayer movement for revival that had been formed by a number of Scottish evangelical ministers. These ministers and their congregations had agreed to spend a part of Saturday evening and Sunday morning each week, as well as the first Tuesday of certain months of the year, in prayer to God for 'an abundant effusion of His Holy Spirit', so as to 'revive true religion in all parts of Christendom' and 'fill the whole earth with His glory'.[2] This 'concert of prayer' ran initially for two years and then was renewed for a further seven.

When Edwards was sent information regarding it, he lost no time in seeking to initiate a similar concert of prayer in the colonies of New England. He encouraged his own congregation to implement the idea and also communicated the concept of such a prayer union to neighbouring ministers whom he felt would be receptive. Although the idea initially met with a poor response, Edwards was not to be put off. In a sermon given in February 1747 on Zechariah 8:20-22, he sought to demonstrate how the text supported his call for a union of praying Christians. Within a year a revised and greatly expanded version of this sermon was ready for publication as the *Humble Attempt*.

The *Humble Attempt* is divided into three parts. The first section opens with a number of observations on Zechariah 8:20-22 and then provides a description of the origin of the concert of prayer in Scotland. Edwards goes on to argue that it is a duty well pleasing to God and incumbent upon God's people in America to assemble and, with 'extraordinary, speedy, fervent, and constant prayer', pray for those 'great effusions of the Holy Spirit' that will dramatically advance the kingdom of Christ.[3]

Part 2 of the treatise cites a number of reasons for participating in the concert of prayer. Among them is the fact that one of God's major purposes in the atoning work of Christ was to secure the blessed presence of the Spirit of Christ for his people. As Edwards puts it:

> The sum of the blessings Christ sought by what He did and suffered in the work of redemption, was the Holy Spirit... The Holy Spirit, in His indwelling, his influences and fruits, is the sum of all grace, holiness, comfort and joy, or in one

word, of all the Spiritual good Christ purchased for men in this world: and is also the sum of all perfection, glory and joy, that He purchased for them in another world...

Now therefore, if this is what Jesus Christ, our great Redeemer and head of the church, did so much desire, and set his heart upon, from all eternity, and for which he did and suffered so much, offering up strong crying and tears (Hebrews 5:7), and his precious blood, to obtain it; surely his disciples and members should also earnestly seek it, and be much in prayer for it.[4]

This link between the atonement and the outpouring of the Spirit was not new to Edwards' thinking, however. It also can be found nearly twenty years earlier, in a series of sermons that a youthful Edwards preached on John 16:8. These sermons were originally delivered in 1729, the year that Edwards became the sole pastor of the church in Northampton and about five years before the start of the first wave of revival in New England.

This series of sermons portrays the Holy Spirit in his threefold work as the convincer of sin, of righteousness and of judgement. The way that Edwards views the interconnections between the atoning work of Christ and the gift of the Holy Spirit is explored and unfolded in this chapter as we see how Edwards' sermons explain the threefold work of the Spirit. Edwards' Christ-centred pneumatology is thus seen as something that was prominent from some of his earliest theological reflections.

THE GIFT OF THE SPIRIT

The Holy Spirit, Edwards told his Northampton congregation, is given by Christ from the Father, because Christ has the office of dispensing salvation, and this office was conferred upon him as his reward for procuring that salvation. He is the dispenser because he is the procurer. In Edwards' words:

> The Holy Trinity saw it meet that he that had been at so great a cost to purchase salvation should also have the disposal of it... It was looked upon but a suitable reward [for Christ's

obedience unto death]... For this reason, God gave Christ 'power over all flesh, that he should give eternal life to as many as he hath given him' (John 17:2) ... 'and hath given him authority to execute judgment also, because he is the Son of man' (John 5:27).[5]

In this view, the giving of the Holy Spirit to the elect is the just reward from the Father to the God-man Christ for his atoning work, and the sending of the Spirit to the elect is Christ's prerogative as the Head of the new creation. The exaltation of the God-man in his kingly office, whereby he gives eternal life to the elect by sending them the Holy Spirit from the Father, is seen as the reward of Christ's priestly work of having fully satisfied the justice of his Father. It was in his own human nature that Christ died and suffered all that was necessary to redeem the elect. It is his prerogative, therefore, as the God-man, to be the sender of the Spirit. Whatever the Holy Spirit does for the salvation of the Father's elect, he does as the messenger of the incarnate Son of God and through his mediation. There is no other way that the Holy Spirit can come to Adam's posterity and continue his operations in them, but by Christ, who is the only mediator between God and fallen humanity.

The Holy Spirit is thus the indispensable and chief agent in the application of the benefits of Christ's priestly work of atonement. In Edwards' view, this work of the Holy Spirit takes effect whenever the Spirit declares the mediatorial glory of Christ and begins to manifest that glory to the elect. Edwards sees a parallel between the threefold work of the Holy Spirit and the threefold mediatorial office of Christ. The work of the Spirit as to sin, righteousness and judgement corresponds in Edwards' view to the activities of the ascended Christ as prophet, priest and king.[6] This threefold correspondence between the mediatorial work of the ascended Christ and the work of the Spirit as his messenger is reflected in the three major divisions of Edwards' discourse.

THE SPIRIT AND THE DEATH OF CHRIST

First, the atonement opens up the way for convincing fallen human beings that they are sinners. They cannot be convinced in any other way, since they are under the sentence of condemnation and therefore spiritually dead in sin. For reversal of that sentence, satisfaction of justice is necessary; and for making that reversal effective, by the awakening of a dead sinner and by regeneration out of spiritual death, nothing less than the omnipotent, life-giving operations of the Holy Spirit will suffice. Edwards stresses that the Holy Spirit brings conviction of sin by means of the law of God. The preaching of the law in the convicting power of the Spirit is thus one of the prophetic activities mediated by Christ by means of the Holy Spirit. With regard to the elect, such preaching may therefore be viewed as one of the particular fruits of the atonement that prepares the way for conversion.[7]

Yet there are some who hear the preaching and experience conviction of the Spirit, but do not come to Christ. This is because the Spirit moves on their hearts as an external agent only, and does not take up his abode in their hearts. They resist the Spirit. If they persist in doing so, they will be hardened in their sin. This hardening does not come about by the direct agency of the Spirit, but by his withdrawing from the sinner. To illustrate his point Edwards refers to the process of hardening iron. 'Fire hardens iron', he says, meaning that iron ceases to be malleable when the fire is withdrawn.[8]

Second, Christ sends the Holy Spirit for the purpose of evangelism, which goes beyond the conviction of sin and of the need for salvation, to the declaration that salvation resides with Jesus Christ alone and is available to anyone who will receive it from him by faith. The central content of the evangelistic message is the atoning work of Christ, that is, the purchasing of salvation by his perfect obedience and sacrifice of himself. Evangelism, viewed as a specific activity of the Spirit sent by the ascended Christ, is that particular fruit of the atonement which results in the conversion of those who are already convicted of sin. Their conversion is achieved by the Spirit's convincing them also of the righteousness that was wrought by Christ and is laid up in him as a free gift from God to be imputed to them and received by them individually through a personal act of faith.[9]

In the case of the elect, evangelism is accompanied or followed by the effectual calling of the awakened sinner. This is the sovereign and efficacious summons of God the Father to the convicted sinner to come to him through Christ in repentance and faith. The key activity of the Holy Spirit in effectual calling is, according to Edwards:

> To make men understand the way of sinners' reconciliation with God through Christ. This is a more exalted operation of the Spirit of God than convincing men of sin. This is by that heavenly and divine light that the Holy Ghost causes to shine into the heart at conversion; this is a primary operation of the Spirit of God when he first enters into the soul, to take up his abode there.[10]

In a similar vein, Edwards says:

> The Holy Ghost convinces of the reality of this way of reconciliation and acceptance [with God through Christ] by the righteousness of Christ... The Holy Ghost causes to see a glorious excellency in this way. It all appears with a cast of glory upon it: there is a charming excellency and wisdom seen in it; it appears now an heavenly and divine way: there are in it the evident shines of divine glory... The manifestation of the perfections of God in Christ which appear in it seem glorious: God's wisdom in this contrivance, his power in overcoming Satan, his majesty, his holiness appears in its purity and beauty, and specially his grace. II Cor. 4:6, 'For God, who commanded the light to shine out of darkness, hath shined in our hearts, to give the light of the knowledge of the glory of God in the face of Jesus Christ.'
>
> When the soul is thus convinced of the reality, suitableness, and glory of this way of acceptance by Christ, the heart and inclination entirely embraces it.
>
> The whole soul accords and consents to it... There is a sweet harmony now between the soul and the gospel; it doth in a lively manner accord and consent to it, and cleave to it... This is that gladly receiving the gospel spoken of, Acts 2:41...

This is accompanied with the soul's committing itself to Jesus Christ...

Upon all this there follows a quiet rest and calmness of the mind ... and I would observe to you that 'tis in these things that saving, justifying faith primarily does consist.[11]

In this way, and by the instrumentality of the Scriptures, the Holy Spirit manifests to the elect the glory of Christ in his priestly work of atonement. He thus brings them to repentance and faith, conversion and vital union with Christ. The Father thus declares them righteous in his sight, an act that is rooted in his election of them to salvation and effectual calling of them to himself.

Closely related to justification is adoption. The Father who justifies also adopts. As Edwards points out, quoting Galatians 4:4-5, the Father's adoption of the elect as sons is on account of Christ's righteousness:

> Gal. 4:4-5, 'God sent forth his Son, made under the law, to redeem them that are under the law, that we might receive the adoption of sons.' By his [being] made under the law, it is fair to understand all manner of subjection, both as requiring his passive and active subjection, and that both were to redeem us, that we might be made partakers of the adoption of sons.[12]

Although Edwards does not mention in this context Galatians 4:6-7, these verses bring to view the work of the Spirit in adoption: 'And because ye are sons, God hath sent forth the Spirit of his Son into your hearts, crying Abba, Father. Wherefore thou art no more a servant but a son; and if a son, then an heir of God through Christ' (KJV). One of the particular fruits of the atonement is the activity of the Spirit in the converted by means of which he convinces them that they are sons of their heavenly Father and heirs of glory as joint heirs with Christ. Put differently, the Spirit produces and maintains in God's children a filial confidence towards the Father. This is yet another interconnection between the atonement and the work of the Spirit.

Finally, the work of the Holy Spirit in convincing the world of judgement has to do with Christ's kingly work of building and perfecting the church. The victory secured by Christ in the atonement is seen by Edwards as going beyond the binding of the strong man (i.e. Satan) by the satisfaction of justice to the spoiling of his goods by the power of the Holy Spirit, whom Christ has given to the elect. In this way, Christ takes up and exercises universal dominion over angels and men in his headship of the new creation. In particular, as Edwards says, 'he condemns, confounds and executes judgement upon Satan'.[13] The Holy Spirit sent by Christ in the exercise of kingly power convinces of sin and righteousness, by which means he rescues the elect from Satan's controlling power and brings them to justifying faith and newness of life in Christ. The Holy Spirit also convinces of judgement, revealing and manifesting to believers the victory over sin and Satan that is theirs in Christ, and the excellency of Christ as their ruler and deliverer. In Edwards' words:

> Christ rules his subjects, not as other princes do theirs, by external force, but he rules their hearts. He governs their wills and inclinations, and turns them as rivers [of waters]. Christ exercises his mighty power this way. Ps. 110:3, 'Thy people shall be willing in the day of thy power.' This power is a gracious, almighty influencer, whereby Christ governs the inclinations and actions of the heart.
>
> By this he powerfully causes a willing obedience to his rules and laws, and evinces subjection to him. He gives laws by his Word, but he causes them to be obeyed by his Spirit and vital influence communicated from himself.[14]

Edwards then makes a searching application of this to his hearers. If they are truly convinced of judgement, they will be submitting to Jesus Christ as their Lord and King and deliverer from sin and from punishment. If not, then they cannot be among those who are convinced of righteousness. In other words, without genuine holiness of life one cannot lay claim to true conversion. As Edwards says:

He that serves God from an high esteem and supreme love and thankfulness, he serves God with the heart.

So that the gospel is so far from being an encouragement to sin, and Christ the minister of sin, that there is nothing else that lays a foundation for a true and upright obedience.

Hence we learn how vain the hopes of such persons are that think that they have trusted in Christ's righteousness and yet don't live a life of universal holiness. There are some such: they pretend that they trust in Christ, and that they depend only on Christ's righteousness and have no dependence on their own righteousness, and yet show by their lives that they were never convinced of judgment... They'll do some things, perhaps, but they live in neglect of others. There is some lust or other that they indulge; there is some sin that they practice and that they plead for.[15]

The excellency of Christ as the deliverer of his people is further expounded in terms of particular spiritual benefits secured for them by the righteousness and sufferings of Christ in his humiliation, and dispensed to them as kingly acts in his ascended glory. In particular, he subdues all their enemies and delivers them from all evil; he overrules their trials and tribulations for their highest good; he enables them by the Spirit to mortify sin, and to grow in grace; he delivers them from death and the grave at the resurrection, and brings them to everlasting glory. These kingly acts and the corresponding work of the Holy Spirit, by which Christ builds his church on the ruins of Satan's kingdom, are thus secured by the atoning work of Christ.

Prayer for the Spirit

Not surprisingly, when Edwards comes to give concrete directions for application of this teaching to the lives of his hearers, he urges prayer for the Spirit, both for his initial converting work and for his ongoing work in the believer:

> Let none content themselves without having his indwelling [presence], without having such a glorious principle of life

and action in their hearts.

And let us strive for greater and greater degrees of it. Let it be considered that he that has most of the Spirit will have most [of God]. He that hath most of the Spirit, hath most of God, is most like Christ, has most comfort and joy in the world, and lives most to God's glory; and not only so, but he that has most of the Spirit here in this world, and has most of the exercises and fruits of it, will have most of it also in the other world...

That we may so be, let us carefully avoid all things by which it may be quenched. Let us long and thirst for it. Let us cherish and yield to and follow all his motions. Let us pray for the Spirit.[16]

To pray for more of the Spirit is to pray for God to communicate himself more fully. In Edwards' words:

> He gives holiness and he gives the happiness purchased; he enlightens [the] understanding and renovates the will, elevates and purifies the affections. He gives the heart all comfort and all spiritual blessing in this world; he preserves to the end and fits for glory.
>
> And not only so, but 'tis he that immediately gives eternal life also. 'Tis he that perfects holiness, and 'tis he that perfects the spiritual happiness of the soul. Then they will be perfectly holy and happy forever, because the Holy Spirit fills them.[17]

The fact that Edwards believed in a filling with the Spirit, over and above the indwelling and activity of the Spirit that are common to all converted persons, and earnestly sought such filling of the Spirit for himself and his hearers, is evident from a letter that he wrote to George Whitefield. Writing on 14 December 1740, several months after Whitefield had preached in Northampton, and at the beginning of the Great Awakening, Edwards says:

> I have joyful tidings to send you concerning the state of religion in this place. It has been gradually reviving and prevailing

more and more, ever since you was here. Religion is become abundantly more the subject of conversation; other things that seemed to impede it, are for the present laid aside. I have reason to think that a considerable number of our young people, some of them children, have already been savingly brought home to Christ. I hope salvation has come to this house since you was in it, with respect to one, if not more, of my children. The Spirit of God seems to be at work with others of the family. That blessed work seems now to be going on in this place, especially amongst those that are young.

And as God seems to have succeeded your labours amongst us, and prayers for us, I desire your fervent prayers for us may yet be continued, that God would not be to us as a wayfaring man, that turns aside to tarry but for a night, but that he would more and more pour out his Spirit upon us, and no more depart from us; and for me in particular, that I may be filled with his Spirit, and may become fervent, as a flame of fire in my work, and may be abundantly succeeded, and that it would please God, however unworthy I am, to improve me as an instrument of his glory, and advancing the kingdom of Christ.[18]

In summary, from Edwards' vantage point as early as 1729, a central purpose of the God's atoning work in Christ is to purchase the Spirit. From this perspective, the purchasing of redemption can be viewed as the purchasing of the Spirit – that is, his indwelling and filling of the elect, and bringing many sons to glory. It is through the atonement, therefore, that God secures and opens up the way to communicate himself to believers. Thus, the elect are brought into union with Christ. For Edwards, not only is the Holy Spirit the chief agent in the *application* of the benefits secured by Christ's redeeming work, but he is *himself* the chief benefit procured. And so Edwards can conclude his discourse with the exhortation: 'Let us pray for the Spirit.'[19]

Our ascended Saviour now and then takes a special occasion to manifest the divinity of this Gospel by a plentiful effusion of his Spirit where it is preached.[1]

– Isaac Watts and John Guyse, *preface to the* Faithful Narrative

Chapter 3

A VERY EXTRAORDINARY DISPENSATION OF PROVIDENCE: THE WORK OF THE HOLY SPIRIT IN THE FAITHFUL NARRATIVE

IAIN MURRAY IS OF the opinion that the *Faithful Narrative* (1737) may well have been 'the most significant book to precede the great evangelical awakening on both sides of the Atlantic'.[2] It was certainly well received by those who would be leaders in that awakening. Philip Doddridge (1792-1751) read it the very week it appeared.[3] John Wesley (1703-1791) read it the following year, only a few months after his conversion. His comments on the book were drawn from Psalm 118:23: 'This is the Lord's doing, and it is marvelous in our eyes.'[4] When Howel Harris, the Welsh Calvinistic Methodist leader, read Edwards' book, he felt his heart 'boiling with love to Christ'.[5]

The revival had originally been described by Edwards in an eight-page letter that he sent in early June 1735 to Benjamin Colman

(1673-1747), described by C. C. Goen as 'the urbane and respected pastor' of Boston's Brattle Street Church.[6] Much of this earliest account of the revival was, in turn, communicated by Colman to an English correspondent, a Congregationalist minister by the name of John Guyse (1680-1761). Guyse promptly shared the exciting news with his congregation in a sermon and also with a common friend, the well-known hymnwriter Isaac Watts (1674-1748). Guyse's congregation was so taken with what their pastor told them about the revival from the pulpit that they requested that his sermon be published. Guyse was quite willing to accede to this request, but felt he needed to obtain Colman's permission to cite extracts from Edwards' letter. When Colman received Guyse's letter seeking this permission, he contacted Edwards through his uncle William Williams (1665-1741), one of the leading pastors in Massachusetts. Colman suggested to Edwards that the latter draw up a more detailed account of the revival. Casting his account in the form of a letter to Colman, Edwards finished this more detailed version in November 1736, and mailed it to Colman in Boston. Colman subsequently sent the entire manuscript to Guyse and Watts in London, where they saw it through the press in the latter months of 1737. They provided a lengthy preface to the work and it was they who gave the work the title by which it has come to be known. Within two years of its publication, the book had gone through three editions and twenty printings.[7]

In the *Faithful Narrative*, as Samuel T. Logan Jr has pointed out, Edwards dons the robe of the historian. He is primarily seeking to narrate what took place during the revival. Unlike his later works on revival, he did not intend to produce a detailed morphology of the way that the Spirit works corporately in revival or individually in conversion. Nevertheless, Logan also warns against reading too little out of this influential account.[8] Edwards can emphasize that there is 'an endless variety in the particular manner and circumstances in which persons are wrought on' by the Spirit in conversion, for he is genuinely convinced that the Spirit's work in this regard cannot be reduced to a rigid pattern that allows for no flexibility.[9] Yet, as Logan shows and others have argued, there is a rough pattern of conversion to be found in the book.[10]

A MORPHOLOGY OF CONVERSION

First, Edwards shows how individuals become aware of the miserable condition in which they actually exist and 'the danger they are in of perishing eternally'. Some of these persons are 'brought to the borders of despair, and it looks as black as midnight to them a little before the day dawns in their souls'.[11] Many of them initially seek to reform their lives – 'to walk more strictly, and confess their sins, and perform many religious duties, with a secret hope of appeasing God's anger and making up for the sins they have committed'. When, Edwards notes, these people 'see unexpected pollution in their own hearts, they go about to wash away their own defilements and make themselves clean'.[12] Invariably, though, such attempts at self-cleaning, reform and self-help fail, and they are led on to the next step by the Spirit of God.

In this 'step' on the pathway to conversion, the 'drift of the Spirit of God' is to bring these persons to a 'conviction of their absolute dependence on his [i.e. God's] sovereign power and grace, and universal necessity of a Mediator'.[13] Coupled with this conviction is a deep sense that God would be entirely just in sending them to hell for ever, the realization of what Edwards calls their 'just desert of hell'. 'Their own exceeding sinfulness and the vileness of all their performances' leads them to 'a conviction of the justice of God in their condemnation'.[14] For Edwards, only when people come to a humble recognition of their complete spiritual destitution in the face of God's righteous demand for a holy life are they in the place where they are ready to embrace the Saviour whom God has graciously provided.[15]

This step is an important one in Edwards' morphology, for it reveals the great importance that the Northampton pastor placed on correct doctrine. Recognition of the sovereignty of God in salvation, one of the main themes at the heart of Calvinism, is for Edwards part and parcel of the Spirit's work in revival.[16] Not surprisingly, Edwards notes that of the sermons which he preached during this period of revival, those which were the 'more remarkably blessed' were those 'in which the doctrine of God's absolute sovereignty with regard to the salvation of sinners, and his just liberty with regard to answering the prayers, or succeeding the pains, of natural men, continuing such, have been insisted on'.[17]

The recognition of their desperate plight as sinners and the consciousness that God alone can save them are what Edwards calls 'legal humiliation' and 'the drift of the Spirit of God in his legal strivings with persons'.[18] These discoveries do not necessarily indicate that saving grace is present. But where that grace is present, it eventually manifests itself 'in earnest longings after God and Christ: to know God, to love him, to be humble before him, to have communion with Christ in his benefits'. And it has been Edwards' observation, he points out, that the source of these longings has been 'a sense of the superlative excellency of divine things, with a spiritual relish and taste of 'em'.[19] At this point in the narrative, Edwards does not develop this way of describing the source of these 'earnest longings', or affections as he will come to call them. As we shall see, however, it will become a very important part of his understanding of the Spirit's work in revival.

A final step was the coming into assurance of salvation. In common with the founders of the Reformed tradition in the sixteenth century and the majority of those who developed it during the following century, namely the Puritans, Edwards held that while assurance did not belong to the essence of saving faith, it was nevertheless both obtainable and desirable. Some of those converted in the revival were actually unaware that they had entered into this most joyful of states. Edwards notes that 'many continue a long time in a course of gracious exercises and experiences, and do not think themselves to be converted, but conclude otherwise'. As the pastor of the church, however, Edwards felt it was his duty to help them to come to an assurance of what God had done for them. 'I should account it a great calamity', he noted, 'to be deprived of the comfort of rejoicing with those of my flock who have been in great distress, whose circumstances I have been acquainted with, when there seems to be good evidence that those who were dead are alive, and that those who were lost are found.'[20]

British historian David Bebbington has argued that the pastoral guidance Edwards gave to these converts from Northampton represents a definite watershed in the history of orthodox English-speaking Protestantism. The seventeenth-century Puritans, he maintains, believed that 'assurance is rare, late and the fruit of struggle in the experience of believers'. By assuring the Northampton converts that they were genuine Christians, however, Edwards initiated a shift in the understanding of this doctrine. For him, as for eighteenth-century evangelicalism in general, confidence in one's own salvation came to be expected as 'normally given at conversion and the result of simple acceptance of the gift of God'.[21]

According to Bebbington, the new note sounded in the revival at Northampton was therefore not in the preaching. Guyse and Watts had been right to assert in their preface to the *Faithful Narrative* that it was 'the common plain Protestant doctrine of the Reformation … that the Spirit of God has been pleased to honour with such illustrious success'.[22] Nor was it in the very phenomenon of revival. After all, Edwards notes in the text that revivals had taken place under his grandfather Stoddard's ministry, works wrought by 'the same Spirit' who had been active in Northampton in 1734 and 1735. The ministry of Timothy Edwards, his own father, had also witnessed 'four or five seasons of the pouring out of the Spirit to the general awakening of the people' in East Windsor.[23] What was fresh and distinctive was the guidance that Edwards gave regarding assurance. In fact, Bebbington avers, the dynamic character of the various revivals of the eighteenth century hinges on the fact that those who were leaders in these revivals were assured of their salvation. Secure in their faith, they could give themselves to winning others to Christ. As such, this shift in understanding about the doctrine of assurance was 'responsible for creating in evangelicalism a new movement', quite distinct from Puritanism.[24]

As we shall see in this chapter, close examination of the text of the *Faithful Narrative* reveals that Edwards is at pains to stress the distinctive nature of the revival at Northampton. He clearly wants to point out what he regards as some significant ways in which it differs from those previously known at Northampton or at East Windsor. The use of the word 'surprising' in the title of his account of the revival is by no means fortuitous. It was obviously meant to convey the impression that God was doing a new thing.

However, Edwards shows no awareness that his doctrine of assurance fundamentally differed from that of the Puritan authors whose writings were for him a lifelong mine of inspiration and instruction. His later classic on the assurance of salvation, the *Religious Affections*, though prompted by problems in the Great Awakening, was the fruit of many years of reflection on the nature of genuine piety and primarily sought 'to establish a firm foundation for personal assurance'.[25] It is noteworthy that in support of his position, portions of which will be examined in Chapter 8, Edwards drew widely upon his knowledge of Anglo-American Puritanism, citing such stalwarts as Thomas Shepard (1605-1649), John Flavel (*c.*1630-1691), John Preston (1587-1628), John Owen and Richard Sibbes (1577-1635).[26] He could cite such authors because his views on assurance were essentially theirs. As Conrad Cherry shows, Edwards had a 'Puritan concept of assurance'.[27]

It should also be noted that upon later reflection Edwards was not uncritical of his pastoral ministry during the Northampton revival. In a very revealing letter that he wrote in 1751 to a correspondent in Scotland, a Presbyterian minister by the name of Thomas Gillespie (1708-1774), Edwards reiterated his conviction that 1734 and 1735 undoubtedly witnessed 'a very glorious work of God wrought in Northampton, and there were numerous instances of saving conversion'. Nevertheless, upon hindsight he was now convinced that 'many were deceived, and deceived others, about their true state' and that 'the number of true converts was not so great as was then imagined'.[28] Much of the problem lay in the fact that many of the congregation had wrong notions about the way of ascertaining a genuine conversion. Too much weight was placed upon 'impressions on the imagination' and specific experiences, and not enough consideration given to what Edwards calls 'the abiding sense and temper of their hearts' and 'fruits of grace'.

Yet, Edwards did not absolve himself of blame. He had the sense that he had not given the proper guidance and advice on occasion, with the result that some of his congregation found themselves defenceless against satanic attack and 'spiritual calamity', even to the extent of the eternal ruination of their souls. But so extraordinary was the Spirit's work at that time, that instead of himself, still but 'a child' in spiritual matters, Edwards told Gillespie, 'there was want of [a] giant in judgment and discretion'.[29] In other words, far from seeing the advice that he gave in 1735 concerning assurance as a paradigm for future ministries, Edwards was later critical of its naïveté.

This should not be taken to mean that Bebbington is mistaken about Puritanism and evangelicalism being distinct movements, nor that he is necessarily wrong in viewing Edwards as one of the 'founding fathers' of the latter. Among other things, Puritanism was profoundly interested in ecclesial precision. Polity and church government were key issues for Puritan authors. Evangelicalism, on the other hand, was far more concerned about soteriology than ecclesiology. And even though Edwards would come to grief in Northampton over an issue of church polity, relatively few of his writings had the church as their main focus. Edwards' doctrine of assurance, however, should not be cited as evidence to distinguish him from his Puritan predecessors.

THE GRACES OF GOD'S HOLY SPIRIT

In the narrative of the Northampton revival that Guyse and Watts supervised for publication in 1737, the first mention of the Holy Spirit comes some way into the account. Not until the twelfth paragraph is the Spirit mentioned by name: 'In the latter part of December,' Edwards writes, 'the Spirit of God began extraordinarily to set in, and wonderfully to work amongst us.'[30] There are thirty-four more explicit references to the Spirit in the narrative, certainly not a preponderance given Edwards' conviction that the revival was without a shadow of a doubt a work of the Spirit.[31] Christ, on the other hand, is mentioned no less than eighty-five times in the *Faithful Narrative*. This fact lines up with a deeply held pneumatological conviction in Edwards' Reformed heritage, namely, that the Spirit is a Christ-centred and Christ-exalting Spirit. It is noteworthy that in five sermons Edwards preached immediately before and during the revival, and which he published under the title *Discourses on Various Important Subjects, Nearly Concerning the Great Affair of the Soul's Eternal Salvation* in 1738, the Spirit of God is but rarely mentioned, though Christ is highly prominent.

Careful reading of those places where Edwards does mention the Spirit leaves the reader in no doubt about the New England theologian's view of the Spirit's work in conversion: it is utterly essential. It is the Spirit who awakens the unconverted to the nature of their fearful estate outside of Christ and convinces them of their insufficiency to save themselves.[32] Conversion – that 'great and glorious work of God's power, at once changing the heart and infusing life into the dead soul'[33] – is also the Spirit's work. It was 'wonderful', Edwards writes, to see the Spirit's 'operations on the hearts of many': The way that they were 'taken from a loose and careless way of living, and seized with strong convictions of their guilt and misery, and in a very little time old things have passed away, and all things have become new with them' [2 Cor. 5:17].[34] Edwards can thus denote expressions used by his contemporaries to describe conversion – expressions such as 'a spiritual sight of Christ, faith in Christ, poverty of spirit, trust in God' – as 'graces of God's Spirit'.[35]

Even those who were believers before the revival experienced 'the renewing, strengthening, edifying, influences of the Spirit of God'.[36] Edwards himself testifies to having received with them 'fresh and extraordinary incomes of the Spirit', which made both him and them more fully alive to God.[37] And for some of these older believers, the Spirit brought deep assurance of their being in Christ. 'Many who before had laboured under difficulties about their own state', Edwards writes, 'had now their doubts removed by more satisfying experience, and more clear discoveries of God's love.'[38]

The most important pneumatological aspect of the *Faithful Narrative*, however, is found in Edwards' use of the phrase the 'pouring out of the Spirit of God', which he well knew was a favourite term of many of his Puritan predecessors. A good number of Edwards' New and Old England contemporaries, also quite familiar with the Puritan tomes in which this term occurred, found Edwards' use of the term startling, for it was coupled with the claim that what had taken place in Northampton, as well as in the other towns in the Connecticut Valley, was nothing less than what those Puritans had longed to see and to taste: 'the Spirit of

God ... poured out on many persons' and 'so remarkably poured out on so many towns at once'.[39]

THIS REMARKABLE POURING OUT OF THE SPIRIT OF GOD

In the two or three decades preceding the Northampton revival, a feeling of inner stagnation, even decline, had been widespread among anglophone Protestants on both sides of the Atlantic. Guyse and Watts noted in their preface that 'a great and just complaint for many years among the ministers and churches in Old England, and in New' had been that 'the work of conversion goes on very slowly, that the Spirit of God in his saving influences is much withdrawn from the ministrations of his Word, and there are few that receive the report of the Gospel, with any eminent success upon their hearts'.[40] On the other side of the Atlantic, William Cooper, the assistant of Benjamin Colman at Brattle Street Church, Boston, could write in his preface to Edwards' *The Distinguishing Marks of a Work of the Spirit of God* (1741):

> What a dead and barren time has it now been, for a great while, with all the churches of the Reformation? The golden showers have been restrained; the influences of the Spirit suspended; and the consequence has been that the Gospel has not had any eminent success; conversions have been rare and dubious; few sons and daughters have been born to God; and the hearts of Christians not so quickened, warmed and refreshed under the ordinances, as they have been.[41]

Among the reasons contributing to this spiritual malaise in the opening decades of the eighteenth century, John Walsh, an Oxford historian, lists the decay of ministerial authority, the growth of rationalism, the spread of material wealth and 'luxury', and the frivolity and spiritual indifference of the young.[42] Pious Anglicans and Calvinist Dissenters in England sought to rectify this situation by the creation of voluntary societies that would combat the spread of vice and promote morality. New England Puritans, on the other hand, saw the solution in zealous civil magistrates who would initiate reform as well as in the maintenance of churches that were solely composed of regenerate individuals. By the 1720s, though, a consensus had been reached by many of these divines, in particular, the heirs of Anglo-American Puritanism. 'Reformation would not be lasting until God poured out his Spirit' in revival and that their responsibility was to pray and to promote prayer for this effusion.[43]

This metaphor of the pouring out of the Holy Spirit – a biblical idea first found in such prophetic Old Testament books as Joel, Isaiah and Ezekiel – had been commonly employed by various Puritan preachers from the 1660s onwards. John Howe (1630-1705), to take but one example, had preached a series of fifteen sermons in 1678 on Ezekiel 39:29: 'Neither will I hide my face any more from them: for I have poured out my Spirit upon the house of Israel, saith the Lord God.'[44] Unless the Spirit is poured forth, Howe asserted, then preaching, or the right form of church government, or even the power to do miracles, would be unable to heal the inner decay that was becoming evident in orthodox congregations.[45] 'We are dead, the Spirit of God is retiring, retired in a very great degree ... even from Christian assemblies', Howe bluntly declared.[46] And in a passage that would be cited in the preface to Edwards' *Distinguishing Marks*, Howe predicted that:

> When the Spirit shall be poured forth plentifully ... I believe you will hear much other kind of sermons, or they will, who shall live to such a time, than you are wont to do now-a-days; souls will surely be dealt withal at another kind of rate. It is plain, too sadly plain, there is a great retraction of the Spirit of God even from us; we do not know how to speak living sense [i.e. felt reality] unto souls, how to get within you; our words die in our mouths, or drop and die between you and us. We even faint, when we speak; long experienced unsuccessfulness makes us despond; we speak not as persons that hope to prevail... When such an effusion of the Spirit shall be as is here signified ... [ministers] shall know how to speak to better purpose, with more compassion and sense, with more seriousness, with more authority and allurement, than we now find we can.[47]

When Edwards, therefore, in the *Faithful Narrative* speaks of the 'remarkable pouring out of the Spirit of God' at Northampton and how the 'Spirit of God began to be so wonderfully poured out in a general way through the town',[48] he is harking back to texts like those cited above from Howe and boldly declaring that what English Dissenters and New England Puritans had long been praying for had finally come.[49]

This explains Edwards' description of the revival as a 'very extraordinary dispensation of Providence', in which 'God has in many respects gone out of, and much beyond, his usual and ordinary way'.[50] Yes, Edwards knows that there were local revivals in Northampton during his grandfather's lengthy ministry,[51] but he emphasizes that there are key differences between what took place then and what had taken place under his ministry. Edwards reckoned that the revival of 1734/1735 was extraordinary for at least five reasons. It made a deep impact upon every class and age in Northampton, even, Edwards notes, upon 'old men and little children'. Of the latter group, Edwards estimated that nearly thirty between the ages of ten and fourteen were saved, two around nine or ten, and one, Phebe Bartlet, who was but four years of age when she was soundly converted.[52] In the revivals under Stoddard, it was mostly the 'young people' who were affected.[53] Then there were the numbers who professed faith in Christ. When he wrote the *Faithful Narrative* in 1736, Edwards estimated that 'more than 300 souls were savingly brought home to Christ'.[54] As we have seen, Edwards later thought this figure was somewhat inflated.

The work was extraordinary also because of 'the swift progress [God's] Spirit has made in his operations on the hearts of many'. Edwards could only conclude that God has 'seemed to have gone out of his usual way in the quickness of his work'.[55] The Northampton pastor also points to the striking depths of emotion experienced by those who were professing converts.[56] Finally, he mentions the extraordinary extent of the revival. Unlike 'former times of the pouring out of the Spirit of God' on Northampton when 'neighbouring towns all around continued unmoved', it was quite different this time. Town after town up and down the Connecticut River Valley experienced revival along with the Northampton community. This was something completely unprecedented.[57]

In the concluding paragraphs of the *Faithful Narrative*, Edwards implicitly returns to this theme of the extraordinary nature of the revival. He speaks of the fact that it was through a relatively unknown pastor, in an obscure 'corner of the world', that God chose to bring the revival.

> A great part of the country have not received the most favourable thoughts of this affair; and to this day many retain a jealousy concerning it, and prejudice against it. I have reason to think that the meanness and weakness of the instrument, that has been made use of in this town, has prejudiced many against it; it don't appear to me strange that it should be so: but yet this circumstance of this great work of God is analogous to other circumstances of it. God has so ordered the manner of the work in many respects, as very signally and remarkably to shew it to be his own peculiar and immediate work, and to secure the glory of it wholly to his own almighty power, and sovereign grace. And whatever the circumstances and means have been, and though we are so unworthy, yet so hath it pleased God to work! And we are evidently a people blessed of the Lord! For here, in this corner of the world, God dwells, and manifests his glory.[58]

Although Edwards is today recognized as 'the greatest Christian theologian of the eighteenth century',[59] this was far from being the case in the 1730s. Moreover, while Northampton in this decade was certainly not what it had been when Edwards' grandfather had first come there in 1669 – 'a rude frontier outpost' was the way that one writer described it[60] – yet it was still on the fringe of transatlantic anglophone society. But it was in such obscure circumstances and with such an unknown pastor that God chose to bring revival.

When the third edition of the *Faithful Narrative* was published in Boston in 1738, it was accompanied by a preface written by four Boston ministers, including Thomas Prince (1687-1758) and William Cooper. It provides a marvellous insight into the way that some of Edwards' fellow pastors concurred with his conviction that what had taken place in the Connecticut Valley was indeed an extraordinary event. The authors of this preface place the 1734/1735 revival in an epic line of great works of the Spirit: 'the extraordinary effusion' of the Spirit at Pentecost; the Reformation; 'the work of God's Spirit stirring up' the Puritans to leave England and to come to settle in New England, with whom 'God was eminently present ... by his Word and Spirit'. Just as significantly, the 'Holy Spirit was in a plentiful and extraordinary manner poured out' in Northampton and in the various other towns in the Connecticut River Valley.[61] Though Edwards is much more subtle in the way that he presents what he sees as the significance of the revival, his repeated use of the term 'extraordinary' with respect to the awakening leaves the impression that he would have been in hearty agreement with these four men. From the point of some of Edwards' contemporaries, this was nothing more than sheer arrogance. From our perspective, more than 250 years later, the remarks of the preface are remarkably prescient.

THE 'WITHDRAWAL' OF THE SPIRIT

Towards the end of May 1735 'it began to be very sensible' to Edwards and his congregation 'that the Spirit of God was gradually withdrawing' from them.[62] Evidence for this assertion Edwards found especially in the suicide of his own uncle, Joseph Hawley (1682-1735), a leading merchant in Northampton. Up until May, Edwards was convinced that the extraordinary work of the Spirit in Northampton had kept Satan at bay. In the words of Edwards, Satan 'seemed to be unusually restrained'.[63] Hawley had long wrestled with depression. Satan, Edwards avers, took advantage of this constitutional weakness of Hawley, keeping him awake at nights in dire distress about the fact that he had no apparent hope of being converted. Eventually, the terror of his seemingly helpless condition proved to be too much for the poor man and on Sunday morning, June 1, he cut his throat and was dead within half an hour. Plunged into shock, the Northampton church observed a day of prayer and fasting.[64]

It was only some time later, during the Great Awakening, that Edwards came to a clear understanding that the problem with which Hawley was wrestling had to do with assurance of salvation. In the early 1740s, some radical leaders in the revival maintained that assurance of salvation belonged to the essence of saving faith. When some who were psychologically unstable heard this, they reasoned thus: 'Only when I face God will I know if I am saved; according to some of the preaching that I have heard, if I am saved I am ready to meet God now; if not, there is every likelihood I never will be, and the longer I am alive the more I sin and the more I increase my guilt; therefore, better to settle the matter now by committing suicide.'[65] Although, as we have seen, Edwards never maintained that assurance was vital to saving faith, it would appear that in the weeks prior to his suicide Hawley's disordered mind reasoned along these lines.

Along with the dreadful shock of the manner of Hawley's death, there were 'two remarkable instances of persons led away with strange enthusiastic delusions', one of which involved the belief that there would be a complete restoration of 'the extraordinary gifts of the Holy Ghost' in Edwards' day.[66] As we shall see in the next chapter, Edwards was firmly opposed to such a view. Here it is sufficient to notice that Edwards explicitly cites what he regards as 'enthusiasm', i.e. fanaticism, as a leading cause for the decline of the revival.

Finally, Edwards notes that there were also various other matters that began to occupy the minds and interest of the people in Northampton instead of matters relating to the revival. There was, for instance, the arrival of the governor of Massachusetts, Jonathan Belcher (1682-1757), in Deerfield, sixteen miles to the north of Northampton, in August, to negotiate a treaty with the Cagnawaga, Housatonic, Scautacook and Mohawk Indians. Nevertheless, those who had been converted continued to have 'a new sense of things, new apprehensions and views of God, of the divine attributes, and Jesus Christ, and the great things of the Gospel'. With regard to all of these, their hearts now knew 'new sweetnesses and delights' and 'an inward ardor and burning of heart'.[67] As we will see, Edwards regards such affections as the evidence of the indwelling of the

Spirit. Thus, his talk about the Spirit 'withdrawing' from Northampton should not be understood literally. It is a metaphor for the waning of what Edwards was surely right to call 'a very extraordinary dispensation of providence'.

He [i.e. the Spirit] comes to give you a sight of the glory of Jesus Christ.[1]

– *Jonathan Edwards, 'The Work of the Spirit of Christ' (1728)*

Chapter 4

THE MOST GLORIOUS OF GOD'S WORKS: SAVING GRACE, NOT THE EXTRAORDINARY GIFTS OF THE SPIRIT

It was an unquestioned theological axiom for most eighteenth-century, English-speaking Protestants that what they called the extraordinary gifts of the Spirit, gifts such as prophecy, glossolalia and miraculous powers, had ceased with the passing of the apostles. The itinerant evangelist George Whitefield, for instance, in his sermon *The Indwelling of the Spirit, the Common Privilege of All Believers* (1739), declares that Christ's promise of the Spirit in John 7:37-39 has nothing to do with receiving power 'to work miracles, or show outward signs and wonders'. Whitefield suggests that such signs and wonders occurred only when 'some new revelation was to be established, as at the first settling of the Mosaic or gospel dispensation'. He is suspicious of 'the spirit of those who insist upon a repetition of such miracles at this time. For the world being now become nominally Christian (though God knows, little of its power is left among us) there need not outward miracles, but only an inward co-operation of the Holy Spirit with the word, to prove that Jesus is the Messiah which was to come into the world'.[2] From Whitefield's point of view, genuine manifestations of these extraordinary gifts of the Spirit occurred only to authenticate the giving of fresh revelation. 'The world being now become nominally Christian' – that is, the 'world' having intellectually accepted the truth of Christianity – the Spirit's work was circumscribed to making this intellectual commitment a reality in heart and life.[3]

It was a few months after the appearance of these remarks in print, when Whitefield was on his second trip to America, that the English preacher wrote his first letter to Edwards. It was to be another year, though, before the two men actually met, for six days, in the autumn of 1740. If Whitefield's pulpit discourse during his time in Northampton is anything to go by, their conversations together would have been centred around the work of the Holy Spirit in revival and the 'plentiful effusion of the Spirit upon believers'.[4] Did they also talk about the gifts of the Spirit and the cessation of those which they and their era described as 'extraordinary'? They may well have done so, for it was an issue that had come to the fore during the final days of the revival in the Connecticut Valley. As we noted in the previous chapter, Edwards records, in the concluding pages of the *Faithful Narrative*, the account of a man from nearby South Hadley, Massachusetts, who 'was possessed with an opinion, that it [i.e. the revival] was the beginning of the glorious times of the church spoken of in Scripture' and that, therefore, 'many in these times ... should be endued with extraordinary gifts of the Holy Ghost'.[5]

Further evidence that Edwards might have raised the subject comes from the two sermons to be examined in this chapter, both a part of *Charity and Its Fruits*, a series of sermons on 1 Corinthians 13 that Edwards preached in 1738.[6] Of the fifteen sermons that comprise this series, two of them, sermons two and fourteen, argue at some length for the cessationist position. Edwards obviously felt there were important reasons to highlight publicly the fact that the extraordinary gifts had ceased once and for all. If the issue did arise, Edwards would have rejoiced to find Whitefield in full agreement with his views. As we shall see, however, the former's reasons for believing that the extraordinary gifts had ceased are somewhat more compelling than the reason offered by Whitefield.

The extraordinary gifts of the Spirit

At Edwards' death in 1758, a considerable number of his writings and sermons remained unpublished. His will, probated on 13 May 1758, bequeathed the manuscripts to his wife, whom he had also named as his executrix.[7] She died later that same year, on October 2. In her will, she specified that ownership of her husband's manuscripts 'should continue to reside in all the children and their heirs'.[8] In 1767, the Edwards children formally committed the manuscripts to Jonathan Edwards Jr (1745-1801), who had them until his death. At that time they passed into the hands of Timothy Dwight (1752-1817), the son of Mary Edwards Dwight (1734-1807) and the president of Yale. Sereno E. Dwight, his son, possessed them after his father's death until the late 1840s, when they became the property of another of Edwards' great-grandsons, Tryon Edwards.

It was Tryon Edwards who decided to undertake the publication of the sermons on 1 Corinthians 13, being rightly convinced that these 'lectures', as he called them, are 'of great interest and value'.[9] However, as Paul Ramsey, the editor of the most recent critical edition of *Charity and Its Fruits*, has clearly shown, Tryon Edwards' edition freely introduces various 'improvements' and abridgements into the text of a number of the sermons, as well as on occasion simplifying Edwards' language. Ramsey's critical edition is primarily based on an early nineteenth-century copy of the original sermons, which are no longer extant.[10] It is this critical edition which has been used in this chapter.

Sermon two, the first of the two sermons to tackle the issue of the gifts of the Spirit, is based on 1 Corinthians 13:1-2. Edwards begins by arguing that two distinctions need to be made when it comes to the gifts of the Spirit. First, those that are 'common' are to be distinguished from those that are saving. For instance, the Spirit can bring about conviction of sin in both the ungodly and the godly, but saving faith and love belong only to the godly. Then, the 'extraordinary or miraculous gifts of the Spirit' must be differentiated from 'the ordinary influences of the Spirit in the saints'. The extraordinary gifts were plentiful in the 'first age of the church till the death of all the apostles', for that was 'the age of miracles'. They are denoted 'extraordinary', since they occur 'only on extraordinary occasions', not in every period of history. They were given in the apostolic era, and certain earlier biblical periods, 'to reveal the mind and will of God before the canon of the Scripture was complete' and to help establish the fledgling church.[11] It should be noted that when Edwards uses the word 'extraordinary' in the earlier *Faithful Narrative*, and in his later *Distinguishing Marks* and *Religious Affections*, he gives the term a somewhat different meaning than in *Charity and Its Fruits*. In this, it is a recognized technical term, part of the standard vocabulary of cessationism. In the writings that relate directly to the revivals of the 1730s and 1740s, however, the word denotes what is unexpected and out of the ordinary.[12]

Edwards does not wish to belittle these extraordinary gifts. Possession of them was indeed a great privilege. After an eloquent passage in which he enumerates a number of biblical characters who were privileged in this regard, men such as Moses and Daniel, Edwards locates their privilege in the fact that Christ himself is a prophet, and thus 'there is in them [i.e. the gifts] a conformity to Christ in his prophetical office'. Edwards also links the 'greatness of the privilege' to the fact that many of those who have been the recipients of these gifts have been 'the most eminent saints'. In these cases, the bestowal of the gifts can only be understood as clear 'tokens of God's extraordinary favor and love'.[13]

The burden of the sermon, though, is to emphasize that though the possession of these gifts is indeed a great privilege, 'the ordinary influences of the Spirit of God working grace in the heart is a far greater privilege'.[14] Edwards is led to this conclusion, first of all, by his exegesis of the text. 1 Corinthians 13, Edwards rightly notes, cannot be divorced from the two chapters on either side of it. From 1 Corinthians 14:1 ['Follow after charity, and desire spiritual gifts'], Edwards observes that love and the gifts are two entirely different things. To determine which of the two is to be preferred, Edwards goes back to 1 Corinthians 12:31. There the apostle Paul has no sooner encouraged his Corinthian readers to desire 'the best gifts' than he urges them to engage themselves wholeheartedly in the pursuit of 'a more excellent way', love, which Paul delineates in chapter 13.[15] Thus, as the New England theologian reads 1 Corinthians 13, the particular question he asks of this text is 'Which is more preferable, the gifts or love?'

When 1 Corinthians 13 and its immediate context is examined in this way, the passage yields the obvious answer that Paul prefers love to the gifts. Paul's actual concern in this passage, however, is somewhat different from the one that Edwards brings to it when he interprets it. Paul is seeking to demonstrate, in this chapter, that love is the criterion that must shape every use of the gifts of the Spirit. Chapter 13 crystallizes Paul's central concern in chapters 12 to 14, which is to maintain that the Corinthians act in love toward one another. Rather than entertaining the choice of either the gifts or love, Paul is insistent that both are necessary.[16]

THE GREATEST PRIVILEGE AND BLESSING[17]

Edwards has sought to magnify these extraordinary gifts in order to offset the far-surpassing blessing of 'the Spirit of God working grace in the heart'. In what constitutes the third major section of the sermon, Edwards proceeds to enumerate nine reasons why the possession of saving grace or holiness is something far greater than 'the spirit of prophecy, or the gift of tongues, or working miracles even to the moving of mountains'.[18] What is significant about this list is that it anticipates many of the same points Edwards will make when he comes to write his spiritual classic, *Religious Affections*, seven or eight years later.

First, the blessing of saving grace 'makes a man's heart and nature excellent'. By it, the believer is constituted a holy person, for 'holiness consists in having grace in the heart'. The extraordinary gifts, on the other hand, have no salvific effect on their possessor's heart and nature. Edwards compares them to garments that a person wears and to 'precious jewels, which a man carries about him'. Neither of these can effect any lasting inner change – unlike grace, 'by which the very soul itself becomes a precious jewel'.[19]

Saving grace effects such a change because it issues from the Spirit's very presence in the believer's heart. Of course, by means of the extraordinary gifts, the Spirit can and does 'produce effects in the man' who possesses them. But these gifts in themselves do not convey holiness. Edwards alludes to Genesis 1:2 to drive home his point: 'The Spirit of God may produce effects on many things to which it does not communicate itself. So the Spirit of God moved on the face of the waters, but not so as to impart himself to the waters.'[20] The Holy Spirit can act upon many things, both animate and inanimate, to which he does not communicate or impart his nature. Thus, in Genesis 1:2, it is stated that the Spirit of God moved upon the face of the waters, but in doing so he did not impart his nature to the watery deep. In the case of an individual human being, a person may be the possessor of powerful, extraordinary gifts and yet not actually be indwelt by the Spirit.

Third, what Edwards calls 'the spiritual image of God' consists not of the 'power to work miracles, and foretell future events', or the possession of any of the Spirit's extraordinary gifts. It lies in being holy, which can result only from having saving grace in the heart.[21] Among Edwards' key theological concepts was the distinction between what he calls the 'natural image of God' and the 'spiritual image of God'.[22] The former consists of 'men's reason and understanding, his natural ability and dominion over the creatures'. The latter, which was lost at the Fall and is restored only in Christ, consists of holiness. Since the 'spiritual image of God' can also be described as 'the amiable image and likeness of Christ',[23] it can readily be seen why Edwards is adamant that saving grace is of far greater value than the extraordinary gifts of the Spirit. Christlikeness has far more to do with 'having the same mind in us which was in Christ, in having the same spirit which he was of, in being meek and lowly of heart' than with doing the miracles that he did.[24]

Then, Edwards takes note of the fact that God bestows the saving grace of his Spirit 'only on his own favorites and children' and that the 'grace of God in the heart is a gift of the Holy Ghost peculiar to the saints'. But it is not so with the various gifts of the Spirit. As Edwards peruses the pages of Scripture he finds that various wicked, unregenerate individuals, such as Balaam, Saul, and Judas Iscariot, prophesied and worked miracles.[25] Though this exercise of the gifts of the Spirit by the unregenerate was unusual, it served to demonstrate that there is no essential link between such extraordinary gifts and genuine spirituality.

In the fifth place, the Spirit's work in the heart of an individual bears an 'infinitely more excellent fruit' than the exercise of the gifts, for the former issues in eternal salvation whereas the latter does not. From scriptural examples such as Judas Iscariot, it is plain that a person may be the recipient of the extraordinary gifts of the Spirit and yet still go to hell. Edwards has Christ's own words in Matthew 7:22-23 to cite as proof in this regard. In this text, Christ predicts that there will be 'many' on the day of judgement who will turn to their exercise of the gifts of prophecy and exorcism, and to the working of wonders, to justify their entry into heaven. But the Lord Christ says he will have to respond to them, 'I never knew you; depart from me, ye that work iniquity.'[26]

Sixth, Edwards asserts that genuine 'happiness consists in holiness', not in the experience of 'extraordinary influences'. Holiness – knowing, serving and loving God, having 'a holy and divine temper of soul' – is sufficient for happiness apart from anything else. As Edwards would later confess in *Distinguishing Marks*, with regard to the possibility of the extraordinary gifts of the Spirit being once more given to the church: 'For my part, I had rather enjoy the sweet influences of the Spirit, shewing Christ's spiritual divine beauty, and infinite grace, and dying love, drawing forth the holy exercises of faith, and divine love, and sweet complacence, and humble joy in God, one quarter of an hour, than to have prophetical visions and revelations for a whole year.'[27]

Moreover, the reason God gave the extraordinary gifts during the apostolic era was the establishment and propagation of the gospel, which in turn would lead men and women to God and promote true holiness in their lives. The extraordinary gifts, then, were designed to serve as the handmaidens, as it were, of saving grace in the history of redemption.[28] This was a conviction Edwards had first expressed a decade earlier, when he wrote in his 'repository for writings on various theological topics', the notebooks called the *Miscellanies*, that the extraordinary gifts were:

… made use of once, only for the introducing of the more perfect way, in which the catholic church of all nations was forever to be instructed. God now communicates himself to his church in a much more excellent and glorious way than that by miracles, etc., by the communications of his Spirit of holiness to the hearts of his people, and his teaching and spiritually instructing us out of the Word. This is infinitely a more excellent way, as the Apostle says (1 Cor. 12:31), 'Covet earnestly the best gifts: and yet I show you a more excellent way. Though I speak with the tongues of men and angels, and have not charity,' etc. This is the end of the other way; it is excellent in itself; but inspiration and miracles are good for nothing without it, as the Apostle plainly tells us in the thirteenth chapter of 1 Corinthians.[29]

It is noteworthy that undergirding both this reflection on the extraordinary gifts subserving saving grace and that in *Charity and Its Fruits* is 1 Corinthians 13. And it is also obvious that this Pauline passage is crucial for the development of Edwards' thinking about the nature of the extraordinary gifts of the Spirit. As we shall see, Edwards develops this specific point at much greater length in the fourteenth sermon of *Charity and Its Fruits*.

Eighth, those who possess the Spirit's extraordinary gifts, yet have no experience of saving grace, will find that this privilege serves only to heighten their hardheartedness and further their ultimate condemnation. Edwards sees such people depicted in the solemn words of Hebrews 6:4-6, especially the phrases that talk of tasting the heavenly gift and being 'made partakers of the Holy Ghost'. These individuals had seen the gifts at work in their lives and had actually felt the power of them in their souls. But they were devoid of 'saving influences of the Spirit', and they found themselves ultimately committing the unpardonable sin, apostasy.[30]

Finally, Edwards points to the eternality of saving grace and divine love as indicative of their greater worth when measured alongside the gifts. Citing 1 Corinthians 13:8 ('Charity never faileth: but whether there be prophecies, they shall fail; whether there be tongues, they shall cease; whether there be knowledge, it shall vanish away'), he concludes that 'divine love will remain throughout all eternity.' The gifts, on the other hand, are but temporary 'means of grace'.[31]

Extraordinary impressions

In what is Edwards' application of this doctrinal teaching, he first of all reiterates that having 'saving grace in the heart' is far greater than any other privilege one can imagine. No other God-given privilege in this world can compare with this, 'the greatest privilege and blessing which God ever bestows on any persons in this world', not even that granted to 'the blessed virgin Mary … that of her should be born the Son of God'.[32] As Edwards would later boldly declare in *Some Thoughts*, 'the work of God in the conversion of one soul … is a more glorious work of God than the creation of the whole material universe: it is the most glorious of God's works'.[33]

Edwards then goes on to deal with a way of thinking that was common to the spirituality of his day. It was thought by many that when spiritual impressions came to the mind with suddenness and force – Edwards refers to them as 'extraordinary impressions' – they were genuinely from God. There were also some who concluded from the fact that when verses of Scripture came 'suddenly, and with ever so great impression', God was revealing something that he was about to do or informing the individual concerned about his or her spiritual state. Thus, if someone was reading Romans 5, and Romans 5:1 ['we have peace with God through our Lord Jesus Christ'] leapt out from the page, as it were, and impressed itself upon the mind of the reader, the reader might conclude from this experience that he or she was regenerate.[34] Edwards believes this thinking to be woefully misguided.

Edwards considers it vital to distinguish between those whom God originally addressed in the biblical record and later readers. Obviously, the two are not identical. Therefore, no reader after the apostolic era, when the canon was completed, is justified in believing that he or she is the recipient of a special divine revelation.[35] Thus, Edwards argues, if these impressions go beyond what the actual text of Scripture says, then they fall into the class of an extraordinary gift of the Spirit. Since these gifts no longer occur, any such revelatory impression after the apostolic era must be a delusion. Moreover, as Edwards has argued to this point in the sermon, such extraordinary gifts in themselves have no salvific value.[36] Yet, it should be noted that Edwards is quite prepared to grant that God can and does use his Word to drive home truth to an individual's mind and conscience. He will later make the distinction in the *Religious Affections* between those impressions that 'arise on occasion of the Scripture', that is, when a portion of the Word of God is being read or heard, and those impressions that 'properly come from the Scripture, as the genuine fruit of the Scripture, and by a right use of it', that is, that are agreeable to the actual meaning of the text being read.[37]

A third point of application concerns the possibility of the gifts being restored in the millennial era. Since this point is covered in greater fullness in Edwards' fourteenth sermon in *Charity and Its Fruits*, we shall leave our discussion of it till later in this chapter. Edwards concludes sermon two with an exhortation to his Christian hearers to consciously live out their lives in the light of the great privilege that is theirs. He urges those who have been the recipients of saving grace to consider 'how great that blessing is which God has bestowed upon them of his mere free love and sovereign grace, and not for any worthiness of theirs; and how great obligations they are under to glorify God: and to glorify Christ, who hath purchased this blessing with his own blood'.[38]

The Holy Spirit, 'the great purchase of Christ'

The fourteenth sermon takes for its text, 1 Corinthians 13:8 ['Charity never faileth; but whether there be prophecies, they shall fail; whether there be tongues, they shall cease; whether there be knowledge, it shall vanish away'], and has for its major theme the eternality of the love that God has given to his church. In exploring this theme, Edwards has more to say about the place that the extraordinary gifts have in the history of redemption and the Spirit's work in that redemptive plan.

In the doctrinal section of the sermon, Edwards begins by emphasizing that 'the great purchase' of Christ's death is the Holy Spirit, an assertion we have seen Edwards develop in his early sermon *The Threefold Work of the Holy Ghost*.[39] In a statement that he will make with increasing frequency in the years to come, Edwards maintains that the 'sum of all those good things in this life, and the life to come, which are purchased for the church is the Holy Spirit'.[40] Adam and Eve had possessed the Spirit prior to the Fall, and he indwelt them. But at the Fall they lost him, an indication to Edwards that they 'had no proper right or sure title to the Spirit'. With Christ's death, however, a fundamental change comes in the way that the Spirit relates to human beings. Those for whom Christ died receive the Spirit on the basis of the 'sure covenant' between Christ and God the Father, a covenant sealed by the blood of Christ. Now the Spirit is not only 'communicated to those who are converted', he is given to them on the basis of this covenant, 'so that he is become theirs'. This section of the sermon concludes with a most telling description of the permanence of the Spirit's indwelling in Christians. Believers need to recognize, Edwards stresses, that 'Christ is become theirs, and therefore his fullness is theirs, his Spirit is theirs, the Spirit of Christ is their purchased and promised possession.'[41]

MIRACULOUS GIFTS OF THE SPIRIT BUT TEMPORARY

The communication of the Spirit to the church during the apostolic era involved the giving of a variety of extraordinary gifts to believers of that day. Unlike the Spirit's indwelling, however, these gifts were but temporary. When those who had enjoyed their use in this world as a 'means of grace' reached heaven, they found that there was neither place nor need for their exercise. Like the 'ordinary' means of grace, such as prayer and the sacraments, the extraordinary gifts were only given for a season. This fact about the realm of the Spirit, Edwards goes on to assert, is analogous to one in the world of agriculture. The fruits of the field 'need tillage, and rain, and the shining of the sun' until they have ripened. But once they have been harvested and 'gathered in', they no longer need these helps for their growth.[42]

Not only were these gifts temporary, as regards the individuals who possessed them, they were also 'but for a season with regard to the church of God as a collective body'. Edwards briefly traces the history of the way in which these gifts have been given since the beginning of the world. Before the writing of Job and the Pentateuch, in Edwards' thinking, the earliest books of the Bible, the Spirit of God had communicated in 'dreams and visions' and 'immediate revelation'. Adam and Eve, Enoch (who had the gift of prophecy according to Jude 14), Noah, the patriarchs (Abraham, Isaac, Jacob and Joseph), Job and his friends were all favoured with 'many immediate revelations'. After a period of time when such gifts were not given, Moses and a succession of Old Testament prophets received these gifts. At the death of the last of these prophets, Malachi, there followed another 'great intermission of several hundred years', until the dawn of the apostolic era, when the Spirit once again began bestowing his extraordinary gifts. Even though these gifts were plentiful in the church at that time, this 'age of miracles' lasted for only 100 years. Once the canon of Scripture was complete, 'an established written revelation of the mind and will of God', which could serve as a 'standing rule' for the church throughout the ages, 'then the miraculous gifts of the Spirit ceased'. And this cessation Edwards sees as a direct fulfilment of Paul's statement in 1 Corinthians 13:8.[43]

At the end of this sermon, Edwards will consider a possible future scenario in which these gifts are fully restored to the church. One of the reasons that he will firmly reject this possibility is that believers 'have no need of another Scripture', they already have 'a perfect rule by which to walk'. If the canon of Scripture were indeed imperfect and needed an addition, then the gifts of revelation would be needed, as well as the power to work miracles, since 'it is requisite that revelation should be confirmed by miracles'.[44]

A further reason Edwards emphasizes the cessation of the gifts with such confidence is that he is employing what Ramsey has called a 'means-end argument'.[45] The extraordinary gifts are but a means to an end, and once that end is reached they no longer have a purpose. As we have seen, Edwards touched on this in his earlier sermon, sermon two. 'Revelations and miracles' were given so as 'to promote the setting up and building up of Christ's kingdom in men's hearts' and for 'revealing and confirming the mind and will of God'. This was achieved with the inscripturation of the canon, which Edwards can describe as 'the great and principal means of grace'. No longer needed by the church, the gifts can thus cease. Divine love, on the other hand, is *the* end that the miraculous and revelatory gifts are ultimately designed to promote. Consequently, it 'remains when the means cease'; indeed, 'it remains forever'.[46]

THE MILLENNIUM AND THE EXTRAORDINARY GIFTS

History's course, though, has not yet finished and it might well be the case that there would be a future restoration of the gifts. In particular, 'some have thought', Edwards says, 'that the extraordinary gifts of the Spirit of God are to be restored in the future glorious times of the church' – that is, in the millennium. Edwards does not specify who the 'some' are that he has in mind at this point, though he does go on to describe them as 'many divines' and 'some now living'.[47] One influential Puritan author who seems to advocate a restoration of the gifts in the millennial era is Thomas Goodwin (1600-1680), the English Congregationalist. In his *A Glimpse of Sions Glory: or, The Churches Beautie specified*, he states that among the characteristics of the church in the millennium is that 'the gift of the saints shall be abundantly raised. He that is weak shall be as David, and he that is strong as the Angel of the Lord, Zech. 12:8, and then shall be accomplished that promise, that God "will pour his Spirit on them; and their young men shall see visions, and their old men shall dream dreams" (Joel 2:28). It was fulfilled in part upon the Apostles, but the full is not till that time knowledge shall be increased'.[48]

Edwards, like many of the seventeenth-century Puritans he admired, firmly believed in a future golden age for the church within the realm of history, a period of unprecedented growth and prosperity for the church immediately prior to the final coming of Christ.[49] Some remarks that were once said of Samuel Hopkins, one of Edwards' closest friends and most influential disciples, could easily have been said of his mentor: 'The millennium was more than a belief to him. It had the freshness of visible things. He was at home in it.'[50] As Edwards envisioned this golden age, it was to be characterized by an outpouring of the Spirit 'in measures so much more abundant than ever were before'. This rich outpouring, though, would not include a restoration of the extraordinary gifts. 1 Corinthians 12:31, Edwards reminds his hearers, had called upon God's people to seek 'a more excellent way' than the pursuit of the gifts. This 'more excellent way' is nothing less than 'the influence of the Spirit of God working charity or divine love in the heart'. Since this future era in the church's history is to be 'vastly more glorious than all that was ever before it', he reasons that the Spirit will be poured out in a way commensurate with the excellency of that era.[51]

Furthermore, 1 Corinthians 13:8 and the next two verses talk of that which is imperfect, the extraordinary gifts, disappearing with the advent of that which is far more perfect, 'the influence of the Spirit of God in love'. The presence of the extraordinary gifts thus bespeaks a time of imperfection in the church's history, a time when the church is in its infancy. Edwards supports this latter remark by citing 1 Corinthians 13:11, a verse that speaks of 'childish things' being put away. The millennial state, on the other hand, is a period when 'the church is come, as it were, to the stature of a man', a clear allusion to Ephesians 4:13, a verse that is cited earlier in the sermon. Presumably the reference to childhood in 1 Corinthians 13:11 suggested it as a good contrast. Thus, the Northampton preacher concludes: 'The Apostle seems to call these gifts of prophecy and working miracles childish things in comparison with that nobler fruit of the Spirit, divine love.'[52]

Nor does God need these miraculous gifts to introduce the 'glorious times of the church'. Explicitly referring to the way that he had seen the Spirit of God work in the revival at Northampton in 1734 and 1735, Edwards is confident that if 'the Spirit of God be poured out only in his gracious influences in converting souls, and infusing divine love into them in such a measure as he may, this will be enough without revelations or miracles to produce all the effects which need to be produced in order to bring about the glorious times'.[53]

The sermon concludes with a renewed warning to be 'exceedingly cautious' about regarding mental impressions as special revelation from God and an exhortation to earnestly seek 'Christian and divine love'. To have the latter, Edwards states in characteristic fashion, is to 'have that within us which will be of an immortal nature, and which will be a sure evidence of our own blessed immortality, and the beginning of eternal life in our souls'.[54]

We live in a day wherein God is doing marvellous things; in that respect we are distinguished from former generations.[1]

– *Jonathan Edwards to William McCulloch*

Chapter 5

THE TRANSATLANTIC EVANGELICAL REVIVAL

THE FINAL DECADES of the seventeenth century witnessed a definite decline of piety and morals in transatlantic British society. Attestation of this fact is found in both public documents and private testimonies. Here, for example, is the witness of the London Baptist author, Benjamin Keach (1640-1704), writing in 1701 about the situation in the English capital:

> Was ever sodomy so common in a christian nation, or so notoriously and frequently committed, as by too palpable evidences it appears to be, in and about this city, notwithstanding the clear light of the gospel which shines therein, and the great pains taken to reform the abominable profaneness

that abounds? Is it not a wonder the patience of God hath not consumed us in his wrath, before this time? Was ever swearing, blasphemy, whoring, drunkenness, gluttony, self-love, and covetousness, at such a height, as at this time here?[2]

Despite the presence of gospel-centred ministries and various societies which were created in the late seventeenth and early eighteenth centuries to bring about moral reform, homosexuality, profanity, sexual immorality, drunkenness and gluttony became increasingly widespread in Great Britain. In New England, this same period saw a decline in the public influence of the clergy, the prevalence of sin, even among church members, and a dearth of conversions. And the next three decades saw little improvement. Increasingly, orthodox ministers on both sides of the Atlantic prayed for and preached about what they saw as the only remedy to this situation: the outpouring of the Holy Spirit.[3] Isaac Watts and John Guyse, the English Dissenters who arranged for the publication of the first edition of Edwards' *Faithful Narrative*, may be considered typical in this regard. 'May a plentiful effusion of the blessed Spirit', they prayed in their preface to this work, 'descend on the British Isles and all their American plantations, to renew the face of religion there.'[4]

Revival comes to Great Britain[5]

Now, it is an amazing fact that when the revival for which this prayer longs actually came to Great Britain, it did not originate among the fellow Dissenters of Watts and Guyse. Though biblical orthodoxy had by and large been kept alive by these heirs of Puritanism, it was from within that body which had actually persecuted the Puritans, namely, the Church of England, that revival broke forth.

The first flames of full-fledged revival in the British Isles were visible in Wales. In 1735, the two men who were to be the leaders of the revival in Wales, Howel Harris and Daniel Rowland (1711-1790), were converted. By 1750, their preaching and spirituality, and that of others such as Howel Davies (d.1770) and William Williams of Pantycelyn (1717-1791), had brought about the creation of 433 religious societies. Known to history as the Calvinistic Methodists, these societies would set the tone and character of the Welsh people for the next century and a half.[6] All of these early Calvinistic Methodist leaders were convinced of the vital importance of having the Holy Spirit's power and anointing on their various ministries. As Harris once asked: 'What is the Bible but a dead letter to us till we do experience the work of the Holy Spirit in us, not one or other separately, but both together?'[7]

Another Celtic land deeply impacted by the revival was Scotland. Local awakenings occurred sporadically during the 1720s and 1730s. Typical of these revivals was one that took place in 1739 at Nigg, Easter Ross, near Cromarty, where forty were converted during this one year.[8] A far more extensive work began at Cambuslang in the Lowlands a few years later in 1742, under the preaching of William McCulloch (1691-1771), the minister of Cambuslang, at that time a rural parish a few miles southeast of Glasgow. McCulloch was far from being an accomplished speaker. In the jargon then current, he was a yill- or ale-minister, a term that was used of ministers whose preaching was so dry that when their turn came to preach at the large outdoor communion gatherings then held once a year by the Scottish churches, many of the audience would leave to quench their thirst from nearby ale barrels provided for refreshment.[9] Yet it was under McCulloch's preaching in mid-February 1742, that, according to the English Nonconformist Philip Doddridge, around 130 people, most of whom had sat under McCulloch's preaching for a number of years, 'were awakened on a sudden to attend to it, as if it had been a new revelation brought down from heaven, and attested by as astonishing miracles as ever were wrought by Peter or Paul'.[10]

In July of the same year, George Whitefield arrived at Cambuslang, where he was soon preaching to huge, receptive audiences. In August, for instance, some 30,000 attended an outdoor communion service, where Whitefield preached a number of sermons over the course of a three-day weekend. Alexander Webster, a minister from Edinburgh, wrote of some of the happenings of that weekend:

During the time of divine worship, solemn, profound reverence overspread every countenance. They hear as for eternity... Thousands are melted into tears. Many cry out in the bitterness of their soul. Some ... from the stoutest man to the tenderest child, shake and tremble and a few fall down as dead. Nor does this happen only when men of warm address alarm them with the terrors of the law, but when the most deliberate preacher speaks of redeeming love.[11]

A number of the Scottish ministers involved in the leadership of this revival – men such as William McCulloch, John McLaurin (1693-1724) of the Ramshorn Church in northwest Glasgow, James Robe (1688-1753) of Kilsyth and John Erskine of Kirkintilloch – would become close correspondents of Edwards.

The ministry of George Whitefield

The man who bound together the British and American dimensions of this revival in his own person was George Whitefield.[12] Whitefield was the youngest son of the proprietor of an inn in Gloucester. At school he had been unremarkable. He left school early, and when his older brother took over running the inn, he became one of his brother's servants. But his mother longed for something better for her son. Her persistence and the kindness of friends enabled him in December 1732 to enter Oxford University. It was here that he first met John Wesley and his younger brother Charles (1707-1788), later co-leaders in the revival, and it was in Oxford that he was subsequently converted in the spring of 1735. The following year he was ordained a deacon in the Church of England and preached his first sermon.

Within months of this sermon he was in great demand as a preacher, as he spoke powerfully and with authority on justification by faith, the new birth and repentance. Such preaching, though, was not well received by the majority of the Anglican clergy, and churches began to be barred to him. Joseph Butler (1692-1752), the bishop of Bristol, criticized Whitefield for what he regarded as nothing less than fanaticism. In an interview with John Wesley on 18 August 1739, Butler accused both of the

George Whitefield

Engraving based on the portrait of George Whitefield by Nathaniel Hone.

evangelists of 'pretending to extraordinary revelations and gifts of the Holy Ghost', which he found 'a horrid thing – a very horrid thing'.[13] Of course, if Whitefield had been present, he would have rightly disputed the accuracy of Butler's accusation. This perception of Whitefield, though, would stick to his name throughout the crest of the revival in the 1740s. For example, John Callender, a Baptist pastor in Newport, Rhode Island, denounced Whitefield as 'a second George Fox', obviously convinced that Whitefield, like Fox, promoted the restoration of the extraordinary gifts of the Spirit.[14]

Whitefield, however, was not to be deterred. On 17 February 1739, he took to the open air and preached to a group of coal miners on the outskirts of Bristol, who lived in dire poverty without any church nearby. There were around 200 at that service. Within weeks, Whitefield was preaching thirty or so times a week to crowds of 10,000 or more! Whitefield's description of his ministry to these coal miners is a classic one. To visualize the scene, picture the green countryside, the piles of coal, the squalid huts, and the deep semicircle of unwashed faces, as we read his words:

> Having no righteousness of their own to renounce, they were glad to hear of a Jesus who was a friend of publicans, and came not to call the righteous, but sinners to repentance. The first discovery of their being affected was to see the white gutters made by their tears which plentifully fell down their black cheeks, as they came out of their coal pits. Hundreds and hundreds of them were soon brought under deep convictions, which, as the event proved, happily ended in a sound and thorough conversion. The change was visible to all, though numbers chose to impute it to anything, rather than the finger of God.[15]

Over the thirty-four years between Whitefield's ordination as deacon and his death in 1770, in Newburyport, Massachusetts, it is calculated that he preached around 18,000 sermons. Actually, if one includes all of the talks that he gave, he probably spoke about 1,000 times a year during his ministry. A pioneer in open-air preaching, many of his sermons were delivered to congregations of 10,000 or so, some to as large a gathering as 20,000. Moreover, in a day of laboriously slow travel, he visited Scotland fifteen times, traversed the Atlantic thirteen times, and crisscrossed much of the English and Welsh countryside.

There are a number of reasons for the key role that Whitefield played in the rapid spread of the revival throughout British society on both sides of the Atlantic. First, the Anglican evangelist addressed his hearers simply as fellow human beings, so that distinctions of rich and poor, educated and uneducated, ceased to matter. The Anglican Church and its ministers had been largely unable to reach the lower classes prior to the revival. But Whitefield spoke in such a way that he was readily understood and appreciated by the poor and uneducated as well as by the wealthy and learned.

He put spiritual issues to his hearers as one who transparently loved them and longed for them to be saved. Many who came to mock the preacher and laugh at his doctrine went away sobered, and ultimately converted, as they heard of the love of God in Christ and felt that love in Whitefield's impassioned preaching. Then, Whitefield spoke as one who sought to awaken and grip the heart. Unlike many of his Anglican contemporaries who preached mere moralism and were lacking in zeal, Whitefield spoke to the whole man with passion and without mincing any words.[16]

There is, however, a more fundamental reason for Whitefield's success: his life and ministry had upon it the anointing of the Holy Spirit, as did other preachers in the revival of his day. This reason is found in a letter that the Welsh evangelist Howel Harris wrote to George Whitefield in 1743, as he gave his friend what can be regarded as a classic description of the eighteenth-century evangelical revival:

> The outpouring of the Blessed Spirit is now so plentiful and common, that I think it was our deliberate observation that not one sent by Him opens his mouth without some remarkable showers. He comes either as a Spirit of wisdom to enlighten the soul, to teach and build up, and set out the works of light and darkness, or else a Spirit of tenderness and

love, sweetly melting the souls like the dew, and watering the graces; or as the Spirit of hot burning zeal, setting their hearts in a flame, so that their eyes sparkle with fire, love, and joy; or also such a Spirit of uncommon power that the heavens seem to be rent, and hell to tremble.[17]

As Edwards would also maintain, the revival was ultimately a sovereign work of God the Holy Spirit, one that could not be manufactured or conjured up, let alone controlled. The Spirit anointed and blessed the labours of various preachers and it was he who enabled them to see such a great work of God, whereby God completely reshaped many facets and sectors of society on both sides of the Atlantic.

Revival in New England

In the middle of the winter of 1740, Jonathan Edwards sat down at his desk to write a letter of invitation to George Whitefield to come and preach for his congregation in Northampton that summer. He had heard, he told Whitefield, that the English evangelist was 'one who has the blessing of heaven' attending him wherever he went, and he hoped that 'such a blessing' might descend on Northampton, enter his house, and even fill his own soul. 'It has been with refreshment of soul', Edwards continued, 'that I have heard of one raised up in the Church of England to revive the mysterious, spiritual, despised and exploded[18] doctrines of the gospel, and full of a Spirit of zeal for the promotion of real, vital piety, whose labours have been attended with such success. Blessed be God that hath done it! who is with you, and helps you, and makes the weapons of your warfare mighty.'[19]

Whitefield had been in America three and a half months at this point, and when Edwards wrote to him he was wintering in Georgia. He arrived in New England, not in the summer as Edwards had hoped, but in mid-September.[20] His coming long anticipated by many of the New England ministers, he quickly threw himself into a breathtaking round of itinerant preaching. In Boston and its neighbourhood, where he preached for twenty-six days, the response to his ministry was overwhelming. His farewell sermon on the city common on 12 October 1741, for instance, drew more than 20,000 listeners, the largest crowd ever assembled in America to that point in history.

After Whitefield left Boston for Northampton, churches in the Boston area continued to be thronged. That winter William Cooper, the assistant pastor of Brattle Street Church, declared that 'more came to him in one week in deep concern about their souls, than had come in the whole twenty-four years of his preceding ministry'.[21] In November 1741, when he wrote the preface for Edwards' *Distinguishing Marks*, Cooper testified that the entire face of Boston had been changed. Taverns and dance halls were much less frequented than before. The Christian faith was more a topic of regular and daily conversation in peoples' homes than Cooper had ever known. 'The doctrines of grace' were 'espoused and relished'; private religious meetings 'greatly multiplied'; opportunities for public worship well attended with 'attentive and serious' auditors. 'There is indeed', Cooper emphasized, 'an extraordinary appetite after the sincere milk of the word.'[22]

Whitefield spent six days with Edwards, from Friday, 17 October, to the following Wednesday, 22 October.[23] As he preached from the Northampton pulpit on Sunday morning, Whitefield later noted in his diary that 'Edwards wept during the whole time of exercise' and that the congregation were 'equally affected'. During the afternoon service, he recorded, 'the power increased yet more'. In all Whitefield spoke on five occasions in the town, and, Edwards later wrote in 1743, 'the congregation was extraordinarily melted by every sermon', with 'almost the whole assembly being in tears' during the preaching.[24] Whitefield's affective preaching had rekindled the fires of revival in the Massachusetts town, as the following months would show.

Not only in Northampton and Boston, though, did the fires of revival burn white hot after the preaching tour of Whitefield, who left New England that November. Revival swept this heartland of Puritan theology for the next two years, yielding a harvest of between 30,000 to 40,000 new church members.[25] Yet, as Edwards and those who promoted this revival were to learn, revivals are inevitably disfigured works of God.

The wildest Enthusiast I ever saw

A key element in the disfigurement of this revival came from 'enthusiasm', one of the great bugbears of the eighteenth century.[26] In the mindset of that era, enthusiasm involved the claim of extraordinary revelations and powers from the Holy Spirit, though the word could be also used more loosely to describe any kind of religious excitement.[27] For instance, in a letter written by the Scottish nobleman James Ramsay (1736-1814) of Ochtertyre to his cousin Elizabeth Graham in 1800, Ramsay quoted with approval the definition of enthusiasm by Edmund Gibson (1669-1748), the bishop of London and an early critic of the evangelical revival. 'Enthusiasm', according to Ramsay's rendering of the bishop's words, 'is a strong persuasion that [one is] guided by immediate impulses and impressions of the Holy Spirit, not distinguishing 'twixt the ordinary and extraordinary operations.' The latter, Ramsay further informed his cousin, were unique to 'the apostles and other first propagators of the gospel' and involved the ability 'to work miracles and speak with tongues'.[28]

Chief among the 'enthusiasts' who troubled the revival in America has to be reckoned James Davenport, who came from a distinguished Puritan forebear and pastored a Congregationalist church in Southhold, Long Island.[29] Davenport became acquainted with Whitefield in 1740 in New York and soon sought to imitate the success of the English evangelist. Itinerating throughout New England he was led, however, into increasingly fanatical attitudes and patterns of behaviour. When he came into a town he would interrogate the minister as to his spiritual state. Those who refused to answer his questions or whose answers did not satisfy him he declared to be unconverted and unfit to be spiritual leaders. He would then encourage the members of their congregations to forsake them and conduct their own meetings. Invariably, he would publicly upbraid those members of the clergy he deemed to be unconverted. For example, at New Haven, he branded the pastor Joseph Noyes 'an unconverted hypocrite and the devil incarnate', a veritable 'Wolf in Sheep's Cloathing', and urged his congregation to desert him.[30] In East Hampton, Long Island, he denounced

Nathanael Huntting (d.1753), the venerable Puritan minister of the town, as 'a carnal old Pharisee' and as 'unconverted'.[31] Moreover, those individuals whom he considered regenerate he would call 'brother' or 'sister', the rest 'neighbour'. Not surprisingly, wherever Davenport went he left divided congregations in his wake.

Davenport – and others like him, such as his friend, Andrew Croswell (1709-1785), the pastor of a Congregationalist church in Groton, Connecticut[32] – began to assure individuals who fell to the ground, or who experienced bodily tremors, or who saw visions while they were preaching that such experiences were a sure sign of the Spirit's converting work.[33] In Croswell's words, only those who have had such 'divine Manifestations … know what true Holiness means'.[34] He asserted that 'God never works powerfully, but men cry out disorder; for God's order differs vastly from their nice and delicate apprehensions' of him.[35] Davenport, for his part, claimed to have the ability to distinguish who was among the elect of God, a 'gift' which he especially sought to exercise when he called into question the spiritual state of those ministers who had refused to allow him to preach from their pulpits.

Prominent also in Davenport's ministry was a devotion to loud, boisterous singing. Davenport's followers would engage in such singing out in the streets, at the top of their lungs, and frequently at night, to the great consternation of others. Moreover, while vibrant singing has regularly been a mark of movements of revival in the history of the church, some of the lyrics written by Davenport were cause for deep concern. For instance, in 'A Song of Praise for Joy in the Holy Ghost' (1742), Davenport wrote the following of the Holy Spirit's work in the believer's life:

> This makes me Abba Father cry,
>   With confidence of soul.
> It makes me cry, My Lord, My God,
>   And that without control.[36]

To profess the loss of self-control as the work of the Spirit of God was worrisome to both advocates and critics of the revival.

The most bizarre episode of Davenport's career took place in March 1743, in the town of New London, Connecticut, where Davenport and a number of his followers had established a seminary known as the Shepherd's Tent.[37] Under the guidance 'received from the Spirit in dreams', Davenport directed his followers in the afternoon of Sunday, 6 March, just as the inhabitants of the town were returning home from public worship, to publicly dissociate themselves from the 'heresy' of Puritan New England by burning in a bonfire a large quantity of books. Among the books burnt that day, there were said to be works by such well-known Puritans as John Flavel, Matthew Henry (1662-1714) and Increase Mather. Davenport's followers then proceeded to dance around the bonfire praising God and shouting 'Hallelujah' and 'Gloria Patri' (Glory to the Father).

The following day a second bonfire was prepared, this time intended to consume the 'idolatry' of Davenport and his followers. Anything that smacked of the 'world' and worldly pride – 'wigs, cloaks and breeches, hood, gowns, rings, jewels and necklaces' – was heaped up, ready to be consumed. Davenport himself stripped off his breeches and hove them onto the pile to be burned. At this point, a bystander said to Davenport that he thought him demonized, to which the latter surprisingly agreed. Smitten with contrition for his actions, Davenport soon quit Connecticut for Long Island, a broken and shattered man.

Although Davenport would later confess that he had been wrong in much of what he had said and done,[38] he had helped to spark a 'wildfire' spirit that in many places made havoc of the revival. Moreover, he had furnished anti-revival forces with ammunition for their attacks. These forces were captained by Charles Chauncy, co-pastor of the most prestigious Congregationalist church in Boston, who could say of Davenport, in particular, 'He is the wildest Enthusiast I ever saw.'[39]

CHARLES CHAUNCY'S ATTACK ON THE REVIVAL

Chauncy had first written of the revival in 1741, when he actually gave thanks for what the Spirit of God was doing. He has no doubt, he writes, that there are 'a number in this land, upon whom God has graciously shed the influence of this blessed Spirit', something for which he and his readers ought to be thankful. Yet, he goes on to note some concerns. There have arisen 'unchristian heats and animosities' along with 'rash, censorious, uncharitable judging. Evil speaking, reviling and slandering' have become all too common.[40] Here, Chauncy clearly has in view the uncharitable way that men such as Davenport often treated those whom they judged to be unconverted.

By the following year, the prominent Boston pastor had become much more critical. In July of that year Davenport had appeared in Boston and specifically sought out Chauncy to pronounce judgement on the latter's spirituality. The encounter, which took place in the doorway of Chauncy's study, decisively turned the latter against the revival. He quickly fired off a sermon, published as *Enthusiasm Described and Cautioned Against*, in which he accused Davenport and his ilk of being 'enthusiasts', who show their true colours by their blatant disregard of the 'dictates of reason'.[41] As a safeguard against their fanaticism, he first encourages his hearers and readers to use the Scriptures – 'the great rule of religion, the grand test in matters of salvation' – to test what was going in New England. He also draws attention to the fact that 'the Spirit of God deals with men as reasonable creatures.' Reason, though not to be set up in place of God's revelation in the Bible, was essential to the Christian life. Failure to use it, as Davenport and his followers appeared to be doing, was a sure way to fall into 'all manner of delusion'.[42]

In particular, Chauncy stresses that the arousal of one's 'passions and affections' needs to be carefully monitored. The 'passions', when properly acted upon by the Spirit, 'tend mightily to awaken the reasonable powers'. If one's passions are set ablaze, but one's reason and understanding are not enlightened, it is all to no avail. Reason and judgement, the 'more noble part' of the human being, must be pre-eminent in all religious experience, otherwise it is but a sham and 'enthusiasm'. Real religion, he concludes, is 'a sober, calm, reasonable thing'.[43]

At the beginning of the following month, Chauncy penned a further attack on the revival in an open letter that he wrote to a minister in Scotland. In it, Chauncy declares: 'There never was such a spirit of superstition and enthusiasm reigning in the land before; never such gross disorders and barefaced affronts to common decency; never such scandalous reproaches on the Blessed Spirit, making him the author of the greatest irregularities and confusions.' Again Chauncy expresses a hope that through the events of the revival 'a good Number ... have settled into a truly Christian temper'. Nevertheless, he is firmly persuaded that in general the revival is nothing more than the 'effect of enthusiastic heat'.

> The goodness that has been so much talked of, 'tis plain to me, is nothing more, in general, than a commotion in the passions. I can't see that Men have been made better, if hereby be meant, their being formed to a nearer resemblance to the divine being in moral holiness. 'Tis not evident to me, that persons, generally, have a better understanding of religion, a better government of their passions, a more Christian love to their neighbour, or that they are more decent and regular in their devotions towards God. I am clearly of the mind, they are worse in all these regards. They place their religion so much in the heat and fervour of their passions, that they too much neglect their reason and judgment.[44]

For Chauncy, the excesses of the revival revealed its true nature: it was not at all a work of God's Holy Spirit, but merely an instance of uncontrolled emotionalism. Viewing the revival through the lens of the antics of Davenport and others like him, it is not at all surprising that Chauncy came to the conclusion that the revival was mostly heat with little light, and therefore to be rejected as spurious.

Chauncy's main attack on the revival was his *Seasonable Thoughts on the State of Religion in New-England* (1743). It continued to press home what Chauncy saw as the main work of the Spirit, the enlightenment of the mind. 'An enlightened mind, and not raised affections', he stated, 'ought always to be the guide of those who call themselves men; and this, in the affairs of religion, as well as other things: And it will be so, where God really works on their hearts, by his Spirit.'[45]

Edwards thus found himself in the unenviable position of giving an answer to both sides in the debate about the nature of the revival. To the 'pious zealots' such as Davenport he would stress the point that biblical Christianity must involve the mind and reason: when God converts a person, light is shed upon the mind. On the other hand, there is much more to conversion than enlightenment. In response to Chauncy and those of his persuasion, he would thus maintain that genuine spirituality flows from a heart aflame with the love of God. There is no genuine Christianity without a warm heart.

Let us turn, then, to look at the first of the books that Edwards penned in charting this *via media*.

I had rather enjoy the sweet influences of the Spirit, shewing Christ's spiritual divine beauty, and infinite grace, and dying love ... one quarter of an hour, than to have prophetical visions and revelations for a whole year.

– *Jonathan Edwards,* Distinguishing Marks of a Work of the Spirit of God

Chapter 6

THE AUTHENTIC SPIRIT [1]

On 10 September 1741, Edwards addressed the faculty and students of Yale College at the school's annual commencement exercises.[2] His address was based on 1 John 4:1 – 'Beloved, believe not every spirit, but try the spirits whether they are of God: because many false prophets are gone out into the world' – and sought to deal with the rising opposition to the revival. A couple of months after the address, Edwards had it published 'with great enlargements'. The published treatise contains an introduction and three main sections. In his introduction, Edwards notes that the main purpose of 1 John 4 is to set forth 'some certain rules, distinguishing and clear marks', whereby the church might discern what is and what is not a genuine work of the Spirit. In the first section of the work,

Edwards enumerates nine 'negative signs' or evidences, which *cannot* be used to determine whether or not the Spirit is at work in an individual's life or corporately in revival. Then come five 'sure, distinguishing Scripture evidences and marks' of a genuine work of the Holy Spirit. Finally, in what amounts to roughly half of the entire work, Edwards provides an application to the situation of his day. It should be noted that this device of enumerating signs of the Spirit's work is not unique to Edwards. Puritan predecessors such as Cotton Mather had also done it on occasion.[3] In the hands of Edwards, though, it will ultimately reach the level of a fine art, as he hones his skill in discernment to produce the refined maturity of the *Religious Affections*. As Perry Miller rightly judged: 'Puritanism is the essence of Protestantism, and Edwards is the quintessence of Puritanism.'[4]

THE NEGATIVE SIGNS

The fact that a work said to be of the Spirit involves what is 'very unusual and extraordinary' says nothing about its spiritual authenticity. True to the Reformation principle of *sola scriptura*, Edwards refuses to allow 'what the church has been used to' as 'a rule by which we are to judge' spiritual phenomena.[5] As he emphasized in his introduction to this work, the Scriptures are 'the great and standing rule which God has given to his church' to discern spiritual authenticity. They and they alone are 'infallible and sufficient'.[6] As long as a phenomenon does not violate Scripture, one cannot say that it is not from God. Here, Edwards wishes to safeguard the sovereignty of the Spirit. As he says: 'We know that he [i.e. the Holy Spirit] uses a great variety; and we can't tell how great a variety he may use, within the compass of the rules he himself has fixed.' Believers must ever be careful not to set up their standards of conduct, their experience or their theological perspectives as *the* criteria by which the Spirit must act. 'We ought not to limit God', Edwards warns, 'where he has not limited himself.'[7]

Nor should a work be judged spurious because men and women are moved to 'tears, trembling, groans, loud outcries, agonies of body, or the failing of bodily strength'. Scripture, nor reason for that matter, does not rule out the possibility of such taking place in a genuine work of God. Edwards believes that there may well be a few instances in the Bible that allude to physical effects accompanying a genuine work of the Holy Spirit. When the Philippian jailor, for example, fell down before Paul and Silas, and asked them what he must do to be saved (Acts 16:29-30), 'his falling down seems to be from the same cause as his trembling' and came from 'real convictions of conscience'.

Later, in his *magnum opus* on what constitutes true spirituality, the *Religious Affections*, Edwards will admit that he knows of no reason why 'a view of God's glory should not cause the body to faint'.[8] Indeed, there are a number of scriptural texts that indicate that 'true divine discoveries, or ideas of God's glory, when given in a great degree, have a tendency, by affecting the mind, to overbear the body'.[9] Edwards refers to passages such as Psalm 119:120, where the psalmist expressly states that his 'flesh trembleth for fear' of God, or Revelation 1:17, here, at the vision of the risen Christ, the apostle John 'fell at his feet as dead'.[10] Were God to display but a little of that which is seen of him by saints and angels in heaven, our frail natures would sink under the weight of the display. Those who say that God cannot or will not 'give the like clear and affecting ideas and apprehensions of the same real glory and majesty of his nature' in his day, Edwards considers 'very bold and daring'.[11]

Underlying all of these remarks is Edwards' deep conviction, as he put it in *Distinguishing Marks*, that the Scriptures are 'the great and standing rule which God has given to his church' to discern spiritual authenticity. They and they alone are 'infallible and sufficient'.[12] As long as a phenomenon does not violate Scripture, one cannot say that it is not from God. Believers must be careful not to set up their standards of conduct, their experience or their theological perspectives as *the* criteria by which the Spirit must act. In the words of Edwards:

> Many are guilty of not taking the Holy Scriptures as a sufficient and whole rule… Scripture rules respect the state of the mind, and persons' moral conduct, and voluntary behaviour, and not the physical state of the body. The design of the

Scripture is to teach us divinity, and not physic and anatomy. Ministers are made the watchmen of men's souls, and not their bodies; and therefore the great rule which God has committed into their hands is to make them divines, and not physicians. Christ knew what instructions and rules his church would stand in need of better than we do; and, if he had seen it needful in order to the church's safety, he doubtless would have given to ministers rules to judge of bodily effects and would have told 'em how the pulse should beat under such and such religious exercises of mind; when men should look pale, and when they should shed tears; when they should tremble, and whether or no they should ever be faint or cry out; or whether the body should ever be put into convulsions... But he has not done it, because he did not see it to be needful.[13]

On the other hand, these physical phenomena ultimately can tell us nothing as to the spiritual state of the one undergoing them. As a guide to spiritual discernment they are valueless, for there is 'no rule of Scripture given us' to determine the Spirit's presence by physical effects.[14] Moreover, as we have already seen in the examination of sermon two of *Charity and Its Fruits*, the Holy Spirit can act upon many things, both animate and inanimate, which he does not indwell.[15] 'The degree of the influence of the Spirit of God', Edwards will conclude in the final section of *Distinguishing Marks*, is never 'to be determined by the degree of effect on men's bodies.'[16]

It is important to note that Edwards' remarks here in *Distinguishing Marks* are drawn from his own personal experience and observation. Only a few months before he wrote these words, in May 1741, Edwards had been speaking to a small group of believers gathered in a private home in Northampton. Just as he was about to conclude, one or two individuals, 'so greatly affected with a sense of the greatness and glory of divine things' were physically overcome. Within minutes many in the room were visibly affected, so that 'the whole room was full of nothing but outcries, faintings, and such like'.[17]

A couple of months later, on 8 July, Edwards preached a sermon that has long been remembered, *Sinners in the Hands of an Angry God*. On the basis of this one sermon, Edwards has been unjustly labelled in the American memory as primarily a hell-fire preacher. In fact, this sermon was atypical for Edwards. He more frequently preached on heaven. But he was never reticent to declare all that Scripture says about the future of the impenitent. As he preached in Enfield, Connecticut, that day, there soon arose in the meeting house, in the words of one then present, 'a great moaning & crying out through the whole house – What shall I do to be saved – oh I am going to hell – what shall I do for Christ, etc. etc. so that the minister was obliged to desist – the shrieks and cries were piercing & amazing'.[18] Although Edwards was hopeful, in both cases, that some of those who underwent the various physical phenomena were actually subject to the regenerating power of the Holy Spirit, it was not the physical effects upon which he based his hope.

Furthermore, the fact that a work occasions controversy and 'a great deal of noise about religion' cannot be used as a criterion to judge the work. 'What a mighty opposition was there in Jerusalem', Edwards rightly notes, 'on occasion of that great effusion of the Spirit!'[19] Nor should the fact that people have 'great impressions [made] on their imaginations' and are subject to visions be used to write off a work as spurious. As we have already seen in the previous chapter, Edwards is certain that interpreting these experiences as 'prophetical visions, divine revelations', and 'significations from heaven' is wrong. Nevertheless, God has made human beings with the faculty of imagination. It should not occasion surprise, therefore, that when the Spirit of God is profoundly at work in people's lives their imaginations will be affected and their minds even be 'carried beyond themselves'.[20]

Then, the fact that people are influenced spiritually, by hearing of the experiences of others, is not a cause to question the legitimacy of the work. There is no doubt that God uses means to advance his kingdom, and among them is the example set by some of his people. Scripture and history inform Edwards that there 'never yet was a time of remarkable pouring out of the Spirit, and great revival of religion, but that example had a main hand' in it. Again, though, God does not need to use the examples of the godly in the furtherance of his cause. It is the Scripture that is 'the principal means of carrying on God's work'.[21] And the fact that people are moved to imitate the example of those who are godly does not necessarily require the influence of the Spirit.

Indiscretions, imprudence and things 'really contrary to the rules of God's holy Word' cannot be used to reject, automatically, a work as false. In fact, a 'thousand imprudences won't prove a work not to be the work of the Spirit of God'. Edwards finds an excellent example in the New Testament congregation at Corinth. 'Blessed with large measures of the Spirit of God', both with respect to the conversion of sinners and the bestowal of extraordinary gifts, but 'what manifold imprudences, and great and sinful irregularities' were also in the church! Even if certain leaders in a work are judgemental and censorious of others they deem to be unconverted – Edwards presumably has in mind some of the tactics of men like Davenport – it is no reason to oppose the work as being not from God. Such practices Edwards laments, but he observes from his study of both Scripture and church history that 'many holy men have erred this way'.[22] After all, Edwards observes in what Michael Jinkins calls 'one of his most memorable and delightful aphorisms',[23] believers must always bear in mind that 'the end for which God pours out his Spirit, is to make men holy, and not to make them politicians'.[24]

Similarly, there have been godly persons who have embraced 'woeful delusions', in particular, the conviction that they could receive infallible teaching like the apostles and 'immediate revelations from God'.[25] Moreover, genuine revivals have invariably been attended with 'whimsical and extravagant errors, and gross enthusiasm'. In the apostolic church there were the Gnostics; at the time of the Reformation there were certain fanatical Anabaptists; in the days of Oliver Cromwell there were such groups as the Quakers and the Ranters. Even 'in the beginning of New England, in her purest days, when vital piety flourished', there were problems of this nature. Here, Edwards is undoubtedly referring to the Antinomian Controversy.[26] As Edwards will state towards the end of *Distinguishing Marks*: 'A work of God without stumbling blocks is never to be expected.'[27] In short, revival is 'always a disfigured work of God, and the more powerful the revival, the more scandalising disfigurements we may expect to see'.[28]

Finally, concentration by some preachers on the 'terrors of God's holy law' and the reality of hell, and 'that with a great deal of pathos and earnestness', are not good reasons to reject a work as invalid. On the contrary, Edwards emphasizes that if hell is real and unregenerate sinners are headed there, they need to be warned of the danger they are in. And such warnings should be given with ardency and fervour. Actions, Edwards incisively notes, 'have a language to convey our minds, as well as words'. If 'a preacher's words represent the sinner's state as infinitely dreadful', while 'his behaviour and manner of speaking contradict it … he defeats his own purpose'.[29]

As Michael Jinkins has observed, the purpose in listing these 'negative signs' is to convince the critics of the revival that the 'Spirit of God is free and unbound by human preferences, but acts as God pleases'.[30] In the words of Edwards himself: there is a 'latitude the Spirit of God uses in the methods of his operations', something which not only the critics, but also some of the champions of the revival failed to recognize.[31]

Sure, distinguishing Scripture evidences and marks

In the second section of the treatise Edwards proceeds to list five definitive signs to recognize the Spirit of God's presence and work in a person's life. As C. C. Goen has noted, if Edwards had not included this section of his treatise and had been content to cite merely the 'negative signs', there may well have been few who would have been convinced by his examination.[32]

The Spirit of God, Edwards first points out, is a Christ-centred Spirit. He leads men and women to confess the true humanity and full deity of Christ, and centres their thinking on Christ as 'the only Saviour' of sinners.

> If the Spirit that is at work among a people is plainly observed to work after that manner, as to convince them of

Christ, and lead them to Christ; more to confirm their minds in the belief of the story of Christ, as he appeared in the flesh, and that he is the Son of God, and was sent of God to save sinners, and that he is the only Saviour, and that they stand in great need of him; and seems to beget in them higher and more honorable thoughts of him than they used to have, and to incline their affections more to him; it is a sure sign that it is the true and right Spirit.[33]

The heart of the Holy Spirit's ministry, as J. I. Packer has aptly put it, is 'to fulfil what we may call a floodlight ministry in relation to the Lord Jesus Christ', that is, focus attention upon Christ, draw the gaze of men and women to the Saviour, and exalt him in their minds and hearts.[34]

Second, the Spirit, who is an implacable foe of the 'interest of Satan's kingdom', seeks to oppose the advance of that realm by turning sinners from sin. He does so by giving them 'a deep concern about a future and eternal happiness in that invisible world, that the Gospel reveals' and drawing them to an 'earnest seeking the kingdom of God and his righteousness'. He reveals the corruption of the human heart and the utter inability of being saved by one's own works, or righteousness, or holiness. In sum, he imparts to sinners a profound sensitivity to sin and their need for salvation. 'If we see persons made sensible of the dreadful nature of sin', Edwards writes, 'and of the displeasure of God against it, and of their own miserable condition as they are in themselves by reason of sin, and earnestly concerned for their eternal salvation, and sensible of their need of God's pity and help, and engaged to seek it in the use of the means that God has appointed, we may certainly conclude that it is from the Spirit of God.'[35]

The third, clear, distinctive mark of a genuine work of the Spirit of God is the inculcation of a great regard for the Scriptures as the infallible Word of God.

> The spirit that operates in such a manner, as to cause in men a greater regard to the Holy Scriptures, and establishes them more in their truth and divinity, is certainly the Spirit of

God... The Devil never would go about to beget in persons a regard to that divine Word, which God has given to be the great and standing rule for the direction of his church in all religious matters and concerns of their souls, in all ages. A spirit of delusion won't incline persons to seek direction at the mouth of God... And accordingly we see it common in enthusiasts, that they depreciate this written rule, and set up the light within, or some other rule above it.[36]

Prominent among the 'enthusiasts' mentioned in the final sentence of this quote would be the Quakers. On a couple of occasions in this treatise Edwards goes out of his way to distance what was taking place in the revival from what had taken place in the Quaker movement of the previous century.[37] This is quite understandable in view of the fact that critics of the revival regularly equated it with Quakerism, which for many eighteenth-century authors was one of the most recent and most notable examples of 'enthusiasm'. It is noteworthy that the *Faithful Narrative* records the opinion of some that the Northampton revival was linked to Quakerism.[38] As T. T. Taylor has rightly observed, Quakerism was quite important to the defenders of the revival as a target to attack and thus reassure their critics that they were indeed orthodox.[39]

The Quaker movement had emerged in the late 1640s when George Fox (1624-1691), a part-time shoemaker and part-time shepherd, began to win converts to a perspective on the Christian faith which rejected much of orthodox Puritan theology. Fox and the early Quakers proclaimed the possibility of salvation for all humanity, and urged men and women to turn to the light within them to find salvation. We 'call All men to look to the Light within their own consciences', wrote Samuel Fisher (1605-1665), a General Baptist turned Quaker; 'by the leadings of that Light ... they may come to God, and work out their Salvation'.[40] This emphasis on the light within, which the Quakers variously called the indwelling Christ or Spirit, often led them to elevate it above the Scriptures. The deep conviction of the Quakers that the Spirit was speaking in them as he had spoken in the apostles also sometimes led to an elevation of their experience of the indwelling Spirit over the written Word of God.

Isaac Penington the Younger (1616-1679) is one early Quaker author who well illustrates this tendency to make the indwelling Spirit rather than the Scriptures the touchstone and final authority for thought and practice. In a letter that he wrote a fellow Quaker by the name of Nathanael Stonar in 1670, Penington tells his correspondent that one of the main differences between themselves and other 'professors' is 'concerning the rule'. While the latter assert that the Scriptures are the rule by which men and women ought to direct their lives and thinking, Penington is convinced that the indwelling Spirit of life is 'nearer and more powerful, than the words, or outward relations concerning those things in the Scriptures'. As Penington states:

> The Lord, in the gospel state, hath promised to be present with his people; not as a wayfaring man, for a night, but to *dwell in them and walk in them*. Yea, if they be tempted and in danger of erring, they shall hear a voice behind them, saying, 'This is the way, walk in it.' Will they not grant this to be a rule, as well as the Scriptures? Nay, is not this a more full direction to the heart, in that state, than it can pick to itself out of the Scriptures? ... the Spirit, which gave forth the words, is greater than the words; therefore we cannot but prize Him himself, and set Him higher in our heart and thoughts, than the words which testify of Him, though they also are very sweet and precious to our taste.[41]

Penington here affirms that the Quakers esteemed the Scriptures as 'sweet and precious', but he is equally adamant that the indwelling Spirit is to be regarded as the supreme authority when it comes to direction for Christian living and thinking.[42] Thus, when Edwards emphasizes that the Holy Spirit brings men and women to view the Scriptures as 'the infallible rule' for doctrine and practice, the Northampton pastor is expressly rejecting the conjecture that the revival is synonymous with Quakerism.

A fourth definitive mark of the Spirit's presence is drawn from the final words of 1 John 4:6, where the apostle John describes the Spirit of God as the 'spirit of truth'. Where people are being led to give heartfelt assent to Christian truth, then the Spirit of God is at work. Thus, for example, if men and women are increasingly convinced that there is a God, 'a great God, and a sin-hating God', that 'life is short, and very uncertain', that men and women are great sinners helpless to rescue themselves from their plight, and that one day they must give an account of themselves to this God, then one may conclude that the 'spirit that works thus, operates as a spirit of truth' and is indeed the Holy Spirit. This criterion for determining the presence of the Holy Spirit is obviously linked to the previous sign. It is as men and women grow in their appreciation of the Word of God that they develop an increasing devotion to the truth of things as they truly are.[43]

Finally, the Spirit of God can be recognized by the love that he produces, as 1 John 4:7-21 implies. When people are brought to have 'high and exalting thoughts' of God and 'his glorious perfections', when their hearts are given an 'admiring, delightful sense of the excellency' of the Lord Jesus and drawn to prize him as 'altogether lovely' and 'precious to the soul', when they cease to be contentious, quarrelsome individuals and long for the salvation of sinners, then the Holy Spirit must indeed be the source of such love.[44] As Edwards notes, 'love and humility are two things the most contrary to the spirit of the Devil'.[45]

SOME PRACTICAL APPLICATION

In the final section of *Distinguishing Marks*, Edwards deals with a number of practical inferences that flow out of what he has delineated. Among them he grapples with what was especially troublesome to many observers of the revival, namely the various physical phenomena that attended it. Edwards begins by noting that he speaks as an eyewitness of many of these phenomena, something that has already been mentioned above. As far as he can determine, there are two main causes for these phenomena: deep, spiritual distress or profound exhilaration as they have been overwhelmed by 'a sweet sense of the greatness, wonderfulness, and excellency of divine things'. Few that Edwards personally observed did he judge to be 'feigning or affecting such manifestations'. Moreover, generally speaking, those who experienced these phenomena retained their ability to reason. Of the 'many hundreds', possibly 'thousands', who had been subject to these manifestations, Edwards knew of none who were 'lastingly deprived of their reason'. This was important to emphasize, since one of the main criticisms that opponents like Charles Chauncy hurled against the revival was that it was nothing but 'enthusiasm', the loss of reason.[46]

The charge of disorder and confusion had also been levelled against the revival. Unlike James Davenport, Edwards did not delight in disorder. Individuals who, during public worship, are 'extraordinarily moved' in their affections and emotions should do all they can to 'refrain from outward manifestations'. But if such 'great outward manifestations' cannot be avoided and even if it means they interrupt the public worship of God's people, then Edwards is quite prepared to condone them. After all, they will achieve what the public worship is also designed to do: the conversion and sanctification of sinners. As Edwards aptly says, the man 'who is going a journey to fetch a treasure, need not be sorry that he is stopped by meeting the treasure in the midst of his journey'.[47]

Convinced that the revival going on in New England at the time he was writing was genuine, Edwards urged all who professed Christ not to oppose it, but to do their utmost to promote it. 'Christ is come down from heaven into this land, in a remarkable and wonderful work of his Spirit', he writes in no uncertain terms, and 'it becomes all his professed disciples to acknowledge him, and give him honor'.[48] In a rare moment of stridency, Edwards expresses the fear that those who continue to oppose it as a genuine work of God may actually be committing the unpardonable sin.[49] It is noteworthy that *Some Thoughts*, published the year following, is just as fervent in its defense of the revival as a great outpouring of the Spirit, but there is no evidence at all of the 'unpardonable sin' line of argument. By the time that Edwards finished writing *Some Thoughts* the wildfire fanaticism of Davenport and others like him was in full flame, and Edwards now recognized that genuine believers might well oppose the work because of the imprudences attending it.[50]

In fact, Edwards' final words of advice were for zealous 'friends' of the revival. He urged them to guard against spiritual pride and be eager to be marked by 'humility and self-diffidence, and an entire dependence on our Lord Jesus Christ'.[51] He was particularly concerned that some of them were seeking the restoration of the extraordinary gifts of the Spirit. In response, Edwards argued that no one since the apostolic era can expect direct inspiration since new revelation ended with that era. In previous sections of *Distinguishing Marks* Edwards had argued that while the apostles and prophets who comprise the foundation of the church in Ephesians 2:20 were 'all the penmen of sacred Scripture',[52] yet:

> However great a pouring out of the Spirit there may be, 'tis not to be expected that the Spirit of God should be given now in the same manner that it was to the apostles, infallibly to guide them in points of Christian doctrine, so that what they taught might be relied on as a rule to the Christian church... Many godly persons have undoubtedly in this and other ages, exposed themselves to woeful delusions, by an aptness to lay too much weight on impulses and impressions, as if they were immediate revelations from God, to signify something future, or to direct them where to go and what to do.[53]

In the final section of practical application, Edwards personalized this caution. Let us not presume, he urged those eager for revival, that we above all others are fit to be regarded as 'the great instructors and censors of this evil generation: and, in a high conceit of our own wisdom and discerning ... assume to ourselves the airs of prophets or extraordinary ambassadors of heaven'.[54]

In arguing against those who would claim to possess the extraordinary gifts of the Spirit, Edwards first employed what one might call the teleological argument, namely, that the sanctifying influences of the Holy Spirit supersede the extraordinary gifts. Second, claiming that latter day extraordinary gifts[55] would bring the church shame rather than glory, Edwards employed hyperbole to drive home his point:

Therefore I don't expect a restoration of these miraculous gifts in the approaching glorious times of the church, nor do I desire it: it appears to me that it would add nothing to the glory of those times, but rather diminish from it. For my part, I had rather enjoy the sweet influences of the Spirit, shewing Christ's spiritual divine beauty, and infinite grace, and dying love, drawing forth the holy exercises of faith, and divine love, and sweet complacence, and humble joy in God, one quarter of an hour, than to have prophetical visions and revelations for a whole year.[56]

Third, he uses an argument from experience. He urged great caution since he states that he had seen 'very many' prophecies fail to be realized.

I would therefore entreat the people of God to be very cautious how they give heed to such things. I have seen 'em fail in very many instances; and know by experience that impressions being made with great power, and upon the minds of true saints, yea eminent saints; and presently after, yea, in the midst of, extraordinary exercises of grace and sweet communion with God, and attended with texts of Scripture strongly impressed on the mind, are no sure signs of their being revelations from heaven: for I have known such impressions [to] fail…[57]

Finally, he plays what Philip Craig calls his trump card. To surrender the sure guidance of canonical revelation for so-called 'new revelation' is to follow what amounts to a will-o'-the wisp.

They that leave the sure word of prophecy [i.e. Scripture], that God has given us as a light shining in a dark place, to follow such impressions and impulses, leave the guidance of the polar star to follow a Jack-with-a-lanthorn. And no wonder therefore that sometimes they are led a dreadful dance, and into woeful extravagances.[58]

As Edwards had said earlier in the work, it is the Scriptures alone that are 'that divine Word, which God hath given to be the great and standing rule for the direction of his church in all religious matters and concerns of their souls, in all ages'.[59]

THE CENTRALITY OF PREACHING

Not surprisingly, Edwards' Word-centredness was yoked to a high view of preaching. Edwards had been reared in an environment – the home of a pastor – where, in the words of Wilson H. Kimnach, 'sermons were always in the making'.[60] His father, Timothy Edwards, was a good preacher in his own right, who, it would appear, would write out most of his sermons in manuscript form and then preach them from his memory of his manuscript. His extant sermons are classic example of solid Puritan divinity, which would have taught the young Edwards as he listened to his father week by week the fundamentals of preaching.[61] Central to his understanding of preaching was the conversion of his hearers. As he stated in his sermon *All the Living Must Surely Die*:

> Let us labour in a very particular, convincing and awakening manner to dispense the Word of God; so to speak as tends most to reach and pierce the Hearts and Consciences, and humble the Souls of them that hear us…[62]

The other important influence on Edwards as a preacher was his grandfather, Solomon Stoddard, one of the last great Puritan preachers in Massachusetts and equally ardent as Edwards' father in his desire to win men and women to Christ through the preaching of the Word. Stoddard was an exceptionally powerful preacher, whose sermons were formally similar to those of Timothy Edwards, but filled with 'pungent, epigrammatic expression', for which it appears Stoddard had a real gift.[63] Here he is, for instance, preaching about the failure of the unregenerate to nurture a proper fear of hell and thus their inability to develop a proper fear of sin. 'If they were afraid of Hell, they would be afraid of Sin. When their Lusts were as Spurs to stir them up to Sin, this fear would be a Bridle to curb them in.'[64]

In addition to the influence of his father and grandfather on his preaching, there were also significant literary influences on his understanding of preaching. One of these was undoubtedly *Manductio ad Ministerium: Direction for a Candidate of the Ministry*, published in Boston in 1726. Although Edwards may have had some qualms about reading Mather's book – it was, after all, Cotton Mather's father who had engaged in a long-running controversy with Solomon Stoddard over the issue of the Half-Way Covenant – he seems to have regularly used this book 'as an authority on matters relating to the education of a preacher'.[65] The work especially emphasized the vital need of the preacher to be spiritually prepared before he preached. 'Go directly from your Knees in your *Study* to the *Pulpit*', Mather urged prospective preachers.

Edwards' high view of preaching and exalted perspective on the status of the preacher is seen clearly in a number of places. In a 1738 preface to some sermons preached during the 1734/1735 revival in Northampton, for example, Edwards could declare, 'have we not reason to think that it ever has been, and ever will be, God's manner to bless the foolishness of preaching to save them that believe?'[66] Similarly, in his *Some Thoughts* (1743), Edwards can state that ministers are:

> [God's] ambassadors and instruments, to awaken and convert sinners, and establish, build up, and comfort saints; 'tis the business they have been solemnly charged with before God, angels and men, and that they have given up themselves to by the most sacred vows. These especially are the officers of Christ's kingdom, that above all other men upon earth do represent his person; into whose hands Christ has committed the sacred oracles and holy ordinances, and all his appointed means of grace, to be administered by them.[67]

Philip Craig accurately sums up Edwards' Word-centredness and its significance for the modern church in the West when he states:

> With his Puritan Reformed heritage, Edwards takes great pains to reaffirm an emphasis sadly lacking in contemporary

evangelicalism, the primacy of the preached word... It is not prophecy, but preaching that God has appointed to 'impress upon sinners their misery and need of a Savior and the glory and sufficiency of Christ'.[68]

The name – 'The Comforter' – seemed to denote that the Holy Spirit was the only and infinite Fountain of comfort and joy.[1]
– Sarah Pierpont Edwards (1742)

An affectionate and prudent Wife
And a very eminent Christian
– On the tombstone of Sarah Pierpont Edwards in Princeton Cemetery

Chapter 7

THE COMFORTER IS COME: SARAH EDWARDS AND THE VISION OF GOD

JONATHAN EDWARDS' SECOND major defence of the revival is his *Some Thoughts*. Written during the course of 1742, it was not actually published until mid-March 1743.[2] During the period of time that Edwards devoted to writing it, the division over the revival was becoming increasingly obvious. Two parties were emerging, the Old Lights and the New Lights, as they came to be called, which, Edwards observes, had the tendency to divide the churches in New England into 'two armies, separated, drawn up in battle array, ready to fight with one another'.[3] In an attempt to bring peace to this situation, Edwards drew up this lengthy work, which ran to 378 pages in its first edition.

While Edwards' basic stance towards the revival remains unchanged, he is increasingly critical of the imprudent excesses committed by 'friends' of the revival. In fact, as Iain Murray has pointed out, the book's structure seems to reflect this change in reflection on the revival.[4] The book is divided into five main parts. In the first part, the Northampton pastor defends the revival as a 'glorious work of God'.[5] The next division of the book outlines the 'obligations that all are under to acknowledge, rejoice in, and promote this work'.[6] The third section seeks to vindicate the 'zealous promoters' of this work.[7] The largest part of the book is Part 4, which focuses on how the friends of the revival need to correct various problems in the work.[8] The final section is devoted to outlining various things that could be done to further promote the revival.[9] The length of the fourth part of the book makes it abundantly clear that Edwards' growing concern is the very real danger of fanaticism. 'One truly zealous person', he observes, 'may do more (through Satan's being too subtle for him) to hinder the work, than an hundred great, and strong, and open opposers.'[10] It is not hard to imagine that he may have had James Davenport in mind at this point.

It is noteworthy that one recent interpreter of the events of the Great Awakening, William DeArteaga, has argued that it was not Davenport's fanaticism but Chauncy's opposition that quenched the Great Awakening. 'In spite of Edwards's own theories', he has maintained, 'it seems that the Great Awakening was not quenched because of its extremists. It was quenched because of its opponents.'[11] But this opinion flies in the face of not only Edwards' *Some Thoughts*, written in the midst of the revival, but also his *Religious Affections* (1746), written a number of years after the revival. By the time that Edwards came to write *Religious Affections*, he had had the time to reflect deeply on the revival and its outcome. And, as we shall see in Chapter 8, instead of toning down his views from *Some Thoughts*, he sharpens them. The greatest quenching force to times of revival is more fanaticism than opposition.

Many of the points made in *Some Thoughts* are made in the other places in the Edwardsean corpus that we have examined in previous chapters or will examine in chapters to come. There is one key feature of the work, though, that is unique and that needs to be looked at. This is the account of Sarah Edwards' spiritual experience, in which Edwards presents his wife as a model of a truly Spirit-filled person.[12]

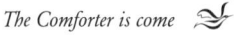

Sarah Edwards

Amanda Porterfield has noted, in a recent historical study of the spirituality of American women, that:

> One of the most striking phenomena about the New England Puritans is that their greatest ministers and governors – Thomas Shepard, John Winthrop, Simon Bradstreet, Edward Taylor, and Jonathan Edwards, for example – loved their wives beyond measure. These men found their wives to be earthly representatives of God's beauty. For these men a loving wife was not only a model Christian but also an expression of the beauty of the world that pointed beyond itself to divine beauty. And the enjoyment of God's beauty was the essence of Puritan spirituality.[13]

The few texts we have from the hand of Edwards that are explicitly about his wife, Sarah, certainly help to substantiate these striking remarks. Unfortunately, Sarah was not a writer and she did not leave behind her an extensive journal or substantial correspondence by which we might outline her spiritual life. But there is the one remarkable text in *Some Thoughts* that provides an insight into the workings of her heart. For much of her life, though, we must rely on the words of others, especially those of her husband and his first biographer, Samuel Hopkins.

In Chapter 1 there has been cited the famous passage Edwards first recorded about his future wife while they were both living in New Haven. We cite it again here for ease of reference. At the time the following text was written, Jonathan would have been twenty and Sarah but thirteen.

> They say there is a young lady in [New Haven] who is beloved of that almighty Being, who made and rules the world,

and that there are certain seasons in which this Great Being, in some way or other invisible, comes to her and fills her mind with exceeding sweet delight, and that she hardly cares for any thing, except to meditate on him – that she expects after a while to be received up where he is, to be raised out of the world and caught up into heaven; being assured that he loves her too well to let her remain at a distance from him always. There she is to dwell with him, and to be ravished with his love, favor and delight forever. Therefore, if you present all the world before her, with the richest of its treasures, she disregards it and cares not for it, and is unmindful of any pain or affliction. She has a strange sweetness in her mind, and sweetness of temper, uncommon purity in her affections; is most just and praiseworthy in all her actions; and you could not persuade her to do anything thought wrong or sinful, if you would give her all the world, lest she should offend this great Being. She is of a wonderful sweetness, calmness and universal benevolence of mind; especially after those times in which this great God has manifested himself to her mind. She will sometimes go about, singing sweetly, from place to [place]; and she seems to be always full of joy and pleasure; and no one know for what. She loves to be alone, and to wander in the fields and on the mountains, and seems to have someone invisible always conversing with her.[14]

There is little doubt that Jonathan was deeply impressed by Sarah's spirituality and Christian maturity. Sarah's sweetness – her sweetness of mind and temper, her sweet singing, and the 'exceeding sweet delight' that she had for God – especially appealed to Edwards, for whom the adjective 'sweet' and its derivatives were frequently on his lips when he spoke of God and divine things.[15]

Sarah, like her future husband, had been born into a family rich in spiritual privileges. Her father, James Pierpont, had been the minister of First Church, New Haven, from 1685 until his death. Her great-grandfather was Thomas Hooker, one of the most influential first-generation Puritans in New England. She herself had come to Christ while a little child. Her husband estimated that she had

Sarah Pierpont Edwards

Circa 1750-1755, by Joseph Badger, Yale University Art Gallery, bequest of Eugene Phelps Edwards, © Reproduced with permission.

been converted before she was five.[16] After their marriage in 1727 Sarah would have been kept extremely busy with domestic concerns, for the couple had eleven children between 1728 and 1750. While Jonathan certainly played a significant role as spiritual mentor to his children,[17] much of the raising of the children fell to Sarah. Understandably the pressure of these parental duties and all of the other chores of running a busy household seems to have weighed heavily on Sarah. To cope, Sarah gave herself and all that she was unreservedly to God on at least a couple of distinct occasions in 1739 and 1740.[18]

These self-dedications – in the Puritan tradition of making a personal covenant with God – were to be the foundation of some extraordinary experiences in late January and early February 1742. Jonathan was away from Northampton for much of this time on a two-week preaching tour that involved at least eight meetings in Massachusetts and Connecticut.[19] While he was away, other ministers – among whom the most notable was Samuel Buell (d.1798), who eventually settled at East Hampton, Long Island, and whose ordination sermon Edwards preached in 1746 – filled the pulpit at Northampton.[20] Sarah was disturbed by a number of things at the time: in particular, a remark that her husband made just before he had left on his preaching tour to the effect that he believed Sarah 'had failed in some measure in point of prudence, in some conversation I had with Mr. [Chester] Williams', the minister in nearby Hadley and a distant cousin. Sarah was distressed that she did not 'have the good opinion of my husband'.[21] Other stresses – 'for example, finances and jealousy with regard to God's blessing upon the ministry of others in Northampton like Buell and Williams' – have led some to suggest that Sarah's experiences were part and parcel of a nervous breakdown. Elisabeth Dodds, for instance, describes Sarah becoming 'grotesque – jabbering, hallucinating, and idiotically fainting'.[22] But Edwards was surely right to see his wife's experiences as a genuine encounter with the triune God and the stresses God's means to bring her to the point of absolute submission to his sweet sovereignty.[23]

Benign, meek, beneficent, beatifical, glorious distraction

When Edwards returned from his preaching trip, he asked Sarah to write down an account of her experiences. Edwards carefully edited Sarah's account so as to remove any indication of the identity and gender of the author and changed each personal pronoun to 'the person', and he then inserted his edited version into *Some Thoughts*.

Sarah was given, we read:

> Such views of the glory of the divine perfections, and Christ's excellencies, that the soul in the meantime has been as it were perfectly overwhelmed, and swallowed up with light and love and a sweet solace, rest and joy of soul, that was altogether unspeakable; and more than once continuing for five or six hours together, without any interruption, in that clear and lively view or sense of the infinite beauty and amiableness of Christ's person, and the heavenly sweetness of his transcendent love; so that (to use the person's own expressions) the soul remained in a kind of heavenly Elysium, and did as it were swim in the rays of Christ's love, like a little mote swimming in the beams of the sun, or beams of his light that come in at a window; and the heart was swallowed up in a kind of glow of Christ's love, coming down from Christ's heart in heaven, as a constant stream of sweet light, at the same time the soul all flowing out in love to him; so that there seemed to be a constant flowing and reflowing from heart to heart.[24]

On the other hand, there were times that Sarah had 'a deep and lively sense' of her 'own exceeding littleness and vileness'.[25] She had:

> ... an extraordinary sense of the awful majesty and greatness of God ... a sense of the holiness of God, as of a flame infinitely pure and bright ... a sense of the piercing all-seeing eye of God ... and an extraordinary view of the infinite terribleness of the wrath of God ... together with a sense of the

ineffable misery of sinners who are exposed to this wrath, that has been overbearing: sometimes the exceeding pollution of the person's own heart, as a sink of all manner of abomination, and a nest of vipers, and the dreadfulness of an eternal hell of God's wrath, opened to view both together.[26]

But foundational to all of these profound experiences was:

A sweet rejoicing of soul at the thoughts of God being infinitely and unchangeably happy, and an exulting gladness of heart that God is self-sufficient, and infinitely above all dependence, and reigns over all, and does his will with absolute and uncontrollable power and sovereignty ... [and the person's] soul often entertained, with unspeakable delight ... the thoughts of heaven, as a world of love, where love shall be the saints' eternal food, and they shall dwell in the light of love, and swim in an ocean of love, and where the very air and breath will be nothing but love; love to the people of God, or God's true saints, as such that have the image of Christ, and as those who will in a very little time shine in his perfect image, that has been attended with that endearment and oneness of heart, and that sweetness and ravishment of soul, that has been altogether inexpressible.[27]

Now, accompanying these various experiences were certain unusual bodily phenomena, over twenty of them by one reckoning.[28] These 'views of divine things', we are told, often deprived her body of 'all ability to stand or speak'.[29] When Sarah was given an 'extraordinary sense of the awful majesty and greatness of God', she lost all bodily strength.[30] Another time, it was the 'overwhelming sense of the glory of the work of redemption, and the way of salvation by Jesus Christ' which caused her body to faint.[31] On yet another occasion, 'a sense of the glory of the Holy Spirit, as the great Comforter', was such 'as to overwhelm both soul and body'.[32] On occasion, she was so taken with the joy of knowing such an awesome God that she had 'to leap with all the might, with joy and mighty exultation of soul'.[33]

Edwards, though, was at pains to point out that Sarah's joy was never attended 'with the least appearance of any laughter or lightness of countenance'. On the contrary, it led to 'a new engagedness of heart to live to God's honor, and watch and fight against sin'.[34] This view of the Christian life as a warfare against sin is typically Puritan. Nor were her experiences attended with any leanings towards sinless perfection, which Edwards notes as being the 'the notion of the Wesleys and their followers, and some other high pretenders to spirituality in these days'.[35] This appears to be the only public reference of Edwards to the Wesley brothers.

Sarah's experiences did not involve 'any enthusiastic [i.e. fanatical] disposition to follow impulses, or any supposed prophetical revelations'.[36] As we have seen in our analysis of *Distinguishing Marks* in Chapter 6, Edwards was ever insistent that the Spirit of God always leads those whom he indwells to view the Scriptures as 'the great and standing rule for the direction of his church in all religious matters, and all concerns of their souls, in all ages'.[37] 'Enthusiasts' or fanatics, on the other hand, regularly 'depreciate this written rule, and set up the light within or some other rule above it'.[38] In other words, Sarah's experiences were proven genuine by her refusal to look for God in any other place but his divine Word.

Moreover, what helped Edwards come to a decision about the divine source of these experiences was their fruit in daily life. Sarah did not feel that her experiences elevated her above others. On the contrary, she had:

> ... a peculiar sensible aversion to judging others that were professing Christians of good standing in the visible church, that they were not converted, or with respect to their degrees of grace; or at all intermeddling with that matter, so much as to determine against and condemn others in the thought of the heart; it appearing hateful, as not agreeing with that lamb-like humility, meekness, gentleness, and charity, which the soul then, above other times, saw the beauty of, and felt a disposition to.[39]

This emphasis on humility and meekness will be something that Edwards will emphasize in his *Religious Affections* as a sure mark of being filled with the Spirit. Then, Edwards noted that his wife had a deepened sense of her need to help the poor.[40] Moreover, as he watched his wife engaged in her daily responsibilities in their home, he saw a person who was now 'eating for God, and working for God, and sleeping for God, and bearing pain and trouble for God, and doing all as the service of love, and so doing it with a continual, uninterrupted cheerfulness, peace and joy'.[41] There was not the slightest desire to neglect 'the necessary business' of her calling as a wife and mother. 'Worldly business has been attended with great alacrity, as part of the service of God.' Sarah told her husband that when she did her work thus it was 'as good as prayer'.[42]

Little wonder then that Edwards can burst out, at the conclusion of his edited account of Sarah's experience:

> Now if such things are enthusiasm, and the fruits of a distempered brain, let my brain be evermore possessed of that happy distemper! If this be distraction, I pray God that the world of mankind may be all seized with this benign, meek, beneficent, beatifical, glorious distraction![43]

But without the presence of this God-centredness, the physical manifestations would have been of no value, and would actually have been detrimental to genuine piety. Sarah thus anonymously became a model of what true revival personally looked like.[44]

Divine benevolence

There is one other statement in this section of *Some Thoughts* of which note needs to be taken. Part of Sarah's experience, Edwards wrote,

> … [was] a universal benevolence to mankind, with a longing as it were to embrace the whole world in the arms of pity and love; ideas of suffering from enemies the utmost conceivable rage and cruelty, with a disposition felt to fervent love and pity in such a case, so far as it could be realized in thought;

fainting with pity to the world that lies in ignorance and wickedness; sometimes a disposition was felt to a life given up to mourning alone in a wilderness over a lost and miserable world; compassion towards them being often to that degree, that would allow of no support or rest, but in going to God, and pouring out the soul in prayer for them; earnest desires that the work of God, that is now in the land, may be carried on, and that with greater purity, and freedom from all bitter zeal, censoriousness, spiritual pride, hot disputes, etc.

A vehement and constant desire for the setting up of Christ's kingdom through the earth, as a kingdom of holiness, purity, love, peace, and happiness to mankind.[45]

What Sarah displayed here was, in her husband's mind, true divine love, which he would later define in *The Nature of True Virtue* (1755, published 1765) as 'love of benevolence', which is that 'affection or propensity of heart to any being, which causes it to incline it to its well-being, or disposes it to desire and take pleasure in its happiness'.[46] This sort of love does not require anything beautiful in its object. On the other hand, love which did require its object to be beautiful was what Edwards called 'love of complacence'.[47] Clearly God's love for sinners was of the first kind. And what thrilled Edwards about his wife's experiences was that this sort of love, this love of benevolence that loves regardless of the beauty of the object, attended them. In the words of James Wm. McClendon, what 'God had given her was love understood as cordial consent, her capacity to say yes to God and to all that was God's'.[48]

And surely it was this sort of love that Edwards was referring to on his deathbed when he spoke of 'the uncommon union', which had so long subsisted between himself and his wife, 'has been of such a nature, as I trust is spiritual, and therefore will continue forever'.[49] Their benevolent love for God and his world – truly uncommon in this selfish, sinful world – had bonded them together during their married lives. It was a 'spiritual' love. As McClendon puts it, they were 'two who have breathed together the breath of the same Spirit'.[50] And as such, it was eternal for it had joined them to the triune God.

There is an inward burning desire that a saint has after holiness ... a holy breathing and panting after the Spirit of God to increase holiness.

– *Jonathan Edwards*, The Religious Affections *(1746)*

Chapter 8

TRUE PIETY ... REACHES THE HEART: THE ADVOCACY OF HEART RELIGION IN THE RELIGIOUS AFFECTIONS

THE CLASSIC QUALITY of Jonathan Edwards' *A Treatise Concerning Religious Affections*, which first saw the light of day in 1746, was soon recognized. For instance, only thirty-five years after its publication, the young Andrew Fuller, an English Calvinistic Baptist who would become one of the most influential theologians of his day, noted the impact of this work by Edwards in his diary:

> I think I have never yet entered into the true idea of the work of the ministry... I think I am by the ministry, as I was by my life as a Christian before I read *Edwards on the Affections*... Oh that the Holy Spirit would open my eyes, and let me into the things that I have never yet seen![1]

A few years later Fuller's closest friend, John Ryland Jr (1753-1825), told a fellow Baptist pastor, Joseph Kinghorn (1766-1832), that if he could keep but three books out of his whole library, Edwards' *Religious Affections* would be one of the three.[2] Similar testimonies over the past 200 years could be cited that would easily confirm, for example, Iain Murray's affirmation that it is 'one of the most important books possessed by the Christian church on the nature of true religion'.[3]

Now, some scholars have argued that a central reason for this impact of Edwards' *Religious Affections* is due to its striking originality and its sharp departure from the Puritan theology and ambience of Edwards' spiritual roots.[4] But as Brad Walton, a Canadian scholar, has argued with great cogency, 'far from representing a discontinuity with Puritan traditions', Edwards' *Religious Affections* is, in fact, 'a reassertion – elicited by the events of the Great Awakening – of traditional Puritan "experimental" spirituality, cast largely in the same form, and using essentially the same language and conceptualization, as seventeenth-century Puritan analyses of true piety, spiritual sensation and heart religion'.[5] Through extensive examination of especially those Puritans who formed what has been termed the Spiritual Brotherhood[6] – running from Richard Greenham (1540-1594), the fountainhead of affective Puritanism, through Richard Sibbes, to Thomas Goodwin and John Howe – Walton shows that writings of these Puritans authors, along with those of a few others such as John Owen contain all the various elements that make up Edwards' *Religious Affections*. The uniqueness of Edwards' book lies in the way that it 'attempts to articulate so thorough, coherent, and systematic a treatment of heart' religion.[7]

As we have seen, before Edwards issued this classic of Christian devotion, the religious situation in New England had polarized between those who took Charles Chauncy's position and rejected the revival as sheer fanaticism and those who defended the revival, excesses and all. The prayer of a Presbyterian named John Moorehead, who was sympathetic to the revival, captured the spiritual danger of this polarity: 'God direct us what to do, particularly with pious zealots and cold, diabolical opposers!'[8] The ultimate answer to Moorhead's prayer came by way of Edwards' *A Treatise Concerning the Religious Affections* (1746). From the theological crucible in New England there was thus brought forth one of the richest books on Christian spirituality in the history of the church.

Yet, it needs to be remembered, to quote Harold P. Simonson, that the *Religious Affections* is the culmination of 'some twenty-five years of thought about the nature of religious experience'.[9] Ever since his conversion in 1721, Edwards had been meditating on and writing about what constituted genuine Christian piety, as he notes in his preface to the *Religious Affections*:

> There is no question whatsoever, that is of greater importance to mankind, and that it more concerns every individual person to be well resolved in, than this, what are the distinguishing qualifications of those that are in favor with God, and entitled to his eternal rewards? Or, which comes to the same thing, What is the nature of true religion?… The consideration of these things has long engaged me to attend to this matter, with the utmost diligence and care, and exactness of search and inquiry, that I have been capable of: it is a subject on which my mind has been peculiarly intent, ever since I first entered on the study of divinity.[10]

HEART RELIGION IN THE RELIGIOUS AFFECTIONS

Edwards' *Religious Affections* seeks to answer both of the positions of Davenport and Chauncy.[11] To 'pious zealots' such as Davenport, he will stress that biblical Christianity must involve the mind and reason. When God converts a person, light is shed upon the mind. On the other hand, there is much more to conversion than enlightenment. In response to Chauncy and those of his persuasion, he will maintain that genuine spirituality flows out from a heart aflame with the love of God. There is no genuine Christianity without a warm heart. It is noteworthy that the longest section of the book is an answer to Davenport's position. As has already been noted, Edwards regarded the misguided zeal of a Davenport as a much more serious hindrance to the advance of the gospel in times of revival than the intellectualism of a Chauncy.

In the early pages of the *Religious Affections*, Edwards provides his readers with a definition of the human constitution and indicates how he uses the word 'affection'. He writes:

> ...the affections are no other, than the more vigorous and sensible exercises of the inclination and will of the soul.
>
> God has indued the soul with two faculties: one is that by which it is capable of perception and speculation, or by which it discerns, and views, and judges of things; which is called the understanding. The other faculty is that by which the soul does not merely perceive and view things, but is some way inclined with respect to the things it views or considers; either is inclined to 'em, or is disinclined, and averse from 'em; or is the faculty by which the soul does not behold things, as an indifferent unaffected spectator, but either as liking or disliking, pleased or displeased, approving or rejecting. This faculty is called by various names; it is sometimes called the *inclination*: and, as it has respect to the actions that are determined and governed by it, is called the *will*: and the *mind*, with regard to the exercises of this faculty, is often called the *heart*.[12]

Before any discussion of Edwards' view of the human person in this text, it is vital to note that the Northampton divine regarded the human person as basically an integrated whole. Edwards has to distinguish between different faculties within the person for the sake of discussion, but it should never be forgotten that it is 'a distinction and not a separation'.[13]

In the above-cited text Edwards argues that within the human person there are two faculties by which he or she interacts with the outside world. There is the understanding by which an individual obtains knowledge and can observe and speculate about things. This faculty is purely intellectual. A good illustration of this may be found in an individual's observation of a table. The shape, dimensions, type of wood from which it is made – all of this knowledge can be processed by the understanding without any sense of liking or disliking of the table. The knowledge thus obtained is purely intellectual.

The other faculty – which Edwards denominates by various names: the inclination, the will, the heart – does not merely observe, but has an attraction towards or away from the object in question. This faculty is not divorced from the process of knowing, since something must be known for there to be approbation or disapproval. Where this approbation or rejection is strong – in Edwards' words, where it is 'vigorous and sensible' – there we have what Edwards terms 'the affections'.

For Edwards, the affections are not primarily related to animal passions, as Chauncy had thought.[14] Nor are they simply to be equated with the emotions[15] or experience. They are an essential part of being human and intimately bound up with the will and the heart. The affections are strong and vigorous inclinations that manifest themselves in thought, feeling and action.[16] By explaining the affections in this way, Edwards is thus able to avoid any sort of opposition between the understanding and the heart. There can be no strong exercise of the will, that is, affections, without the understanding being involved. Moreover, as John Smith, the editor of the critical edition of the *Religious Affections* in the Yale series of Edwards' works, puts it: 'The essential point is that the affections manifest the center and unity of the self; they express the whole man and give insight into the basic orientation of his life.'[17]

With this explanation of terms in hand, as it were, Edwards can now argue against Chauncy that 'true religion, in great part, consists in holy affections'.[18] As Edwards notes, 'The Holy Scriptures do everywhere place religion very much in the affections; such as fear, hope, love, hatred, desire, joy, sorrow, gratitude, compassion and zeal.'[19] True faith is never found in a state of indifference to the things of God and Christ. Such a state is what the Scriptures call lukewarmness, which to God is revolting. Rather, the Christian life is a Spirit-wrought passionate engagement of the entire person in living for Christ. In Edwards' words:

> The Spirit of God, in those that have sound and solid religion, is a spirit of powerful holy affection; and therefore, God is said to have given them the spirit of power, and of love, and of a sound mind (2 Tim. 1:7). And such, when they receive

the Spirit of God, in his sanctifying and saving influences, are said to be baptized with the Holy Ghost, and with fire; by reason of the power and fervor of those exercises the Spirit of God excites in their hearts, whereby their hearts, when grace is in exercise, may be said to burn within them; as is said of the disciples (Luke 24:32).[20]

Or as he had declared in an ordination sermon preached on 30 August 1744:

True piety is not a thing remaining only in the head, or consisting in any speculative knowledge or opinions, or outward morality, or forms of religion; it reaches the heart, is chiefly seated there, and burns there. There is a holy ardor in every thing that belongs to true grace: true faith is an ardent thing.[21]

False diamonds and rubies

By the time that Edwards wrote the *Religious Affections* in 1746, he was very conscious that in addition to the work of the Holy Spirit in the Great Awakening Satan had also been powerfully active in producing a counterfeit religion. The latter was a religion that made much of experience, 'discoveries of Christ' and certain aspects of the work of the Holy Spirit. Knowing that some of his readers would be shocked at such assertions, Edwards rightly reasoned that the devil would never trouble himself to counterfeit valueless things. 'There are many more counterfeits of silver and gold, than of iron and copper', he wrote in Part II of the *Religious Affections*, 'there are many false diamonds and rubies, but who goes about to counterfeit common stones?'[22] Satan, ever the master of cunning and lies, employs his subtlety in making imitations of the most excellent things.

Thus, in Part II of the work, Edwards delineated a variety of things that did not necessarily indicate the indwelling presence of the Spirit — some of which he had dealt with in his previous treatises on revival — before he turned, in Part III, to a positive presentation of the nature of true piety under twelve signs or marks.[23]

THE INDWELLING OF THE SPIRIT

First, Edwards sees, in passages such as 1 Corinthians 3:16 and John 14:16-17, that the Holy Spirit indwells believers as his 'proper lasting abode'.[24] By means of this indwelling, he imparts his character, which consists of holiness and godliness, to the Christian.[25] In other words, Edwards is convinced that genuine Christian character is ultimately not a matter of human achievement. It has its root in the indwelling grace of the Holy Spirit. Genuine Christian spirituality begins with God.

In fact, in the words of Edwards' later *Humble Attempt*, the indwelling of the Spirit is 'the sum of the blessings Christ sought by what he did and suffered in the work of redemption'. The Spirit is not simply the One who applies the work of the Lord Jesus Christ to individual believers. He himself is the treasure Christ's death secured for his people. As Edwards argued in the *Humble Attempt*: 'The Holy Spirit, in his indwelling, his influences and fruits, is the sum of all grace, holiness, comfort and joy, or in one word, of all the spiritual good Christ purchased for men in this world: and is also the sum of all perfection, glory and eternal joy, that he purchased for them in another world.'[26] Patricia Wilson-Kastner sums up Edwards' views thus:

> In Edwards' view, not only does the Holy Spirit act on the soul, but the Spirit dwells in the soul and is itself the grace of salvation. Divine love in the soul of the saints is the Holy Spirit himself, who becomes the well-spring of activity and the divine life itself for us.[27]

LOVING GOD PRIMARILY FOR WHO HE IS

Second, at the heart of true piety is a love for God that is based ultimately upon who God is in himself and not on what he does for us. This second sign has been the subject of much discussion over the years since some readers have understood Edwards to be implying that self-love is totally excluded from the elect's relationship with God. This is not at all the case. Rather, Edwards is pressing home the fact that if their love for God were simply a loving of

God for what he does on their behalf, namely saving them from the eternal horror of hell, then Christianity would simply be a subtle form of self-love. If people love God chiefly because of what he does for them, then, instead of God being the end of their existence, he becomes a means to an end, namely their happiness and self-fulfilment. But a biblical Christian loves God because he is altogether loveable and lovely.[28]

Edwards does not rule out entirely elements of self-love in a person's love for God.[29] But he rightly argues that love for God for who he is in himself must ultimately be primary. Christianity that is real and possesses spiritual power is rooted in a love that does not primarily seek its own advantage.

Then, this love for God for who he is in himself is above all a love for God's holiness.[30] In the midst of his discussion of this third sign of genuine spirituality, Edwards states that the Holy Spirit imparts to sinners at their conversion a new way of perceiving spiritual reality. This sense is more than simply an awareness of God and belief in God. It is nothing less than 'a taste' for God's beauty and glory. In Edwards' words:

> [S]piritual understanding consists ... in a sense of the heart, of the supreme beauty and sweetness of the holiness or moral perfection of divine things, together with all that discerning and knowledge of things of religion, that depends upon, and flows from such a sense.
>
> Spiritual understanding consists primarily in a sense of heart of that spiritual beauty.[31]

In the words of the American historian John E. Smith, 'A love of God which does not include the taste and relish of the divine beauty is not the love which reveals the saints.'[32] From Edwards' perspective, the Christian does not merely rationally believe that God is glorious; he has a sense of the gloriousness of God in his heart.

LIGHT AND CONVICTION

One of Edwards' favourite statements was that genuine spiritual affections are 'not heat without light'.[33] The fourth sign of genuine piety is therefore a spiritually enlightened mind.[34] True Christians have a healthy respect for their minds and reason. Trust in the Scriptures as the supreme authority when it comes to truth and error does not entail, for Edwards, the casting aside of the use of one's mind. It is noteworthy that in contrast to much of later American evangelicalism that emphasized the 'religion of the heart' over theological reflection, Edwards was firmly committed to an 'affectionate knowledge' that avoided both 'an anti-intellectual enthusiasm' as well as 'an unfeeling rationalism'. In particular, Conrad Cherry has rightly argued, Edwards, 'unlike the revivalists of a later America … avoided the sanctimonious conclusion that religious intuition is sufficient unto itself and that theology is a waste of time'.[35]

Fifth, Edwards emphasizes that genuine religious affections are accompanied by deep-seated conviction, 'a solid, full, thorough and effectual conviction of the truth of the great things of the gospel'.[36] For examples of such conviction, Edwards adduces a string of biblical examples, including Peter's confession of faith in Matthew 16:17, his similar assertion in John 6:68-69 and Paul's confident assertion in 2 Corinthians 5:1,6-8 regarding the life to come.[37]

Evangelical humility

Edwards' sixth sign is that no affections are genuinely spiritual unless they are accompanied by what he calls 'evangelical humiliation' – what today we would call 'evangelical humility'.[38] By the term 'evangelical humiliation', Edwards had in mind 'a sense that a Christian has of his own utter insufficiency, despicableness, and odiousness, with an answerable frame of heart'.[39] Edwards saw spiritual pride as *the* major reason for serious blockage in the Christian life. In a letter that Edwards wrote in 1741 to Deborah Hatheway, an eighteen-year-old Christian from Suffield, Massachusetts, who had asked for advice on how to live the Christian life, he told her:

> Remember that pride is the worst viper that is in the heart, the greatest disturber of the soul's peace and sweet communion with Christ; it was the first sin that ever was, and lies lowest in the foundation of Satan's whole building, and is the most

difficultly rooted out, and is the most hidden, secret and deceitful of all lust, and often creeps in, insensibly, into the midst of religion and sometimes under the disguise of humility.[40]

Having had long experience in unravelling the labyrinth of the human heart, Edwards is very aware of how deeply self-righteousness and self-exaltation are wedded to the faculty of the human heart. And it is precisely the man who is anxious to be a vital Christian, in contrast to those who seem lifeless and indifferent, who is most at risk to falling prey to spiritual pride. It is the zealous who are prone to comparing themselves with others so that they appear in a good and glorious light.[41]

Genuine piety, though, sees its own poverty and its need for grace and for God. The person 'whose heart is under the power of Christian humility ... is apt to think his attainments in religion to be comparatively mean, and to esteem himself low among the saints, and one of the least of saints'.[42] A mark of true spirituality is thus the renunciation of the personal desire for glory. The truly awakened heart is not one that rests in its own spiritual attainments or great spiritual experiences. Rather, with loving acknowledgement and self-abandon, it rests in the glory of God and of his Son.

This was true to Scripture – among other texts, Edwards refers to Psalm 34:18; 51:17 and Isaiah 66:1-2[43] – and attested by Edwards' own experience. As he once wrote in a personal document never intended for public view:

> I have often since I lived in this town [i.e. Northampton], had very affecting views of my own sinfulness and vileness; very frequently so as to hold me in a kind of loud weeping, sometimes for a considerable time together; so that I have often been forced to shut myself up. I have had a vastly greater sense of my own wickedness, and the badness of my heart, since my conversion, than ever I had before. It has often appeared to me, that if God should mark iniquity against me, I should appear the very worst of all mankind; of all that have been since the beginning of the world to this time: and that I should have by far the lowest place in hell... And it appears

to me, that were it not for free grace, exalted and raised up to the infinite height of all the fullness and glory of the great Jehovah, and the arm of his power and grace stretched forth, in all the majesty of his power, and in all the glory of his sovereignty; I should appear sunk down in my sins infinitely below hell itself, far beyond sight of everything, but the piercing eye of God's grace, that can pierce even down to such a depth, and to the bottom of such an abyss.[44]

ROOTED IN CONVERSION

The seventh sign is very similar to the first: authentic Christian spirituality has its roots in conversion.[45] Truly gracious affections depend totally upon this radical event that turns sinners towards God and away from their corrupt nature, and that changes their goals, motivations and outlook on life. In discussing this topic of conversion, it is noteworthy that Edwards does not touch on that which evangelicals in more recent days have tended to focus on: 'the exact moment' when an individual is saved. Like the Puritans, Edwards is more concerned about discerning whether this great change has taken place or not than dating it.[46]

Moreover, Edwards stresses that conversion does not bring immediate perfection.[47] Past patterns of sinning and sinful inclinations do not all totally disappear, but their dominion is now broken, for the very reason that these sinful patterns now stand in relationship to a new self, which, in virtue of its permanent place in the believer's life, must reveal itself over the course of time. 'Conversion', Edwards wrote, 'don't entirely root out ... those sins which a man by his natural constitution was most inclined to before his conversion.' But 'it is of great power and efficacy ... to correct' them.[48] Edwards thus wants to stress that genuine spirituality not only has its roots in a new nature, but in an *abiding*, new nature.

CHRISTLIKE GENTLENESS AND CHRISTIAN TENDERNESS

Edwards' eighth sign is that where there has been a genuine conversion, it is accompanied by a Christlike character, 'the lamblike, dovelike spirit and temper of Jesus Christ'.[49] This does not mean that boldness for Christ or Christian zeal is wrong *per se*, or that

Christian spirituality is wimpish. But Edwards is concerned that sometimes 'a pretended boldness for Christ ... arises from no better principle than pride' and that zeal for Christ can be marked by 'bitterness against the persons of men'.[50] Christian boldness and zeal are 'indeed a flame, but a sweet one'.[51]

He points to Christ in his fiercest battle against the forces of darkness, namely at the cross and in the events leading up to it. What temper marked him then, he asks. His holy boldness and valour were not shown in 'fierce and violent speeches', displaying 'sharp and bitter passions'. On the contrary, there was an 'all-conquering patience', love and prayer for his enemies: 'never did he appear so much a Lamb, and never did he show so much of the dovelike spirit, as at that time'.[52]

LIKE A BURNT CHILD THAT DREADS THE FIRE

Ninth, Christians have tender hearts, especially towards God. They are sensitive to all that displeases him.[53] They are 'like a burnt child that dreads the fire'.[54] They are very conscious of how sin separates them from the God they love, and so they strive not to readmit it to their lives and press on to be as godlike in behaviour and conduct as they can. Such tenderness of conscience, Edwards affirms, is the only proper attitude for one trying to respond to the heart-work of the Spirit. Referring to verses such as Psalm 2:11 and Psalm 147:11, Edwards maintains that while the believer no longer fears hell, he is increasingly fearful of causing God pain by indulging in sin. There is a 'diminishing of the fear of hell, with an increase of the fear of sin'. Such a believer 'has the firmest comfort, but the softest heart'.[55]

CONSISTENCY AND CONSTANCY

The next sign deals with the aesthetic side of the Christian life. Edwards never tires of emphasizing that God's holiness is beautiful in the most profound sense of that term. This beauty is expressed by the harmony and balance in the life of the believer.[56] Where there is true piety, there is balance. Why is this so? Because the Spirit of Christ, who is the source of all genuine Christian affections, now indwells them. It is the Holy Spirit who brings this balance.

Moreover, the Holy Spirit is transforming the believer into the image of God, who is himself beauty and harmony. So one can rightly expect that Christians reflect this in their own personhood.

Hypocrites, on the other hand, are bound to reveal a disharmony and disproportion in their affections. In some of them there is 'the most confident hope, while they are void of reverence, self-jealousy and caution'. While 'many hypocrites rejoice without trembling', in the saints 'joy and holy fear go together'.[57]

Here Edwards is being critical of those whose religion consists of what he calls 'fits and starts', who are committed only at certain seasons, or who focus on this or that virtue to the neglect of all else.[58] Such men and women fail to exhibit the symmetry that is the shape of true spirituality. Edwards compares them to 'waters in the time of a shower of rain, which during the shower, and a little after, run like a brook and flow abundantly, but are presently quite dry'. The true saint, on the other hand, is 'like a stream from a living spring; which, though it may be greatly increased by a shower of rain, and diminished in time of drought, yet constantly runs'.[59]

A HOLY BREATHING AND PANTING

Edwards' eleventh sign is that a truly Christian spirituality is marked by a longing for more of God.[60] He ties this sign in closely with one he has enumerated earlier on in the treatise, namely that of evangelical humility. The more grace believers receive, 'the more they see their imperfection and emptiness, and distance from what ought to be'.[61] Marked by a consciousness of how far they have yet to go in the Christian life, true believers long after God for more of him. For proof, Edwards turns to Paul's words in Philippians 3:13-15 and declares: 'the greatest eminence and perfection, that the saints arrive at in this world, has no tendency to satiety, or to abate their desires after more; but on the contrary, makes 'em more eager to press forwards' and know more of God.[62]

Moreover, Edwards emphasizes that the more persons have of holy affections, the more they have of that spiritual taste for God's beauty and glory that he had mentioned earlier in his discussion of the third sign. Edwards writes:

Spiritual good is of a satisfying nature; and for that very reason, the soul that tastes, and knows its nature, will thirst after it, and a fullness of it, that it may be satisfied. And the more he experiences, and the more he knows this excellent, unparalleled, exquisite, and satisfying sweetness, the more earnestly will he hunger and thirst for more, till he comes to perfection.[63]

As Edwards puts it in a remarkable turn of phrase, there is in the true believer 'a holy breathing and panting after the Spirit of God, to increase holiness'.[64]

The acid test – the fruit of the Spirit

To the twelfth and final sign Edwards devotes more space than to any of the others, a fact that indicates that it loomed largest in his mind. For Edwards, true spirituality bears visible fruit in Christian practice and living in the world.[65] Both to others and to oneself, holy practice is the main evidence of sincere Christianity.[66] This holy life has three major characteristics. First, it is shaped by what Edwards calls 'Christian rules', that is 'the laws of Christ, laws that he and his apostles did abundantly insist on, as of the greatest importance and necessity'.[67] Second, the living of the Christian life is the believer's main business in this world. As Edwards notes on the basis of Titus 2:14, Christ's people 'not only do good works, but are zealous of good works'.[68] Third, genuine Christian spirituality has in it the crucial quality of perseverance. The real believer makes Christianity his main business not only on Sundays, or at certain extraordinary seasons, but that 'business which he perseveres in through all changes, and under all trials, as long as he lives'.[69]

Some might see this emphasis on a holy life as legalistic, but Edwards rightly insists that while works do not save us, we cannot be saved without them.[70] Stephen Holmes accurately sums up the core emphasis of this classic work of Edwards:

Edwards traces the true work of the Spirit of God in the converted heart, a work that is not, fundamentally, to do with emotional reaction and extraordinary response, although these things might well be present, but is about a humble, cheerful love for God and growth in holiness that lasts a lifetime.[71]

Yea, who can tell, how far the prayers of the saints, & of a few saints, may prevail with heaven to obtain that grace, that shall win whole peoples and kingdoms to serve the Lord?

– *Cotton Mather,* The Nets of Salvation *(1704)*

I am persuaded that ... an agreement of the people of God in different parts, to unite together, to pray for the Holy Spirit, is lovely in the eyes of Jesus Christ the glorious head of the church.[1]

– *Jonathan Edwards, letter to a Scottish correspondent (1745)*

Chapter 9

THE HUMBLE ATTEMPT AND PRAYING FOR REVIVAL

IN AN ESSAY PUBLISHED in the mid-1960s, before the sizable resurgence of interest in Jonathan Edwards and his theology, Peter Gay, a historian with little sympathy for Edwards' theological vision, contrasted Charles Chauncy and Edwards. The former, he said, embraced fully the perspective of eighteenth-century modernity, while the latter, in all of the essential areas of his world-view and piety, clung to the Puritanism of the previous century. Chauncy and others like him, though, 'paid a price for their modernity: they surrendered the citadel of their Puritan faith'.[2] While not agreeing with Gay's sympathies, one has to admit that he has rightly understood the theological scene in mid-eighteenth-century New England. In so many ways, Jonathan Edwards held fast to his

Puritan heritage, and nowhere is this more evident than in his view of prayer.

Edwards and the Puritan view of prayer

Central to any expression of biblical spirituality is prayer. It is not surprising, therefore, that the Puritans, men and women who sought to frame their lives according to God's Word,[3] wrote a great deal about this subject and were themselves, in the words of John Geree (c.1601-1649), 'much in prayer'.[4] As the Congregationalist theologian Thomas Goodwin remarked, 'our speaking to God by prayers, and his speaking to us by answers thereunto, is one great part of our walking with God'.[5] John Bunyan (1628-1688) made a similar judgement about prayer's vital importance when he told those gathered to hear his final words as he lay dying in London: 'The Spirit of Prayer is more precious than treasure of gold and silver.'[6]

Edwards, very much a part of this stream of Reformed piety, also highly prized prayer. There can be found, for example, among his *Resolutions*, this one dated 23 July and 10 August 1723, which declares his awareness of the believer's lifelong duty to pray:

> Resolved, very much to exercise myself in this, all my life long, viz. with the greatest openness, of which I am capable of, to declare my ways to God, and lay open my soul to him: all my sins, temptations, difficulties, sorrows, fears, hopes, desires, and every thing, and every circumstance; according to Dr. Manton's 27th Sermon on Psalm 119.[7]

The statement to which he is referring from the Puritan author Thomas Manton (1620-1677) can be found in the doctrinal assertion of his twenty-seventh sermon on Psalm 119, in which he states: 'They that would speed with God, should learn this point of Christian ingenuity, unfeignedly to lay open their whole case to him.'[8]

Early in his ministry, Edwards addressed in his sermon *The Most High A Prayer-Hearing God* (1736) the subject of why God had instituted prayer.[9] First, Edwards takes note that of the fact that the institution of prayer is not because God is ignorant of our wants or desires. 'He is omniscient', Edwards reminds his hearers of a basic theological point, 'and with respect to his knowledge, unchangeable.'[10] Nor do we pray in order to alter God's sovereign will. Edwards is well aware of the anthropomorphic language of Scripture and admits:

> God is sometimes represented as if he were moved and persuaded by the prayers of his people; yet it is not to be thought that God is properly moved or made willing by our prayers; for it is no more possible that there should be any new inclination or will in God, than new knowledge.[11]

Why then are Christians commanded to pray? Well, working from the Reformation principle that God alone can do the work of God,[12] Edwards states that 'God has been pleased to constitute prayer to be antecedent to the bestowment of mercy, and he is pleased to bestow mercy in consequence of prayer, as though he were prevailed upon by prayer'. As Stephen J. Nichols writes with regard to this passage:

> In other words, God ordains the end or the results, and he also ordains the means. Prayer is a God-ordained means to carrying out his will. Although this humbles us, God ordains the means of the prayers of his people in the carrying out of his will. We don't pray to change his mind; we pray so that we can be used of him.[13]

Sincere prayer also furthers the glorification of God, the goal of all creation. As Edwards puts it, 'prayer is but a sensible acknowledgment of our dependence on him to his glory'.

Prayer is also designed to put those who pray in a proper frame of mind and heart to receive answers to their requests. Prayer changes those who pray, preparing them to be the sort of people through whom God can work.

> Fervent prayer many ways tends to prepare the heart. Hereby is excited a sense of our need, and of the value of the mercy

which we seek, and at the same time earnest desires for it, whereby the mind is more prepared to prize it, to rejoice in it when bestowed, and to be thankful for it. Prayer, with suitable confession, may excite a sense of our unworthiness of the mercy we seek. And the placing of ourselves in the immediate presence of God, may make us sensible of his majesty, and in a sense fit to receive mercy of him. Our prayer to God may excite in us a suitable sense and consideration of our dependence on God for the mercy we ask, and a suitable exercise of faith in God's sufficiency, that so we may be prepared to glorify his name when the mercy is received.[14]

Finally, due to the fact that Edwards was persuaded that 'the great duty of secret prayer ... is more expressly required in the Word of God than any other kind' of prayer he believed it was the duty of Christians to:

Be much employed in the duty of prayer. Let us pray with all prayer and supplication. Let us live prayerful lives, continuing instant in prayer, watching thereunto with all perseverance. Praying always, without ceasing, earnestly, and not fainting.[15]

THE CONCERT OF PRAYER

Now, one area of prayer that Edwards came to increasingly believe was vital for the expansion of God's kingdom was corporate prayer. While in some respects he was an innovator in his own time with regard to corporate prayer meetings, what he called 'concerts of prayer', there was some Puritan precedent. For example, the New England Puritan Cotton Mather believed that the vitality of the church in any era is in the final analysis dependent on the Holy Spirit's sovereign power. He thus maintained that the most significant practical response to the spiritual decline of his day was concerted prayer. As he stated in *The Nets of Salvation* (1704):

Praying for souls is a main stroke in the winning of souls. If once the Spirit of Grace be poured out upon a soul, that soul is won immediately... Yea, who can tell, how far the prayers of the saints, & of a few saints, may prevail with heaven to obtain that grace, that shall win whole peoples and kingdoms to serve the Lord? ... It may be, the nations of the world, would quickly be won from the idolatries of paganism, and the impostures of Mahomet, if a Spirit of Prayer, were at work among the people of God.[16]

A later booklet from the pen of Mather, *Private Meetings Animated & Regulated*, which was published in 1706, encouraged believers to meet in small groups so that, among other things, 'their fervent supplications' would hopefully result in 'the Spirit of Grace [being] mightily poured out upon the rising generation'. Mather recommended bimonthly meetings in which the whole evening could be devoted 'unto Supplications for the Conversion and Salvation of the Rising Generation in the Land; and particularly for the Success of the Gospel in that Congregation' to which the members of the prayer-meeting belonged.[17] It is noteworthy that though Mather prayed long and hard for revival, he never personally saw it. He died in 1728, a few years before it came to New England and Great Britain. Yet, he typifies a rising hunger among God's people in the transatlantic British community to see God move in revival in their society, and who translated that longing into prayer.

Jonathan Edwards' involvement in the Northampton revival of 1734/1735 and the Great Awakening of 1740 to 1742 left him with the keen conviction that the advance of God's kingdom in history was intimately connected to such times of spiritual blessing. The New England divine was also certain that prayer for these times of spiritual awakening was central to seeing them take place. Thus he drew up and published, in 1748, a treatise that sought to encourage believers to gather together regularly to pray for the pouring out of God's Spirit. Entitled *An Humble Attempt to Promote Explicit Agreement and Visible Union of God's People in Extraordinary Prayer, For the Revival of Religion and the Advancement of Christ's Kingdom on Earth, pursuant to Scripture-Promises and Prophecies concerning the Last Time* (henceforth referred to simply as the *Humble Attempt*), the treatise can be summed up by a sentence near the beginning of the work:

It is a very suitable thing, and well-pleasing to God, for many people, in different parts of the world, by express agreement, to come into a visible union in extraordinary, speedy, fervent, and constant prayer, for those great effusions of the Holy Spirit, which shall bring on that advancement of Christ's church and kingdom, that God has so often promised shall be in the latter ages of the world.[18]

This treatise would have some impact during Edwards' own lifetime, but its main influence came during the final decades of the eighteenth century, when it was instrumental in kindling a profoundly significant revival among the Calvinistic Baptists of Great Britain and initiating the modern missionary movement.[19]

The *Humble Attempt* itself was inspired by information that Edwards received during the course of 1745 about a prayer movement for revival which had been formed by a number of Scottish evangelical ministers, including such regular correspondents of Edwards as John McLaurin of the Ramshorn Church, Glasgow, William McCulloch of Cambuslang, James Robe of Kilsyth and John Erskine, then of Kirkintilloch. These ministers and their congregations had agreed to spend a part of Saturday evening and Sunday morning each week, as well as the first Tuesdays of February, May, August and November, in prayer to God for 'an abundant effusion of his Holy Spirit', so as to 'revive true religion in all parts of Christendom, and to deliver all nations from their great and manifold spiritual calamities and miseries, and bless them with the unspeakable benefits of the kingdom of our glorious Redeemer, and fill the whole earth with his glory'.[20] This 'concert of prayer' ran for an initial two years, and then was renewed for a further seven.

When Edwards was sent information regarding it, he lost no time in seeking to implement a similar concert of prayer in the New England colonies. He encouraged his own congregation to get involved, and also communicated the concept of such a prayer union to neighbouring ministers whom he felt would be receptive to the idea. Although the idea initially met with a poor response, Edwards was not to be put off. In a sermon given in

February 1747, on Zechariah 8:20-22, he sought to demonstrate how the text supported his call for a union of praying Christians. Within the year, a revised and greatly expanded version of this sermon was ready for publication as the *Humble Attempt*.

The *Humble Attempt* is divided into three parts. The first section opens with a number of observations on Zechariah 8:20-22 and then goes on to provide a description of the origin of the concert of prayer in Scotland. From the text in Zechariah, Edwards infers that 'there shall be given much of a spirit of prayer to God's people, in many places, disposing them to come into an express agreement, unitedly to pray to God in an extraordinary manner, that he would appear for the help of his church, and in mercy to mankind, and pour out his Spirit, revive his work, and advance his spiritual kingdom in the world, as he has promised.'[21] Edwards thus concludes that it is a duty well-pleasing to God and incumbent upon God's people in America to assemble and, with 'extraordinary, speedy, fervent and constant prayer', pray for those 'great effusions of the Holy Spirit' which will dramatically advance the kingdom of Christ.

Part II of the treatise cites a number of reasons for participating in the concert of prayer. Our Lord Jesus shed his blood and tears, and poured out his prayers to secure the blessed presence of his Spirit for his people. 'The sum of the blessings Christ sought', writes Edwards, 'by what he did and suffered in the work of redemption, was the Holy Spirit.' He then continues: 'The Holy Spirit, in his indwelling, his influences and fruits, is the sum of all grace, holiness, comfort and joy, or in one word, of all the spiritual good Christ purchased for men in this world: and is also the sum of all perfection, glory and eternal joy, that he purchased for them in another world.'[22] Therefore, Edwards rightly concludes, if this is what Christ longed for and 'set his heart upon, from all eternity, and which he did and suffered so much for, offering up "strong crying and tears" [Heb. 5:7], and his precious blood to obtain it; surely his disciples and members should also earnestly seek it, and be much and earnest in prayer for it'.[23]

Scripture, moreover, is replete with commands, incentives and illustrations regarding prayer for the Holy Spirit. There is, for example, the encouragement given in Luke 11:13.[24] These words of Christ, Edwards observes, imply that prayer for the Holy Spirit is one request that God the Father is particularly pleased to answer in the affirmative. Or one might consider the example of the early disciples who devoted themselves to 'united fervent prayer and supplication ... till the Spirit came down in a wonderful manner upon them', as is related in Acts 1-2.[25]

Additional incentives to take part in the concert of prayer are provided by what Edwards terms 'the spiritual calamities and miseries of the present time'. Among them are the disastrous attempt by Charles Edward Stuart ('Bonnie Prince Charlie') to seize the British throne for his father only a couple of years before (1745-1746), the persecution of the Calvinistic Huguenots in France, the decay of vital piety, the deluge of vice and immorality, the loss of respect for those in vocational ministry and the prevalence of religious fanaticism.[26] Edwards also sees in the drift of the intellectual and theological currents of his day a further reason for prayer, as men and women rejected Puritan theology so as to embrace theologies shaped by the rationalistic world-view of the Enlightenment.

> Never was an age wherein so many learned and elaborate treatises have been written, in proof of the truth and divinity of the Christian religion; yet never were there so many infidels, among those that were brought up under the light of the gospel. It is an age, as is supposed, of great light, freedom of thought, and discovery of truth in matters of religion, and detection of the weakness and bigotry of our ancestors, and of the folly and absurdity of the notions of those that were accounted eminent divines in former generations; which notions, it is imagined, did destroy the very foundations of virtue and religion, and enervate all precepts of morality, and in effect annul all difference between virtue and vice; and yet vice and wickedness did never so prevail, like an overflowing deluge. 'Tis an age wherein those mean and stingy principles (as they are called) of our forefathers, which (as is supposed) deformed religion, and led to unworthy thoughts of God, are very much discarded, and grown out of credit, and supposed

more free, noble and generous thoughts of the nature of religion, and of the Christian scheme, are entertained; but yet never was an age, wherein religion in general was so much despised and trampled on, and Jesus Christ and God Almighty so blasphemed and treated with open daring contempt.[27]

Yet, Edwards can list a number of events which show that, though his time is a 'day of great apostasy', it is also a 'day of the wonderful works of God; wonders of power and mercy' that should move believers to united prayer just as much as distresses and calamities.[28] Edwards especially highlights such 'wonders of power and mercy' as the various spiritual revivals on the European continent – including one in Rotterdam in which a Scottish pastor, Hugh Kennedy (1698-1764), played a key role[29] – and in Great Britain, and among the New England colonies. These 'late remarkable religious awakenings', Edwards observes, 'may justly encourage us in prayer for the promised glorious and universal outpouring of the Spirit of God'.[30]

The beauty and benefits involved in a visible union for prayer is yet another motive Edwards gives for complying with his proposal. Unity, Edwards maintains, is regarded by the Scriptures as 'the peculiar beauty of the church of Christ'.[31] In support of this statement, Edwards refers his readers to the Song of Songs 6:9, Psalm 122:3 and Ephesians 4:3-6,16. Union in prayer would also prove to be beneficial for the church in that it would tend to promote closer rapport between the members of different denominational bodies. In Edwards' words: 'Union in religious duties, especially in the duty of prayer, in praying one with and for another, and jointly for their common welfare, above almost all other things, tends to promote mutual affection and endearment.'[32]

Part III is the longest portion of the *Humble Attempt* and is devoted to answering various objections to the idea of a concert of prayer. Much of this section of the *Humble Attempt* is devoted to proving his case from a postmillennial reading of New Testament eschatology.[33] But it was also charged that the concert of prayer was something previously unknown in the history of the church. It was thus suspect. In actual fact, there had been advocates for such meetings from the early years of the eighteenth century, for instance, Cotton Mather, as we have seen. Edwards makes no mention of Mather, but he does recall that in 1712 a group of London Dissenters had issued *A Serious Call from the City to the Country*, in which it was urged that an extra hour be set aside every week to beseech God to 'appear for the Deliverance and Enlargement of His Church'.[34]

Philip Gura has observed that the *Humble Attempt* 'is an important signpost' in Edwards' thinking about revival. Despite the problems that emerged in the revival, which we have examined in previous chapters, the book displays Edwards' 'unshakable belief in the advancement of religion through an even greater outpouring of the Spirit of God than the world had yet seen'.[35] By and large, though, the congregations of New England were not deeply impacted by the book at the time. A number of congregations in America and Scotland did observe concerts of prayer throughout the 1750s. Especially during the French and Indian War (1755-1760), when the British and the French were fighting for the hegemony of North America, the concert of prayer was in wide use among American Calvinists. In 1759, for instance, Robert Smith informed fellow Presbyterians in Pennsylvania that the concert of prayer would prove to be far more effective in hastening the 'brightest period of the militant Church's glory' than the military victories won by British forces.[36] Yet, as has been noted, the *Humble Attempt* would bear its greatest fruit some twenty-five years after the death of its author.

In essence, the *Humble Attempt* is a call for a practical expression of Reformation theology, which maintains that only God is able to do the work of God.[37] Believing this, the church has only one posture: prayer.

CONCLUDING THOUGHTS

IN THE PAST, the reading of Jonathan Edwards' written corpus has been a rich source of spiritual revival.[1] As was mentioned in the introduction, for instance, Edwards was the leading theological mentor, after Scripture, for English Calvinistic Baptists at the close of the eighteenth century and played a central role in leading them from ecclesial insularity to epochal outreach and renewal.[2] Yet, the theological mantle of Edwards has also often been disputed. Who are his true heirs? There were significant debates about the answer to this question in the nineteenth century,[3] as there have been in more recent days.

For example, in his book *Catch the Fire*, a defence of the experience of the so-called Toronto Blessing in the 1990s, Guy Chevreau concludes a lengthy chapter of citations from the works of Jonathan Edwards by answering the question, 'With all of the manifestations that have characterized the meetings at the Airport Vineyard, what assessment would Jonathan Edwards bring to bear?' His answer, using another couple of quotes from Edwards, is that the New England theologian would undoubtedly throw his support behind the Airport Vineyard.[4] On the other hand, the well-known California pastor John MacArthur, who has come out in strong opposition to the Toronto Blessing and other charismatic movements, employed Edwards' works in his 1994 book, *Reckless Faith*, to arrive at a very different evaluation of the Toronto Blessing. Would Edwards, he also asked, defend what happened at the Toronto Airport Vineyard as a true work of God? 'The historical facts', MacArthur answered, 'actually suggest he would be appalled by the movement. He would almost certainly label it fanaticism.'[5]

This study has not primarily sought to answer this recent debate about Edwards' legacy.[6] In an earlier work I did seek to answer this question, and while I have reservations about the format of that work and some of its tone, I would still generally affirm what was written in its conclusion.[7] Largely because of Edwards' Calvinism, his strong commitment to cessationism, his high regard for rigorous intellectual reflection and theological analysis, his passion for preaching and his Christocentric piety, I argued that Edwards would not have supported the Toronto Blessing. The present study has done nothing to alter substantially my convictions in this regard. Edwards' theological bent in this regard is well seen in some remarks made by Samuel Davies (1723-1761) in a letter to Edwards' friend Joseph Bellamy. Davies, who was instrumental in promoting revival in Virginia and was Edwards' successor as president of the College of New Jersey, was seeking to convince Bellamy to help him secure Edwards' presence in Virginia after his dismissal from Northampton:

> Of all the men I know in America, he [i.e. Edwards] appears to me the most fit for this place... Fiery, superficial ministers will never do in these parts: they might do good; but they

would do much more harm. We need the deep judgement and calm temper of Mr. Edwards among us.[8]

But what this present study has really sought to do is to present an Edwardsean morphology of revival from his key works on the subject and indicate something of the historical context that gave rise to this morphology. All of the details of how this morphology is to be appropriated by the church in the present day would really take another monograph. In the course of this study I have indicated from time to time where contemporary application can be made since I am convinced that by and large Edwards' Calvinistic Augustinian vision of revival has much to teach us and we would do well to take him as our mentor. Of course, Edwards would be the first to affirm that his writings are not to be regarded as oracular. But equally faulty would be to act as if God had not given the church the gift of what George Marsden has called Edwards' 'breathtaking' vision of the triune God, his ineffable beauty, and the triumph of his sovereign love in this fallen world.[9]

Appendix 1

JONATHAN EDWARDS, DIRECTIONS FOR JUDGING OF PERSONS' EXPERIENCES

ALEXANDER BALLOCH GROSART (1827-1899), a Scottish author and theologian, made a reputation as an Elizabethan and Jacobean scholar by scouring many of the great libraries of Europe for rare volumes to edit and reprint.[1] It was probably his reputation in this regard that led to his involvement in the early stages of a mid-nineteenth-century biography of Edwards, planned by a Scottish publishing house, that never materialized.[2] Grosart came across the Atlantic to the United States in order to consult Edwards' manuscripts that, at the time, were in the possession of Tryon Edwards, Jonathan's great-grandson.[3] He transcribed a number of them and, according to Tryon Edwards, clandestinely took a number of them with him back to Scotland. Subsequently, Grosart had privately printed a 300-copy edition of what he called *Selections from the Unpublished Writings of Jonathan Edwards, of America* ([Edinburgh]: Printed for private circulation [by Ballantyne and Co.], 1865). The following item is taken from this volume, pages 183-185. The copy from which it has been taken is in the Montgomery Library of Westminster Theological Seminary, Philadelphia. It may also be found in *Writings on the Trinity, Grace, and Faith*, ed. Sang Hyun Lee (*The Works of Jonathan Edwards*, vol. 21; New Haven/London: Yale University Press, 2003), 522-524.

Sang Hyun Lee notes that the only text we have for this document is that reproduced in Grosart's *Selections*. The first part of the document focuses on conviction of sin and, in Lee's words, bears 'some resemblance, in miniature, to Edwards' detailed study of the experiences of his parishioners in his *Faithful Narrative*'. The second part, on the other hand, is more concerned with holiness and Christian practice and may well reflect Edwards' pastoral counsel from the time of the Great Awakening in 1740 to 1742.[4]

See to it

That the operation be much upon the Will or Heart, not on the Imagination, nor on the speculative understanding or motions of the mind, though they draw great affections after 'em as the consequence.

That the trouble of mind be reasonable, that the mind be troubled about those things that it has reason to be troubled about; and that the trouble seems mainly to operate in such a manner, with such a kind of trouble and exercise as is reasonable: founded on reasonable, solid consideration; a solid sense and conviction of truth, as of things as they are indeed.

That it be because their state appears terrible on the account of those things, wherein its dreadfulness indeed consists; and that their concern be solid, not operating very much by pangs and sudden passions, freaks and frights, and a capriciousness of mind.

That under their seeming convictions it be sin indeed; that they are convinced of their guilt, in offending and affronting so great a God: One that so hates sin, and is so set against it, to punish it, etc.

That they be convinced both of sins of heart and life: that their pretences of sense of sin of heart ben't [ie. be not] without reflection on their wicked practice; and also that they are not only convinced of sin of practice, but sin of heart. And in both, that what troubles 'em be those things wherein their wretchedness has really chiefly consisted.

That they are convinced of their spiritual sins, consisting in their sinful defects, living without love to God, without accepting Christ, gratitude to Him, etc.

That the convictions they have of the insufficiency and vanity of their own doings, ben't only from some sense of wanderings of mind, and other sinful behaviour mixed; but from a conviction of the sinful defects of their duties, their not being done from a right principle; and so as having no goodness at all mixed with the bad, but altogether corrupt.

That it is truly conviction of sin that convinces them of the Justice of God in their damnation, in rejecting their prayers, disregarding their sorrowful case, and all desires and endeavours after deliverance, etc., and not merely any imagination or pang, and melting of affection through some real or supposed instance of Divine Goodness.

That they be so convinced of sin as not in the inward thought and habit of their minds to excuse themselves, and impliedly quarrel with God, because of their impotency: for instance, that they don't excuse their slight of Christ, and want of love to Him, because they can't esteem and love Him.

That they don't evidently themselves look on their convictions [as] great, and ben't taken with their own humiliation.

That which should be chiefly looked at should be *evangelical*. If this be sound, we have no warrant to insist upon it, that there be manifest a remarkable work, purely legal, wherein was nothing of grace. So with regard to Convictions and Humiliation; only seeing to it that the mind is indeed convinced of these things, and sees 'em [sees] that [which] many Divines insisted should be seen, under a purely legal work. And also seeing to it that the convictions there are, seem to be deep and fixed, and to have a powerful governing influence on the temper of the mind, and a very direct respect to practice.

See to it

That they have not only pretended convictions of sin; but a proper mourning for sin. And also, that sin is burdensome to them and that their hearts are tender and sensible with respect to it… the object of their care and dread.

That God and Divine things are admirable on account of the beauty of their moral perfection.

That there is to be discerned in their sense of the sufficiency of Christ, a sense of that Divine, supreme, and spiritual excellency of Christ, wherein this sufficiency fundamentally consists; and that the sight of this excellency is really the foundation of their satisfaction as to His sufficiency.

That their conviction of the truth of Divine things be discerned to be truly some way or other primarily built on a sense of their Divine excellency.

That their discoveries and illuminations and experiences in

general, are not superficial pangs, flashes, imaginations, freaks, but solid, substantial, deep, inwrought into the frame and temper of their minds, and discovered to have respect to practice.

That they long after HOLINESS, and that all their experiences increase their longing.

Let 'em be inquired of concerning their disposition and willingness to bear the Cross, sell all for Christ, choosing their portion in heaven, etc.

Whether their experiences have a respect to PRACTICE in these ways. That their behaviour at present seems to be agreeable to such experiences.

Whether it inclines 'em much to think of Practice, and more and more for past ill practice.

Makes a disposition to ill practices dreadful.

Makes 'em long after perfect freedom from sin, and after those things wherein *Holiness* consists; and by fixed and strong resolutions, attended with fear and jealously of their own hearts.

Whether, when they tell of their experiences, it is not with such an air that you as it were feel that they expect to be admired and applauded, and [whether they] won't be disappointed if they fail of discerning in you something of that nature; and shocked and displeased if they discover the contrary.

Enquire whether their joy be truly and properly joy in God and in Christ; joy in Divine Good; or whether it ben't wholly joy in themselves, joy in their own excellencies or privilege, in their experiences; what God has done for them, or what He has promised He will do for them; and whether they ben't affected with their own discoveries and affections.

Appendix 2

BEAUTY AS A DIVINE ATTRIBUTE: THE WESTERN TRADITION AND JONATHAN EDWARDS[1]

UP UNTIL THE eighteenth century, beauty was the most important concept in aesthetics. Plato's *Hippias Major*, one of the earliest works in the history of aesthetics, was focused on the question, 'What is beauty?' and it was this question that informed much of aesthetic thought for the next 2,000 years. With the emergence of the notion of the fine arts as well as the systematic formulation of the idea of aesthetic appreciation in the eighteenth century, however, the question about the nature of beauty lost its traditional centrality in aesthetics and has never regained it.[2] An interesting parallel to this development is the way in which modern philosophical theology since the eighteenth century has by and large neglected discussion of beauty as a divine attribute. Philosophers and theologians in the patristic and mediaeval eras, as well as a number of later thinkers down to and including the eighteenth century, had considered the concept of beauty to be central to any discussion of the divine nature.[3]

In what follows, the two main sources for this philosophical discussion of divine beauty in the western tradition are briefly explored, an overview of the development of the discussion given, some problems with regard to attributing beauty to God looked at, and finally some solutions suggested. As we shall see, Jonathan Edwards plays a key role in this tradition of aesthetic thought.

Two sources

The designation of beauty as a divine attribute in the Western philosophical tradition ultimately has two main sources, Platonic thought and the Bible. Plato's most significant discussions of beauty in this regard occur in the concluding section of his *Philebus* and in a small portion of his *Symposium*.

Central to the *Philebus* is the discussion of a question that is not primarily one of aesthetics, namely, whether pleasure or knowledge is to be regarded as humanity's supreme good. Seeking to distinguish 'pure' from 'mixed' pleasures, Socrates adduces one example of the former, namely, pleasures evoked by objects that are intrinsically beautiful. Simple geometrical shapes – 'something straight or round and what is constructed out of these with a compass, rule, and square, such as plane figures and solids'[4] – single colours and musical notes are cited as examples.[5] The existence of beauty in such objects is considered to be independent of, nor affected by, external perception. They are intrinsically beautiful precisely because they are 'by their very nature forever beautiful'.[6] This concept of the intrinsic is clearly being used to secure the stability of the experience of beauty.

This perspective on the intrinsically beautiful is logically developed in the *Symposium*, where there is an overt hypostatization of beauty. There the priestess Diotima tells Socrates:

> First … [Beauty] always is and neither comes to be nor passes away, neither waxes nor wanes. Second, it is not beautiful

this way and ugly that way, nor beautiful at one time and ugly at another, nor beautiful in relation to one thing and ugly in relation to another; nor is it beautiful here but ugly there, as it would be if it were beautiful for some people and ugly for others… [it is] itself by itself with itself, it is always one in form; and all the other beautiful things share in it, in such a way that when those others come to be or pass away, this does not become the least bit smaller or greater nor suffer any change.[7]

On the basis of this ontological understanding of beauty, Socrates is urged by Diotima to climb the so-called 'ladder of beauty', ascending from examples of beauty in this world – physical and moral beauty, and the beauty of various fields of knowledge – till he finally comes to absolute beauty, and so spend his life in contemplation of what is supremely beautiful.[8]

The other key source in the western tradition for the description of God as beautiful is the Bible. Most of the texts in the Hebrew Bible that ascribe beauty to God are to be found in the Psalms. For example, in Psalm 27:4, the psalmist asserts, 'one thing have I asked of the Lord, that will I seek after: that I may dwell in the house of the Lord all the days of my life, to gaze upon the beauty of the Lord' (ESV). Here, beauty is ascribed to God as a way of expressing the psalmist's conviction that the face-to-face vision of God is the profoundest experience available to a human being. Again, in Psalm 145:5 the psalmist states, that he will meditate 'on the glorious splendour' or beauty of God's majesty (ESV). Similarly, the eighth century B.C. prophet Isaiah can predict that there is coming a day when God will be 'a crown of glory and a diadem of beauty' to his people (Isa. 28:5, ESV).

The most important biblical concept in this connection is probably that of 'glory'. When used with reference to God, it emphasizes his greatness and transcendence, splendour and holiness.[9] God is thus said to be clothed with glory (Ps. 104:1), and his works full of his glory (Ps. 111:3). The created realm, the product of his hands, speaks of this glory day after day (Ps. 19:1-2). But it is especially in his redemptive activity on the plane of history that his glory is revealed. The glory manifested in this activity is to be proclaimed throughout all the earth (Ps. 96:3), so that one day 'the earth will be filled with the knowledge of the glory of the Lord' (Hab. 2:14, ESV). In other words, it was their encounter with God on the plane of history that enabled the biblical authors to see God's beauty and loveliness shining through the created realm.

The development of a tradition

It is well known that Platonism played a significant role in the formulation of a number of aspects of early Christian thought. This is especially evident in those texts of the western tradition that ascribe beauty to God. The fourth-century North African author Augustine (354-430), for example, identifies God and beauty in a famous prayer from his *Confessions*:

> I have learnt to love you late, Beauty at once so ancient and so new! I have learnt to love you late! You were within me, and I was in the world outside myself. I searched for you outside myself and, disfigured as I was, I fell upon the lovely things of your creation... The beautiful things of this world kept me from you and yet, if they had not been in you, they would have had no being at all.[10]

The material realm is only beautiful because it derives both its being and beauty from the One who is Beauty itself, namely, God. Augustine intimates, that if he had been properly attendant to the derivative beauty of the world, he would have been led to its divine source.

Like many of the ancients, Augustine appears to have been fascinated by beauty and, following Plato, used his love of beauty in its many aspects to help him love the beauty of God. But Augustine stressed that the two should not be confused. Thus, speaking about God's creation of the heavens and the earth, Augustine can state again in the *Confessions*:

> It was you, then, O Lord, who made them, you who are beautiful, for they too are beautiful; you who are good, for

they too are good; you who are, for they too are. But they are not beautiful and good as you are beautiful and good, nor do they have their being as you, their Creator, have your being. In comparison with you they have neither beauty nor goodness nor being at all.[11]

There is a tension here. On the one hand, there is Augustine's desire to maintain a clear distinction between the beauty of God and the beauty of creation, a distinction that derives from the emphasis of the Bible on the otherness and uniqueness of God. On the other hand, his imbibing of Plato leads to the argument that what is beautiful in creation derives its beauty solely from its participation in ultimate Beauty.

The same tension is found in one of the most influential of these early discussions of God as beautiful, namely, *The Divine Names*, a treatise written in the early sixth century by a Syrian monk known nowadays as Pseudo-Dionysius. In it, he says that the Good, which is one of the ways that he designates God, is called beauty because it imparts beauty to all things. Furthermore, in a statement that is clearly dependent upon Plato's *Symposium*, the Good/God is:

> ...the all-beautiful and the beautiful beyond all. It is forever so, unvaryingly, unchangeably so ... beautiful but not as something coming to birth and death, to growth or decay, not lovely in one respect while ugly in some other way. It is not beautiful 'now' but otherwise 'then', beautiful in relation to one thing but not to another. It is not beautiful in one place and not so in another, as though it could be beautiful for some and not for others. Ah no! In itself and by itself it is the uniquely and the eternally beautiful. It is the superabundant source in itself of the beauty of every beautiful thing... From this beauty comes the existence of everything, each being exhibiting its own way of beauty. For beauty is the cause of harmony, of sympathy, of community. Beauty unites all things and is the source of all things.[12]

In the words of the Italian philosopher Umberto Eco, Pseudo-Dionysius views 'the universe as an inexhaustible irradiation of beauty, a grandiose expression of the ubiquity of First Beauty'.[13] Yet, there is still the consciousness that one must affirm a distinction between that Beauty which is God and the beauty of the universe.

This philosophical discussion comes to full flower in the mediaeval era. For instance, Thomas Aquinas (c.1225-1274), the quintessential mediaeval philosopher and theologian, carries on this discussion in relation to a two-pronged argument for ascribing all perfections to God. He must have all perfections since he possesses the attribute of aseity, that is, he is a self-subsistent being. Moreover, he must have them because he is the cause of perfection in his creatures, and any cause must always possess the perfections of its effects.[14]

In his commentary on Pseudo-Dionysius' *The Divine Names*, Aquinas applies this argument specifically to beauty as a divine attribute. There he argues that God is called Beauty because, as Aquinas comments, 'he gives beauty to all created beings, according to the properties of each'. He is, Aquinas goes on, most beautiful and super-beautiful, both because of his exceeding greatness (like the sun in relation to hot things) and because of his causality, as the source of all that is beautiful in the universe. He is thus beautiful in himself and not in respect of anything else. And since God has beauty as his own, he can communicate it to his creation. He is, therefore, the exemplary cause of all that is beautiful.[15] Or, as Aquinas puts it elsewhere: 'Things are beautiful by the indwelling of God.'[16]

EDWARDS AND DIVINE BEAUTY

As one enters the modern era, a profound reconstruction takes place in aesthetic thought. The watershed is the eighteenth century, when there is a dramatic shift away from the question of the nature of beauty to a focus upon the perceiver's experience of the beautiful and the determination of those conditions under which beauty is appreciated. Aesthetic perception now becomes the basic concept in aesthetics.[17] And it is intriguing that there is a corresponding diminution of interest in the ascription of beauty to God. Nevertheless, one can still find vital representatives of the older tradition. One such figure is the New England philosopher and theologian, Jonathan Edwards.

There is no doubt that beauty is a central and defining category in Edwards' thinking about God. He regards beauty as a key distinguishing feature of the divine being: 'God is God,' he writes in his *Religious Affections*, 'and distinguished from all other beings, and exalted above 'em, chiefly by his divine beauty, which is infinitely diverse from all other beauty.'[18] Unlike creatures who receive their beauty from another, namely God, it is 'peculiar to God', Edwards writes elsewhere, 'that He has beauty within Himself'.[19] Edwards' conception of divine beauty thus serves to accentuate the biblical idea of the uniqueness and transcendence of God. Typical of the older tradition in aesthetics, his central interest is not in what he calls 'secondary beauty', the beauty of created things, but 'primary beauty', that of God. His writings contain no extended discussion of the nature of the fine arts or of human beauty. Even his occasional rhapsodies regarding the beauties of nature function chiefly as a foil to a deeper reflection on the divine beauty. Secondary beauty holds interest for him basically because it mirrors the primary beauty of spiritual realities.[20]

Yet, in distinction from the Platonic emphasis on ascending from derivative beauty to that of the ultimate, Edwards moves in the opposite direction. In his *Personal Narrative*, for example, where he is describing his conversion to Christianity, he indicates that his conversion wrought a change in his entire outlook on the world:

> The appearance of everything was altered: there seemed to be, as it were, a calm, sweet cast, or appearance of divine glory, in almost everything. God's excellency, his wisdom, his purity and love, seemed to appear in everything; in the sun, moon, and stars; in the clouds, and blue sky; in the grass, flowers, trees; in the water, and all nature; which used greatly to fix my mind. I often used to sit and view the moon, for a long time; and so in the daytime, spent much time in viewing the clouds and sky, to behold the sweet glory of God in these things.[21]

What is striking about this passage is what Michael McClymond calls 'Edwards' mysticism, his capacity for seeing God in and through the world of nature'.[22] As McClymond goes on to note, this mysticism could be explained in terms of the Platonic ascent to the archetype of beauty. Yet, as he rightly points out, Edwards' experience of God precedes his transformed view of nature. The New England philosopher travels from the primary beauty of God to the secondary beauty of the created realm.[23] This recasting of the traditional perspective is typical, though, of a thinker who was consciously seeking to undo what Hans Frei has called the 'great reversal' characteristic of early modernity, in which a theocentric world-view was replaced by an anthropocentric one.[24]

Problems and issues[25]

This traditional attribution of beauty to God raises various problems for contemporary philosophers and theologians. For some, the very concept of beauty is considered outmoded since they would regard beauty as simply a matter of taste, something that varies from person to person and from culture to culture. The idea of divine beauty itself presents further difficulties for others. Beauty is commonly understood in terms of colours, shapes, sounds, and so forth – things experienced through the senses. But how can God, who by definition is without spatial dimensions or a body of any sort, be described as beautiful? Similar problems can, of course, be raised with regard to other divine attributes, such as wisdom, power and love. But theists are able to get around these problems by explaining these attributes in terms of the relevant divine actions, i.e. God's wise governance of the world, the manifestation of his power in natural phenomena, and his love shown in providence. In the case of beauty, however, it is difficult to find any corresponding actions beyond God's creation of beauty in the world. Those who attempt to go further than this tend to say that God's beauty is ultimately inexpressible. Or else they produce an analysis similar to that of Aquinas, for whom God's beauty could be defined as the integrity, harmony and radiance of his being.[26]

At the root of these problems is the fact that we lack a proper vocabulary to support our ascriptions of beauty to God. Contemporary western culture usually employs the term 'beautiful' in one of two ways: either as an overall verdict on a work of art or a natural phenomenon, or to qualify another term, as in the phrase 'beautifully reasoned'. In either case, the term is supported by a vast array of concepts: by other aesthetic terms such as 'elegant' and 'graceful', or by particular words describing the qualities of colours, sounds, and so on. Most of these terms, however, are inappropriate for describing God – what would a pretty, handsome, or elegant God be like?

In the case of divine beauty, the neighbouring or supporting concepts are drawn from other sources. From the language of power, there is, for instance, the biblical term 'glory', which speaks of God's omnipotence and transcendence. From the realm of ethics, there are terms that relate to moral and spiritual qualities – goodness and holiness and the like. God's beauty is also often linked to light, in the sense of intellectual or spiritual illumination, and thus to wisdom, knowledge and truth. It would, appear, therefore, that the idea of divine beauty is obscure both in itself and also in its relation to more familiar types of beauty.

Some suggested solutions

These various difficulties with the concept of divine beauty are formidable, but by no means insurmountable. Although currently aesthetics is not as interested in 'beauty' as earlier centuries, the concept is still the subject of much philosophical reflection and writing. Moreover, it is not true that beauty is ascribed only to colours, lines, sounds, and so forth. We commonly speak of the beauty of a scientific theory or the elegance of a mathematical proof, of beautiful personalities, sweetness of character, or moral deformity. If, therefore, we still recognize moral and intellectual beauty, there seems to be no good reason to exclude discussing beauty in relation to God. As Patrick Sherry admits, though, it is difficult to see how one might go on from this point, given the paucity of recent reflection on divine beauty in both philosophical and popular literature.

Sherry goes on to suggest that there are, in principle, two other possible starting points for a philosopher or theologian here: the divine nature itself and the beauty of creation. As regards the first, one might discuss God's beauty in terms of the relationship between his various attributes.

With regard to the second, a discussion of the topic that begins with our apprehension of beauty in nature would need to answer some common objections. Some have argued that modern thinkers have found the ascription of beauty to God more problematical than, say, power or wisdom. This is not exactly true, though. Gerard Manley Hopkins (1844-1889), the Roman Catholic poet of the Victorian era, certainly did not think so when he penned the following words:

> The world is charged with the grandeur of God.
> It will flame out, like shining from shook foil…[27]

And one finds similar thoughts in the writings of Simone Weil (1909-1943), the French philosopher and social activist, who can describe the beauty of the world as the appearance of divine beauty.

Jonathan Edwards' writings, written in response to early modernity, are also of enormous value in this regard. For him, the beauty of creation exhibited, expressed and communicated God's beauty and glory to men and women. In nature, God's beauty is visible. Thus, he could state with regard to Christ:

> The beauties of nature are really emanations or shadows of the excellencies the Son of God.
>
> So that, when we are delighted with flowery meadows, and gentle breezes of wind, we may consider that we see only the emanations of the sweet benevolence of Jesus Christ. When we behold the fragrant rose and lily, we see His love and purity. So the green trees, and fields, and singing of birds are the emanations of His infinite joy and benignity. The easiness and naturalness of trees and vines are shadows of His beauty and loveliness. The crystal rivers and murmuring streams are the footsteps of His favor, grace, and beauty. When we behold the light and brightness of the sun, the golden edges of an evening cloud, or the beauteous bow, we behold the adumbrations of His glory and goodness; and, in

the blue sky, of His mildness and gentleness. There are also many things wherein we may behold His awful majesty, in the sun in his strength, in comets, in thunder, in the hovering thunder-clouds, in ragged rocks, and the brows of mountains.[28]

Edwards' approach could also be helpful in that it explains why aesthetic experience is for many people also a religious experience. Moreover, by emphasizing that the beauty we perceive in the created realm is a mode of God's presence, he avoids the seeming nebulousness of much of the discussion about divine beauty.

It follows, of course, for Edwards, that those who ignore the beauty of God in creation are committing a religious fault. For Edwards, 'the beatific was basic' to God and the universe.[29] Moreover, Edwards is convinced that men and women uniformly fail in this regard, for they have lost the faculty to see the visible beauty of God in his creation. They perceive the secondary beauty, but fail to see the divine beauty that saturates nature. This faculty can only be restored through the indwelling of the Holy Spirit, 'the agent of conversion and of all our good'.[30]

Appendix 3

ESTHER EDWARDS BURR (1732-1758) AND EDWARDSEAN PIETY

ESTHER EDWARDS BURR was born in Northampton on 13 February 1732, the third child of Jonathan and Sarah Edwards. Samuel Hopkins remembered her as having 'a lively, sprightly imagination, a quick and penetrating thought'.[1] Her childhood years coincided with the years of the Great Awakening. She was eight when the Great Awakening began, and ten when it ended in 1742. All of this would have made a deep impression on her.[2] The revival would, no doubt, have reinforced in her mind that genuine Christianity was a religion of the heart and that 'the only true religion was indeed heartfelt, nothing short of a total and joyous submission to the will of God'.[3] She herself made a profession of faith when she was 'about fifteen'.[4]

On 29 June 1752, at the age of twenty, Esther married Aaron Burr Sr, a minister whose evangelical cast of mind was much like her own and who was deeply respected by her father.[5] Aaron was the pastor of the Presbyterian church in Newark, New Jersey, and the second president of the newly formed College of New Jersey (later to be called Princeton). He was considerably older than Esther, which occasioned some gossip. One of the students at the college, Joseph Shippen, reckoned Esther a 'great beauty' when he saw her, but far 'too young for the president'.[6] Later, though, Shippen was positively glowing in his appreciation of the Burrs' marriage and he called Esther a woman of 'very good Sense, of a Genteel & virtuous education, amiable in her person, of great affability & agreeableness in Conversation & a very excellent Economist'.[7] Also Aaron Burr had last seen Esther when she was fourteen, but it took only a few days of courtship for Esther to agree to marry Aaron. The apparent suddenness of her decision may well have had something to do with the financial strains on the Edwards family at the time, since Jonathan Edwards had been removed from the Northampton pastorate in 1750, two years earlier.[8] But there is every evidence that she deeply loved Aaron. As she said in her *Journal*, 'Do you think I would change my *good Mr Burr* for any person, or thing, or all things on the Earth? *No sure!* Not for a Million such Worlds as this that had *no Mr Burr in it*.'[9]

Esther's move to Newark meant that she was some 150 miles away from her parents and family in Stockbridge, a considerable distance to travel at that time. Moreover, New Jersey was quite different from either Massachusetts or Connecticut. While not as developed, it was far more cosmopolitan, which occasionally made Esther homesick for her roots in New England.[10] All of this was exacerbated by the fact that her husband, as president of the college, was frequently away preaching and raising funds. Esther felt sufficiently 'isolated' and hungry for the fellowship of 'young women with spiritual and intellectual interests similar to her own'[11] to covenant with a close Boston friend, Sarah Prince (1728-1771) – the daughter of Thomas Prince, pastor of Boston's Old South Church and a close friend of Edwards – to maintain their friendship by writing journals for one another.

Esther's *Journal* reveals a woman imbued with an Edwardsean theology of revival.[12]

Esther's piety – Edwardsean

It should come as no surprise that Esther's piety is quite Edwardsean. Her delight in her father as a spiritual mentor is evident in a *Journal* entry for 19 September 1756, when she wrote, during a visit to her parents in Stockbridge:

> Last eve I had some free discourse with My Father on the great things that concern my best intrest – I opend my diffeculties to him very freely and he as freely advised and directed. The conversation has removed some distressing doubts that discouraged me much in my Christian warfare – He gave me some excellent directions to be observed in secret that tend to keep the soul near to God, as well as others to be observed in a more publick way – what a mercy that I have such a Father! Such a Guide!'[13]

Like her father, she was committed to a God who had revealed himself in salvation and history as a God of mercy[14] and sovereignty[15]: 'Mercyfull, Wise, Powerfull, Good God that he was from Eternity, and so will continue to Eternity – altho all things Change, yet our God is what he always was.'[16] And like her father, she emphasized the necessity of 'heart religion'. As she wrote on 14 June 1755:

> That knowledge of God that does not produce a love to him and a desire to be like him is not a true knowledge – that knowledge of any things that produces love will also produce a desire to be like what we know and *Love* – that the fallen Angels know much of God is sertain, and that the more they know of him, the more they hate him is as sertain, and that because their hearts are filled with enmity to all good.[17]

Again, we see this Edwardsean view of the necessity of the engagement of the heart in religious activities when Esther exclaims:

I felt something better than I did yesterday, but did not feel alive in Gods service. O to live always near to God! This might be called life – But I am dead whiles I live![18]

Prayer was essential in living near to God. After hearing her husband preach a sermon that exhorted the congregation to 'faith and praier', Esther noted in her diary, 'O! if a praying spirit was to be seen amongst Gods people things would look incouraging.'[19]

Nearly as much as prayer, Esther prized spiritual conversation with close friends such as Sarah Prince:

> I should highly value (as you my dear do) such *charming friends* as you have about *you* – *friends* that one might unbosom their whole soul too… I esteem *religious conversation* one of the best helps to keep up religion in the soul, excepting secret devotion, I don't know but the very best – Then what a lamentable thing that 'tis so neglected by Gods own children.[20]

Note the connection between friendship and what Esther calls 'religious conversation'. For the Christian, true friends are those with whom one can share the deepest things of one's life. They are people with whom one can be transparent and open. In Esther's words, they are people to whom one can 'unbosom [one's] whole soul'. And in the course of conversation about spiritual things, the believer can find strength and encouragement for living the Christian life. In referring to spiritual conversation with friends as 'one of the best helps to keep up religion in the soul', Esther obviously views it as a means of grace, one of the ways that God the Holy Spirit keeps Christians in fellowship with the Saviour. As another New England Christian, Nathanael Emmons (1745-1840), a theologian who was mentored by close followers of Jonathan Edwards, put it in one of his favourite maxims, 'a man is made by his friends'.[21]

Esther's convictions regarding friendship as such a means of grace were challenged in 1756, when one of the college tutors, a John Ewing, told her that 'he did not think women knew what friendship was', since they 'were hardly capable of anything so cool and rational as friendship'! Esther lost no time in refuting his views. As she wrote in her *Journal*, 'I retorted several severe things upon him before he had time to speak again. He blushed and seemed confused... We carried on the dispute for an hour – I talked him quite silent'.[22] He probably never forgot this encounter with Edwards' formidable daughter.[23]

Submission to the sweet sovereignty of God is also prominent in Esther's *Diary*. During the late summer visit to her parents' home in Stockbridge in 1756, Esther spent much of her time terrified about the possibility of an Indian attack. It was in the early days of the French and Indian War, and Stockbridge was right on the frontier in what Esther judged to be a 'very defenseless condition'. On 10 September 1756, after much fretting and fear, Esther wrote in her *Journal*:

> I want to be made willing to die in any way God pleases, but I am not willing to be Buchered by a barbarous enemy nor cant make my self willing – I slept a little better last night then usual – but feel no easier this noon – *The Lord Reighns*, and why ant I sattisfied, he will order all for the best of the publick and for me, and he will be glorified let all the powers of Earth and Hell do their worst.[24]

Less than a month later, with her son, young Aaron Burr Jr – the future vice-president of the United States – quite ill, 'on the borders of Eternity', in the words of Esther, she felt:

> Here was the greatest tryal that ever I meet with in my life – I may compare the struggles with my self to the *Agonies of Death* – but O God made me submit! He made me say the Lord gave, and the Lord may *take*, and I will bless his name – He shewed me that he had the first right, that the Child was not mine he was only lent, and I could freely return him and say Lord do as seemeth good in thy sight... What obligations are we laid under to bring up this Child in a peculiar manner for God?[25]

It is noteworthy that when her husband died the following year, she wrote to her mother in the following strain, words that were deeply rooted in an Edwardsean understanding of divine sovereignty:

> God has not utterly forsaken, although he has cast down. I would speak it to the glory of God's name, that I think he has in an uncommon degree discovered himself to be an all-sufficient God, a full fountain of all good. Although all streams were cut off, yet the fountain is left full.[26]

A CLOUD OF GLORY: GOD AND REVIVAL

During her time with her family in Stockbridge in 1756 – the last time she was with them – she heard her father preach on Amos 8:11. Later that day – 12 September 1756 – she wrote in her *Journal*:

> We have been entertained today with a discourse[e] from those words, Amos 8 chapter and 11 vers, 'Behold I send a Famin in the Land, not a famin of Bread nor a Thirst for water, but of hearing of the words of the Lord' – a very propper subject for this day – It looks to me that God is about to deprive this Land of his word and ordinances for their shamefull abuse of them, and just and right will he be in so doing – some times today I have felt oprest with the dark aspect of our Publick affairs, but at night when retired felt calmed with the thought that God would be glorified – and O my dear this is refreshing that the ever blessed God will loose none of his glory lett men or Devils do their worst.[27]

Instead of judgement, though, there was revival, at least at the College of New Jersey in its new locale in Princeton, where it had moved in November 1756. According to Aaron Burr, not one student remained untouched.[28]

What was revival for Esther? It was a 'pouring out of the Spirit',[29] in which God displayed his sovereignty over human hearts. As she wrote on 18 February 1757, just as the revival was beginning, 'who knows what the Lord may be about to do! Nothing is beyound his power'.[30] It was also preceded by prayer:

> O my dear who knows what God may do for the poor youth of this College if we pray ernestly for them! O it would be a Heaven upon Erth if he should shower down plentifully… O lets us pray ernestly for a universal rivival.[31]

It involved a deep concern for salvation on the part of those outside of Christ,[32] an openness to Scriptures[33] and an increased esteem of the Lord Jesus.[34] Fortunately, the revival was spared any wildfire fanaticism. Speaking of the impact of the revival upon the hearts of some of the students, Esther noted:

> It is not a Noisy distress but a deep concern, not a flight of fancy but their judgements are thorougly convinced, and they are deeply wounded at Heart with a sense of their sin and need of Christ. No need now of Mr Burrs sending to rooms to see if the schollars keep good hours and mind their studdies. Never was there so much studdying in the College since it has had a being as now.
>
> This wonderfull pouring out of spirit at this time just as the College is finnished and things a little settled looks to me exactly like Gods desending into the Temple in a Cloud of glory, there by signifying that he did except of the House for his dwelling place and would Bless it – but I fear and tremble, for fear that Sattan will get an advantage and obstruct by sowing Tares amongst the Wheat… But stay, why do I distrust God, he is as able to Carry on this work as to begin it – I will hope and pray that it may become universal – O that this might be the dawn of the glorious day! O I am transported at the thought? Come Lord Jesus come quickly! Make no tarry but come now![35]

The revival did not become universal, as Esther had hoped. It remained very much a local affair, one of a few scattered revivals in the American colonies in the late 1750s.[36] Edwardsean piety would not be productive of revival again till after the American War of Independence.

A CONCLUDING PRAYER

I WOULD LIKE to give Jonathan Edwards the last word and conclude with one of his prayers. This prayer is taken from his funeral sermon for David Brainerd, a young missionary to native North American Indians in New York, Pennsylvania and New Jersey, who died of tuberculosis in Edwards' own home. This young man made a deep impression on Edwards, for in him Edwards saw a model of the piety he had so earnestly recommended in his *Religious Affections*. In the words of Mark A. Noll, Brainerd 'exemplified what Edwards considered an ideal form of revitalized spirituality'.[1] Brainerd was a man, in Edwards' words, 'who had indeed sold all for Christ and had entirely devoted himself to God, and made his glory his highest end'.[2] As he concluded the sermon he prayed these words (we can substitute Edwards for Brainerd):

> Oh, that the things that were seen and heard in this extraordinary person, his holiness, heavenliness, labor and self-denial in life, his so remarkable devoting himself and his all, in heart and practice, to the glory of God ... may excite in us all, both ministers and people, a due sense of the greatness of the work we have to do in the world, the excellency and amiableness of thorough religion in experience and practice, and the blessedness of the end of such whose death finishes such a life, and the infinite value of their eternal reward, when absent from the body and present with the Lord; and effectually stir us up to endeavors that in the way of such an holy life we may at last come to so blessed an end. Amen.[3]

NOTES

ACKNOWLEDGEMENTS
1 'Books & Critics: New & Noteworthy', *The Atlantic Monthly* (April 2003), 91-92.
2 For recent bibliographical studies of the ever-burgeoning corpus of books and articles on Edwards, see Sean Michael Lucas, 'Jonathan Edwards between Church and Academy: A Bibliographic Essay' in D. G. Hart, Sean Michael Lucas and Stephen J. Nichols, eds., *The Legacy of Jonathan Edwards: American Religion and the Evangelical Tradition* (Grand Rapids: Baker, 2003), 228-247; Kenneth P. Minkema, 'Jonathan Edwards in the Twentieth Century', *Journal of the Evangelical Theological Society*, 47 (2004), 659-687; and M. X. Lesser, '"So the people rescued Jonathan": Edwards and his Readers' (unpublished paper presented to the American Society of Church History conference, Seattle, January 2005). For a good overview of the history of Edwards scholarship in the last century, see Kenneth

P. Minkema, 'Jonathan Edwards in the Twentieth Century', *Journal of the Evangelical Theological Society*, 47 (2004), 659-687.

3   *Jonathan Edwards: The Man, his Experience and his Theology* (Richmond Hill, Ontario: Canadian Christian Publications, 1995). This work was done with the help of Gary W. McHale.

4   The Jonathan Edwards Center at Yale University is seeking to provide a complete online resource of those Edwards manuscripts not included in the Yale edition. Information may be found at http://edwards.yale.edu.

CHRONOLOGY

1   This chronology is based on 'A Jonathan Edwards Chronology', compiled Kenneth P. Minkema (http://www.yale.edu). Used by permission. Unless otherwise noted, the entries pertain to Jonathan Edwards.

INTRODUCTION

1   'Jonathan Edwards and the Crucial Importance of Revival', in his *The Puritans: Their Origins and Successors* (Edinburgh: The Banner of Truth Trust, 1987), 361. In the words of J. I. Packer, Edwards' theology of revival 'is, perhaps, the most important single contribution that Edwards has to make to evangelical thinking today' [*A Quest for Godliness. The Puritan Vision of the Christian Life* (Wheaton, Illinois: Crossway Books, 1990), 316]. See also the remarks in this regard by R. E. Davies, *I Will Pour Out My Spirit: A History and Theology of Revivals and Evangelical Awakenings* (Tunbridge Wells, Kent: Monarch Publications, 1992), 26: 'No one who studies the topic of revival will dispute the statement that Jonathan Edwards, the eighteenth-century American preacher and writer, is the classic theologian on the subject.'

2   Letter to Mary Edwards, 10 May 1716 [*Letters and Personal Writings*, ed. George S. Claghorn (*The Works of Jonathan Edwards*, vol. 16; New Haven/London: Yale University Press, 1998), 29]. See also 'The Earliest Known Letter of Jonathan Edwards', *Christian History*, 4, No. 4 (1985), 34.

3   John E. Smith, *Jonathan Edwards: Puritan, Preacher, Philosopher* (Notre Dame: University of Notre Dame Press, 1992), 5.

4   Helen Westra, *The Minister's Task and Calling in the Sermons of Jonathan Edwards* (Lewiston, New York/Queenston, Ontario: The Edwin Mellen Press, 1986), 34.

5   In his recent collection of selections from Christian classics, one of the two that Tony Lane includes from Edwards is taken from his *Religious Affections*. See *The Lion Christian Classics Collection*, compiled by Tony Lane (Oxford: Lion Publishing, 2004), 354-358. There is also a selection from Edwards' life of David Brainerd.

6   *The Spider Letter* in John E. Smith, Harry S. Stout and Kenneth P. Minkema, eds., *A Jonathan Edwards Reader* (New Haven/London: Yale University Press, 1995), 1-8.

7   'Memoirs of Jonathan Edwards, A.M.' [*The Works of Jonathan Edwards* (1834

ed.; repr. Edinburgh: The Banner of Truth Trust, 1987), 1:CLXXXIX]. I owe this reference to John Piper, *The Supremacy of God in Preaching* (Grand Rapids: Baker Book House, 1990), 95-96. Piper offers some interesting comments on this aspect of Edwards' ministry; see *Supremacy of God*, 95-98.

8   'Jonathan Edwards and the Crucial Importance of Revival', 361.

9   *Two Dissertations, I. Concerning the End for which God Created the World* [*Ethical Writings*, ed. Paul Ramsey (*The Works of Jonathan Edwards*, vol. 8; New Haven/London: Yale University Press, 1989), 530]. For an excellent study of this work, see John Piper, *God's Passion for His Glory: Living the Vision of Jonathan Edwards* (Wheaton, Illinois: Crossway Books, 1998). See also the small study by George M. Marsden, 'Challenging the Presumptions of the Age: The Two Dissertations', in D. G. Hart, Sean Michael Lucas and Stephen J. Nichols, eds., *The Legacy of Jonathan Edwards: American Religion and the Evangelical Tradition* (Grand Rapids: Baker, 2003), 99-104.

10   Joseph G. Haroutunian, 'Jonathan Edwards: Theologian of the Great Commandment', *Theology Today*, 1 (1944), 361.

11   *Ruth's Resolution* [*Sermons and Discourses 1734-1738*, ed. M. X. Lesser (*The Works of Jonathan Edwards*, vol. 19; New Haven/London: Yale University Press, 2001) 310].

12   'Jonathan Edwards: Theologian of the Great Commandment', 362.

13   'Edwards, Jonathan', in Alister E. McGrath, ed., *The Blackwell Encyclopedia of Modern Christian Thought* (Oxford/Cambridge, Massachusetts: Blackwell, 1993), 145.

14   Mark A. Noll, *The Scandal of the Evangelical Mind* (Grand Rapids: William B. Eerdmans Publishing Co./Leicester: Inter-Varsity Press, 1994), 77-80.

15   Davies, *I Will Pour Out My Spirit*, 36-39.

16   Noll, 'Edwards, Jonathan', in McGrath, ed., *Modern Christian Thought*, 145.

17   This call to prayer is known as the Prayer Call of 1784 and may be found in John Ryland Jr, *The Nature, Evidences, and Advantages of Humility* (circular letter of the Northamptonshire Association, 1784), 12.

18   Cited John Ryland, *The Indwelling and Righteousness of Christ no Security against Corporeal Death, but the Source of Spiritual and Eternal Life* (London: W. Button & Son, 1815), 34.

19   For the story of this revival, and the life and ministry of Sutcliff, in particular, see Michael A. G. Haykin, *One heart and one soul: John Sutcliff of Olney, his friends and his times* (Darlington, Co. Durham: Evangelical Press, 1994). See also Tom J. Nettles, 'Edwards and His Impact on Baptists', *The Founders Journal*, 53 (Summer 2003), 1-18. For some general remarks on the influence of Edwards, see Douglas Sweeney and Steve Farish, 'Jonathan Edwards at Home and Abroad', *Trinity Magazine*, (Spring 2004), 18-21.

20   This phrase is taken from the title of Robert W. Jenson, *America's Theologian. A Recommendation of Jonathan Edwards* (New York/Oxford: Oxford University Press, 1988).

CHAPTER I

1   George M. Marsden, *Jonathan Edwards: A Life* (New Haven/London: Yale University Press, 2003), 495.

2   Especially helpful in preparing this chapter on Edwards' life and legacy has been Iain H. Murray, *Jonathan Edwards – A New Biography* (Edinburgh: The Banner of Truth Trust, 1987) and George M. Marsden, *Jonathan Edwards: A Life* (New Haven/London: Yale University Press, 2003). Some of this chapter was originally given at the Canadian Carey Family Conference on 29 August 1990, and subsequently appeared as 'Jonathan Edwards (1703-1758) and His Legacy', in *Evangel*, (Autumn 1991), 17-23. Some of it has also appeared as 'Un profilo biografico di Jonathan Edwards', *Studi di teologia*, 29 (2003), 3-17, and 'Advancing the Kingdom of Christ: Jonathan Edwards, the Missionary Theologian', *The Banner of Truth*, 482 (November 2003), 2-10. Used by permission.

3   Marsden, *Jonathan Edwards*, 32. This remark is attributed to the Boston pastor Cotton Mather.

4   *Personal Narrative* [*Letters and Personal Writings*, ed. George S. Claghorn (*The Works of Jonathan Edwards*, vol. 16; New Haven/London: Yale University Press, 1998), 790-791].

5   *Personal Narrative* (*Letters and Personal Writings*, ed. Claghorn, 791).

6   *Personal Narrative* (*Letters and Personal Writings*, ed. Claghorn, 791-792).

7   For the date of Edwards's conversion, see Murray, *Jonathan Edwards*, 35. See also Marsden, *Jonathan Edwards*, 39-43.

8   'Now unto the king eternal, immortal, invisible, the only wise God, be honour and glory for ever and ever, Amen' (KJV).

9   *Personal Narrative* (*Letters and Personal Writings*, ed. Claghorn, 792, 793).

10   Samuel Hopkins, *Memoirs of the Life, Experience and Character of the Late Rev. Jonathan Edwards, A.M.* in *The Works of President Edwards* (1817 London ed.; repr. New York: Burt Franklin, 1968), I, 43. This work of Hopkins has been reprinted as 'The Life and Character of the Late Reverend Mr. Jonathan Edwards', in David Levin, ed., *Jonathan Edwards: A Profile* (New York: Hill and Wang, 1969), 1-86. See also Donald S. Whitney, 'Pursuing a Passion for God through Spiritual Disciplines: Learning from Jonathan Edwards', in John Piper and Justin Taylor, eds., *A God Entranced Vision of All Things: The Legacy of Jonathan Edwards* (Wheaton, Illinois: Crossway Books, 2004), 112-114. Before her early death, Jerusha Edwards (1710-1729), one of Jonathan's younger daughters, was known for her 'solitary meditations, contemplative walks in the woods, and late-night Scripture readings' [Kenneth P. Minkema, 'Hannah and Her Sisters: Sisterhood, Courtship, and Marriage in the Edwards Family in the Early Eighteenth Century', *The New England Historical and Genealogical Register*, 146 (January 1992), 38].

11   For a recent edition of the *Resolutions*, see *Jonathan Edwards' Resolutions And Advice to Young Converts*, ed. Stephen J. Nichols (Phillipsburg, New Jersey: P&R Publishing, 2001).

12   Hopkins, *Memoirs of the Life, Experience and Character of the Late Rev.*

Jonathan Edwards (*Works of President Edwards*, I, 12).
13 *Letters and Personal Writings*, ed. Claghorn, 753, 759, 757.
14 Marsden, *Jonathan Edwards*, 93.
15 *Some Thoughts Concerning the present Revival of Religion in New-England* [*The Great Awakening*, ed. C. C. Goen (*The Works of Jonathan Edwards*, vol. 4; New Haven/London: Yale University Press, 1972), 334].
16 *Letters and Personal Writings*, ed. Claghorn, 789-790.
17 Minkema, 'Hannah and Her Sisters', 45.
18 'A short Sketch of Mrs. Edwards's Life and Character', Appendix 1 to his *Memoirs of the Life, Experience and Character of the Late Rev. Jonathan Edwards* (*Works of President Edwards*, I, 94).
19 On Edwards's conception of beauty, see Appendix 2: Beauty as a divine attribute: The western tradition and Jonathan Edwards. See also the remarks of Amanda Porterfield, *Feminine Spirituality in America: From Sarah Edwards to Martha Graham* (Philadelphia: Temple University Press, 1980), 39-41.
20 Elisabeth Dodds, *Marriage to a Difficult Man: The Uncommon Union of Jonathan & Sarah Edwards* (1971 ed.; repr. Laurel, Mississippi: Audubon Press, 2004), 27. In a recent exhibition of Edwards memorabilia, though, was a square of blue damask, reputedly from the dress worn by Sarah on her wedding day. See *Jonathan Edwards Tercentennial Exhibition: Selected Objects from the Yale Collections 1703-2003* (New Haven, Connecticut: Jonathan Edwards College, Yale University, 2003), 16.
21 Cited Stephen J. Stein, 'Jonathan Edwards and the Rainbow', *New England Quarterly*, 47 (September 1974), 444.
22 Cited Murray, *Jonathan Edwards*, 91. For a recent study of their marriage, see Doreen Moore, *Good Christians, Good Husbands? Leaving a Legacy in Marriage & Ministry* (Fearn, Ross-shire: Christian Focus Publications, 2004), 96-127.
23 'A short Sketch of Mrs. Edwards's Life and Character', Appendix 1 to his *Memoirs of the Life, Experience and Character of the Late Rev. Jonathan Edwards* (*Works of President Edwards*, I, 95).
24 Letter to John Erskine, 5 July 1750 (*Letters and Personal Writings*, ed. Claghorn, 355).
25 See also the account of Samuel Hopkins, 'Short Sketch of Mrs. Edwards's Life and Character', (*Works of President Edwards*, I, 93-97) and Chapter 7.
26 Allen C. Guelzo, 'John Owen, Puritan Pacesetter', *Christianity Today*, 20, No. 17 (21 May 1976), 14.
27 'The Laughter of One: Sweetness and Light in Franklin and Edwards', in Barbara B. Oberg and Harry S. Stout, eds., *Benjamin Franklin, Jonathan Edwards, and the Representation of American Culture* (New York/Oxford: Oxford University Press, 1993), 121 and 131, n. 58. For the days and times of the birth of the eleven children, see Marsden, *Jonathan Edwards*, 511-512.
28 Dodds, *Marriage to a Difficult Man*, 1.
29 Hopkins, *Memoirs of the Life, Experience and Character of the Late Rev. Jonathan Edwards* (*Works of President Edwards*, I, 46-47).

30   *A Faithful Narrative of the Surprising Work of God* (*Great Awakening*, ed. Goen, 146).
31   Murray, *Jonathan Edwards*, 87.
32   *Dynamics of Spiritual Life. An Evangelical Theology of Renewal* (Downers Grove, Illinois: Inter-Varsity Press, 1978), 38.
33   *Great Awakening*, ed. Goen, 147-149.
34   *Justification by Faith Alone* [*Sermons and Discourses 1734-1738*, ed. M. X. Lesser (*The Works of Jonathan Edwards*, vol. 19; New Haven/London: Yale University Press, 2001), 147]. For a study of Edwards' doctrine of justification, see Samuel T. Logan, Jr., 'The Doctrine of Justification in the Theology of Jonathan Edwards', *The Westminster Theological Journal*, 46 (Spring 1984), 26-52; Randall E. Otto, 'Justification and Justice: An Edwardsean Proposal', *The Evangelical Quarterly*, 65 (1993), 131-145; George Hunsinger, 'Dispositional Soteriology: Jonathan Edwards on Justification by Faith Alone', *Westminster Theological Journal*, 66 (2004), 107-120. Also see Chapter 2.
35   *Great Awakening*, ed. Goen, 148-149. For a discussion of other subsidiary causes of the revival, see Samuel T. Logan Jr, 'Jonathan Edwards and the 1734-35 Northampton Revival', *Preaching and Revival* (London: The Westminster Conference, 1984), 63-65. This article can also be found in Peter A. Lillback, ed., *The Practical Calvinist: An Introduction to the Presbyterian & Reformed Heritage In Honor of Dr. D. Clair Davis* (Fearn, Ross-Shire: Christian Focus Publications, 2002), 233-266.
36   *Great Awakening*, ed. Goen, 149.
37   *Great Awakening*, ed. Goen, 150.
38   *Great Awakening*, ed. Goen, 157-158.
39   *Great Awakening*, ed. Goen, 159.
40   Jonathan Edwards, Letter to Thomas Gillespie, 1 July 1751 (*Great Awakening*, ed. Goen, 565).
41   *Great Awakening*, ed. Goen, 151.
42   Eifion Evans, *Daniel Rowland and the Great Evangelical Awakening in Wales* (Edinburgh: The Banner of Truth Trust, 1985), 72.
43   Graham D. Harrison, 'Ferment in New England: Reactions to the Great Awakening', in *Faith and Ferment* ([London]: The Westminster Conference, 1982), 72.
44   Preface to Jonathan Edwards, *The Distinguishing Marks Of a Work of the Spirit of God* (*Great Awakening*, ed. Goen, 217-219). See also the comments of Thomas Templeton Taylor, 'The spirit of the awakening: The pneumatology of New England's Great Awakening in historical and theological context (unpublished Ph.D. thesis, University of Illinois at Urbana-Champaign, 1988), 233-235. On William Cooper, see William B. Sprague, *Annals of the American Pulpit* (New York: Robert Carter and Brothers, 1857), I, 288-291.
45   Preface (*Great Awakening*, ed. Goen, 219-220).
46   *George Whitefield's Journals* ([London]: The Banner of Truth Trust, 1960), 476-477.

47 Cited *Great Awakening*, ed. Goen, 64. For more details on Davenport and Chauncy, see Chapter 5.

48 Murray, *Jonathan Edwards*, 267.

49 *An Humble Attempt to Promote Explicit Agreement and Visible Union of God's People in Extraordinary Prayer, For the Revival of Religion and the Advancement of Christ's Kingdom on Earth, pursuant to Scripture-Promises and Prophecies concerning the Last Time* [*Apocalyptic Writings*, ed. Stephen J. Stein (*The Works of Jonathan Edwards*, vol. 5; New Haven/London: Yale University Press, 1977), 320].

50 *Some Thoughts Concerning the present Revival of Religion in New-England* (*Great Awakening*, ed. Goen, 516).

51 For an interesting discussion of this controversy, see Murray, *Jonathan Edwards*, 311-349; Marsden, *Jonathan Edwards*, 341-374; Mark Dever, 'How Jonathan Edwards Got Fired, and Why It's Important for Us Today', in John Piper and Justin Taylor, eds., *A God Entranced Vision of All Things: The Legacy of Jonathan Edwards* (Wheaton, Illinois: Crossway Books, 2004), 129-144.

52 Increase Mather, *A Discourse Concerning the Danger of Apostasy* (Boston, 1679), 84.

53 Letter to John Erskine, 20 May 1749 (*Letters and Personal Writings*, ed. Claghorn, 271).

54 Letter to Joseph Bellamy, 6 December 1749 (*Letters and Personal Writings*, ed. Claghorn, 309).

55 Murray, *Jonathan Edwards*, 342-343.

56 *A Farewell Sermon* [in Wilson H. Kimnach, Kenneth P. Minkema and Douglas A. Sweeney, eds., *The Sermons of Jonathan Edwards: A Reader* (New Haven/London: Yale University Press, 1999), 228]. See also Marsden, *Jonathan Edwards*, 370.

57 Marsden, *Jonathan Edwards*, 360.

58 Cited Marsden, *Jonathan Edwards*, 361.

59 Letter to John Erskine, 5 July 1750 (*Letters and Personal Writings*, ed. Claghorn, 355).

60 *Farewell Sermon* (Kimnach, Minkema and Sweeney, eds., *Sermons of Jonathan Edwards*, 238).

61 See Stephen J. Nichols, 'Last of the Mohican Missionaries: Jonathan Edwards at Stockbridge', in D. G. Hart, Sean Michael Lucas and Stephen J. Nichols, eds., *The Legacy of Jonathan Edwards: American Religion and the Evangelical Tradition* (Grand Rapids, Michigan: Baker, 2003), 47-63.

62 Miklós Vetö, 'Book Reviews: America's Theologian. A Recommendation of Jonathan Edwards. By Robert W. Jenson', *Church History*, 58 (1989), 522. See also John F. Wilson, 'Jonathan Edwards's Notebooks for "A History of the Work of Redemption"' in R. Buick Knox, ed., *Reformation, Conformity and Dissent* (London: Epworth Press, 1977), 240.

63 For example, William B. Sprague, *Annals of the American Pulpit* (New York: Robert Carter and Brothers, 1857), I, 333: Edwards' 'more important labours' during his Stockbridge sojourn were 'undoubtedly those that were performed in his study'.

64 For two of the sermons to the Stockbridge Indians that have been published, see 'To the Mohawks at the Treaty, August 16, 1751' and 'He That Believeth Shall Be Saved' (Kimnach, Minkema and Sweeney, eds., *Sermons of Jonathan Edwards*, 105-120).

65 Marsden, *Jonathan Edwards*, 408-409.

66 'The Coming of Britain's Age of Empire and Protestant Mission Theology, 1750-1839', *Zeitschrift für Missionswissenschaft und Religionswissenschaft*, 61 (1977), 43. Manor devotes five pages to the examination of Edwards' thought in this regard (39-43).

67 See his 'Prepare Ye the Way of the Lord: The Missiological Thought and Practice of Jonathan Edwards (1703-1758)' (unpublished Ph.D. thesis, Fuller Theological Seminary, 1989); 'Jonathan Edwards: Missionary Biographer, Theologian, Strategist, Administrator, Advocate – and Missionary', *International Bulletin of Missionary Research*, 21, No. 2 (April 1997), 60-67; 'Jonathan Edwards, theologian of the missionary awakening' [EMA occasional paper, No. 3 (Spring 1999)] in *Evangel*, 17, No. 1 (Spring 1999); *A Heart for Mission: Five Pioneer Thinkers* (Fearn, Tain, Ross-Shire: Christian Focus, 2002), 79-96.

68 *Personal Narrative* (*Letters and Personal Writings*, ed. Claghorn, 797). For the date of the *Personal Narrative*, see *Letters and Personal Writings*, ed. Claghorn, 747.

69 *Personal Narrative* (*Letters and Personal Writings*, ed. Claghorn, 800).

70 Davies, *Heart for Mission*, 82.

71 For studies of this work, see Joseph Conforti, 'Jonathan Edwards's Most Popular Work: "The Life of David Brainerd" and Nineteenth-Century Evangelical Culture', *Church History*, 54 (1985), 188-201; David B. Calhoun, 'David Brainerd: "A Constant Stream"', *Presbyterion*, 13 (1987), 44-50; [Gray Brady], 'Books in History: Edwards on David Brainerd,' *The Evangelical Library Bulletin* 97 (Winter 1996), 6-8.

72 Conforti, 'Jonathan Edwards's Most Popular Work', 197. See also Davies, *Heart for Mission*, 85.

73 Conforti, 'Jonathan Edwards's Most Popular Work', 196.

74 *A Sermon Preached on the Day of the Funeral of the Rev. Mr. David Brainerd* [*The Life of David Brainerd*, ed. Norman Pettit (*The Works of Jonathan Edwards*, vol. 7; New Haven/London: Yale University Press, 1985), 548].

75 Hopkins, *Memoirs of the Life, Experience and Character of the Late Rev. Jonathan Edwards* (*Works of President Edwards*, I, 84).

76 Cited Hopkins, *Memoirs of the Life, Experience and Character of the Late Rev. Jonathan Edwards* (*Works of President Edwards*, I, 84).

77 See the remarks of Hopkins, *Memoirs of the Life, Experience and Character of the Late Rev. Jonathan Edwards* (*Works of President Edwards*, I, 84).

78 Cited Murray, *Jonathan Edwards*, 442.

CHAPTER 2

1 For a more detailed examination of this treatise, see Chapter 9.

2 *An Humble Attempt to Promote Explicit Agreement and Visible Union of God's*

People in Extraordinary Prayer, for the Revival of Religion and the Advancement of Christ's Kingdom on Earth, pursuant to Scripture-Promises and Prophecies concerning the Last Time [*Apocalyptic Writings*, ed. Stephen J. Stein (*The Works of Jonathan Edwards*, vol. 5; New Haven/London: Yale University Press, 1977), 321]

   3 *Apocalyptic Writings*, ed. Stein, 320.
   4 *Apocalyptic Writings*, ed. Stein, 320.
   5 *The Threefold Work of the Holy Ghost* [*Sermons and Discourses 1723-1729*, ed. Kenneth P. Minkema (*The Works of Jonathan Edwards*, vol. 14; New Haven/London: Yale University Press, 1997), 380].
   6 *Sermons and Discourses 1723-1729*, ed. Minkema, 381, 394, 420.
   7 *Sermons and Discourses 1723-1729*, ed. Minkema, 381-383.
   8 *Sermons and Discourses 1723-1729*, ed. Minkema, 385.
   9 *Sermons and Discourses 1723-1729*, ed. Minkema, 395-402.
  10 *Sermons and Discourses 1723-1729*, ed. Minkema, 394.
  11 *Sermons and Discourses 1723-1729*, ed. Minkema, 406-409, passim.
  12 *Sermons and Discourses 1723-1729*, ed. Minkema, 398-399.
  13 *Sermons and Discourses 1723-1729*, ed. Minkema, 418.
  14 *Sermons and Discourses 1723-1729*, ed. Minkema, 422.
  15 *Sermons and Discourses 1723-1729*, ed. Minkema, 429.
  16 *Sermons and Discourses 1723-1729*, ed. Minkema, 436.
  17 *Sermons and Discourses 1723-1729*, ed. Minkema, 435.
  18 *Letters and Personal Writings*, ed. Claghorn, 16:87.
  19 *Sermons and Discourses 1723-1729*, ed. Minkema, 436.

CHAPTER 3

   1 *The Great Awakening*, ed. C. C. Goen (*The Works of Jonathan Edwards*, vol. 4; New Haven/London: Yale University Press, 1972), 131.

   2 Iain H. Murray, *Jonathan Edwards – A New Biography* (Edinburgh: The Banner of Truth Trust, 1987), 122. Thomas Prince, pastor of Boston's Old South Church, noted that Edwards' *Faithful Narrative* played an instrumental role in preparing the way for the Great Awakening in the 1740s (*Great Awakening*, ed. Goen, 27, no. 6).

   3 Mark Noll, *The Rise of Evangelicalism: The Age of Edwards, Whitefield and the Wesleys* (*A History of Evangelicalism*, vol. 1; Downers Grove, Illinois: InterVarsity Press, 2003), 90.

   4 Cited Murray, *Jonathan Edwards*, 122.

   5 Eifion Evans, *Daniel Rowland and the Great Evangelical Awakening in Wales* (Edinburgh: The Banner of Truth Trust, 1985), 72.

   6 *Great Awakening*, ed. Goen, 32. The details regarding the publishing history of the *Faithful Narrative* are to be conveniently found in *Great Awakening*, ed. Goen, 32-46. Also see Murray, *Jonathan Edwards*, 117-122, who differs with Goen at certain points, and Noll, *Rise of Evangelicalism*, 90-92.

   7 John E. Smith, *Jonathan Edwards: Puritan, Preacher, Philosopher* (Notre

Dame: University of Notre Dame Press, 1992), 5.

8 'Jonathan Edwards and the 1734-35 Northampton Revival', *Preaching and Revival* (London: The Westminster Conference, 1984), 67.

9 *Great Awakening*, ed. Goen, 185. For other references, see *Great Awakening*, ed. Goen, 160, 166, 177-178. On Edwards' concern for flexibility when the Spirit's work in conversion is being considered, see Conrad Cherry, *The Theology of Jonathan Edwards. A Reappraisal* (1966 ed.; repr. Bloomington/Indianapolis: Indiana University Press, 1990), 63-65; Goen, *Great Awakening*, 29.

10 'Jonathan Edwards and the 1734-35 Northampton Revival', 69-72; Goen, *Great Awakening*, 28-29; Karl Dietrich Pfisterer, *The Prism of Scripture: Studies on history and historicity in the work of Jonathan Edwards* (Bern: Hebert Lang/Frankfurt: Peter Lang, 1975), 189; Michael J. Crawford, *Seasons of Grace: Colonial New England's Revival Tradition in Its British Context* (New York/Oxford: Oxford University Press, 1991), 180-195; Michael Jinkins, *A Comparative Study in the Theology of Atonement in Jonathan Edwards and John McLeod Campbell: Atonement and the Character of God* (San Francisco: Mellen Research University Press, 1993), 149-150.

11 *Great Awakening*, ed. Goen, 160, 162.

12 *Great Awakening*, ed. Goen, 164, 166.

13 *Great Awakening*, ed. Goen, 163.

14 *Great Awakening*, ed. Goen, 171, 168.

15 Jinkins, *Theology of Atonement*, 153.

16 Logan, 'Jonathan Edwards and the 1734-35 Northampton Revival', 69.

17 *Great Awakening*, ed. Goen, 168. In his *Personal Narrative*, Edwards wrote that the 'doctrines of God's absolute sovereignty, and free grace, in showing mercy to whom he would show mercy; and man's absolute dependence on the operation of God's Holy Spirit, have very often appeared to me as sweet and glorious doctrines. These doctrines have been much my delight. God's sovereignty has ever appeared to me, as great part of his glory. It has often been sweet to me to go to God, and adore him as a sovereign God, and ask sovereign mercy of him'. [*Letters and Personal Writings*, ed. George S. Claghorn (*The Works of Jonathan Edwards*, vol. 16; New Haven/London: Yale University Press, 1998), 799].

18 *Great Awakening*, ed. Goen, 172, 163.

19 *Great Awakening*, ed. Goen, 172.

20 *Great Awakening*, ed. Goen, 176.

21 *Evangelicalism in Modern Britain. A History from the 1730s to the 1980s* (1989 ed.; repr. Grand Rapids: Baker Book House, 1992), 42-50.

22 *Great Awakening*, ed. Goen, 132.

23 *Great Awakening*, ed. Goen, 190, 154. See also 145-146.

24 *Evangelicalism in Modern Britain*, 43. See also David Bebbington, 'Revival and Enlightenment in Eighteenth-Century England', in Edith L. Blumhofer and Randall Balmer, eds., *Modern Christian Revivals* (Urbana/Chicago: University of Illinois Press, 1993), 22-24.

25 Ava Chamberlain, 'Self-Deception as a Theological Problem in Jonathan

Edwards's Treatise Concerning Religious Affections', *Church History*, 63 (1994), 546.

26 For a useful discussion of the authors whom Edwards quotes in the *Religious Affections*, see John E. Smith, editor's introduction in *Religious Affections*, ed. John E. Smith (*The Works of Jonathan Edwards*, vol. 2; New Haven: Yale University Press, 1959), 52-73. For a listing of most of the authors used by Edwards, see Ralph G. Turnbull, *Jonathan Edwards The Preacher* (Grand Rapids: Baker Book House, 1958), 33-41.

27 *Theology of Jonathan Edwards*, 151. In the words of Thomas A. Schafer, 'Edwards not only accepted Reformed theology in its English Puritan form, he energetically defended it' [The 'Miscellanies' (*The Works of Jonathan Edwards*, vol. 13; New Haven/London: Yale University Press, 1994), 39]. Chamberlain notes that Edwards did not merely recommend a return to the Puritan pattern of piety. Instead, he sought to wed traditional Puritan thinking about assurance with the experience of revival ['Self-deception as a Theological Problem', 541-556]. For a good study of Edwards' view of assurance, see Cherry, *Theology of Jonathan Edwards*, 143-158.

28 Letter to Thomas Gillespie, 1 July 1751 (*Great Awakening*, ed. Goen, 565).

29 Letter to Thomas Gillespie, 1 July 1751 (*Great Awakening*, ed. Goen, 565).

30 *Great Awakening*, ed. Goen, 149.

31 For similar remarks on Edwards' first account of the revival, see Thomas Templeton Taylor, 'The spirit of the awakening: The pneumatology of New England's Great Awakening in historical and theological context' (unpublished Ph.D. thesis, University of Illinois at Urbana-Champaign, 1988), 227.

32 *Great Awakening*, ed. Goen, 160, 164, 166, 167.

33 *Great Awakening*, ed. Goen, 177.

34 *Great Awakening*, ed. Goen, 159. For mention of the Spirit's work in conversion, see also page 158, where Edwards refers to the Spirit's 'regenerating influences', and page 190, where he alludes to the Spirit's 'converting influences'. In his first account of the revival, the letter that Edwards initially sent to Colman, he speaks of the Spirit's 'saving influences' ['Unpublished Letter of May 30, 1735' (*Great Awakening*, ed. Goen, 101)], a phrase that does not occur in the *Faithful Narrative*.

35 *Great Awakening*, ed. Goen, 174.

36 *Great Awakening*, ed. Goen, 190.

37 *Great Awakening*, ed. Goen, 152.

38 *Great Awakening*, ed. Goen, 152.

39 Edwards, 'Unpublished Letter of May 30, 1735' (*Great Awakening*, ed. Goen, 107).

40 *Great Awakening*, ed. Goen, 131.

41 *Great Awakening*, ed. Goen, 216-217.

42 '"Methodism" and the Origins of English-Speaking Evangelicalism' in Mark A. Noll, David W. Bebbington and George A. Rawlyk, eds., *Evangelicalism: Comparative Studies of Popular Protestantism in North America, the British Isles, and Beyond, 1700-1990* (New York/Oxford: Oxford University Press, 1994), 20-21.

43 Crawford, *Seasons of Grace*, 37-51.

44 *The Prosperous State of the Christian Interest Before the End of Time, by a Plentiful Effusion of the Holy Spirit* [*The Works of the Rev. John Howe, M.A.* (London: Frederick Westley/A. H. Davis, 1832), 562-607]. Though preached in 1678, these sermons were not actually published until 1725.

45 *Prosperous State of the Christian Interest* (*Works*, 603-604).

46 *Prosperous State of the Christian Interest* (*Works*, 604).

47 *Prosperous State of the Christian Interest* (*Works*, 575). For the explanation of 'living sense' as 'felt reality', I am indebted to J. I. Packer, *God In Our Midst. Seeking and Receiving Ongoing Revival* (Ann Arbor, Michigan: Servant Books, 1987), 33.

48 *Great Awakening*, ed. Goen, 154, 161.

49 For Edwards' knowledge of Howe's sermons on Ezekiel 39:29, see, for example, his *Treatise on Grace and An Essay on the Trinity* [Jonathan Edwards, *Treatise on Grace and other posthumously published writings*, ed. Paul Helm (Cambridge/London: James Clarke & Co. Ltd., 1971), 59, 112]. The very text of Howe cited above is quoted by William Cooper in his preface to Edwards' *Distinguishing Marks* (*Great Awakening*, ed. Goen, 217-218).

50 *Great Awakening*, ed. Goen, 157. In the letter that he wrote to Colman in 1735, he simply called it 'an extraordinary dispensation of providence' (*Great Awakening*, ed. Goen, 107).

51 *Great Awakening*, ed. Goen, 145-146, 190.

52 Many years later, Edwards' son, Jonathan Edwards Jr (1745-1801), noted in a letter written in 1789 to John Ryland Jr that Phebe was at that time 'yet living, and has uniformly maintained the character of a true convert' [cited Samuel Hopkins, *Memoirs of the Life, Experience and Character of the Late Rev. Jonathan Edwards, A.M. in The Works of President Edwards* (1817 London ed.; repr. New York: Burt Franklin, 1968), I, 114].

53 *Great Awakening*, ed. Goen, 157, 158. For the story of Phebe's conversion, see *Great Awakening*, ed. Goen, 199-205.

54 *Great Awakening*, ed. Goen, 157-158.

55 *Great Awakening*, ed. Goen, 159.

56 *Great Awakening*, ed. Goen, 159.

57 *Great Awakening*, ed. Goen, 159. For a list of these towns, see pages 152-156. For comments on these towns and villages, see pages 21-25.

58 *Great Awakening*, ed. Goen, 209-210.

59 Miklós Vetö, 'Book Reviews: America's Theologian: A Recommendation of Jonathan Edwards. By Robert W. Jenson', *Church History*, 58 (1989), 522.

60 Patricia J. Tracy, *Jonathan Edwards: Religion and Society in Eighteenth-Century Northampton* (New York: Hill and Wang, 1980), 18-20.

61 *Great Awakening*, ed. Goen, 138-141.

62 *Great Awakening*, ed. Goen, 206. For the withdrawing of the Spirit, see pages 162, 207.

63 *Great Awakening*, ed. Goen, 205.

64 *Great Awakening*, ed. Goen, 206-297. See also the discussion of Goen, *Great*

Awakening, 46-47, and George M. Marsden, *Jonathan Edwards: A Life* (New Haven/London: Yale University Press, 2003), 162-163.
  65 *Great Awakening*, ed. Goen, 47.
  66 *Great Awakening*, ed. Goen, 207.
  67 *Great Awakening*, ed. Goen, 207-208.

CHAPTER 4

  1 This sermon has not been published in the Yale edition. For references to it, see Stephen J. Nichols, *An Absolute Sort of Certainty: The Holy Spirit and the Apologetics of Jonathan Edwards* (Phillipsburg, New Jersey: P&R Publishing, 2003), 168-171. The quote can be found on page 173.
  2 *Sermons on Important Subjects* (London: Thomas Tegg, 1833), 432.
  3 For brief discussions of Whitefield's perspective on the gifts of the Spirit, see Victor Budgen, *The Charismatics and the Word of God. A biblical and historical perspective on the charismatic movement* (Welwyn, Hertfordshire: Evangelical Press, 1985), 162-163; Thomas Templeton Taylor, 'The spirit of the awakening: The pneumatology of New England's Great Awakening in historical and theological context' (unpublished Ph.D. thesis, University of Illinois at Urbana-Champaign, 1988), 299, 317-318.
  4 For Whitefield's own account of what he preached on during this time, see Iain H. Murray, *Jonathan Edwards – A New Biography* (Edinburgh: The Banner of Truth Trust, 1987), 161. See also George M. Marsden, *Jonathan Edwards: A Life* (New Haven/London: Yale University Press, 2003), 209-213.
  5 *The Great Awakening*, ed. C. C. Goen (*The Works of Jonathan Edwards*, vol. 4; New Haven/London: Yale University Press, 1972), 207.
  6 For the historical context, see Marsden, *Jonathan Edwards*, 189-192.
  7 'Jonathan Edwards' Last Will, and the Inventory of his Estate', *The Bibliotheca Sacra*, 33 (1876), 441-443.
  8 'Copyright of President Edwards' Works', *New England Puritan*, 4 (November 4, 1843), [2].
  9 Tryon Edwards, Introduction to Jonathan Edwards, *Charity and Its Fruits. Christian love as manifested in the heart and life* (1852 ed.; repr. Edinburgh: The Banner of Truth Trust, 1969), iv. For the history of Edwards' manuscripts, see Murray, *Jonathan Edwards*, 481-484,
  10 *Ethical Writings*, ed. Paul Ramsey (*The Works of Jonathan Edwards*, vol. 8; New Haven/London: Yale University Press, 1989), 104-111. This early nineteenth-century copy is now housed in the Franklin Trask Library at the Andover-Newton Theological School, Newton Center, Massachusetts. It should be noted that because of various lacunae in this copy, especially in sermons three, five, six, and eight, Ramsey had to make use of Tryon Edwards' edition to construct the critical edition of *Charity and Its Fruits* (*Ethical Writings*, ed. Ramsey, 110-111).
  11 *Ethical Writings*, ed. Ramsey, 149-154.
  12 *Ethical Writings*, ed. Ramsey, 157, n. 8.

13 *Ethical Writings*, ed. Ramsey, 154-157.
14 *Ethical Writings*, ed. Ramsey, 157.
15 *Ethical Writings*, ed. Ramsey, 151.
16 Gordon D. Fee, *The First Epistle to the Corinthians* (Grand Rapids: William B. Eerdmans Publ. Co., 1987), 625.
17 *Ethical Writings*, ed. Ramsey, 166.
18 *Ethical Writings*, ed. Ramsey, 157.
19 *Ethical Writings*, ed. Ramsey, 157-158.
20 *Ethical Writings*, ed. Ramsey, 158. Edwards used the same verse to make a similar point a few years before in one of his most notable sermons, *A Divine and Supernatural Light, Immediately Imparted to the Soul by the Spirit of God*, preached in August 1733, a year and a half before the Northampton revival. There, Edwards observed near the beginning of the sermon: 'The Spirit of God may act upon a creature, and yet not in acting communicate himself. The Spirit of God may act upon inanimate creatures; as "The Spirit moved upon the face of the waters," in the beginning of the creation [Gen. 1:2]; so the Spirit of God may act upon the minds of men, many ways, and communicate himself no more than when he acts upon an inanimate creature.' [*Sermons and Discourses 1730-1733*, ed. Mark Valeri (*The Works of Jonathan Edwards*, vol. 17; New Haven/London: Yale University Press, 1999), 411].
21 *Ethical Writings*, ed. Ramsey, 159.
22 *Religious Affections*, ed. John E. Smith (*The Works of Jonathan Edwards*, vol. 2; New Haven: Yale University Press, 1959), 256. For other passages in Edwards' corpus, see Jonathan Edwards, *Freedom of the Will*, ed. Paul Ramsey (*The Works of Jonathan Edwards*, vol. 1; New Haven: Yale University Press, 1957), 166-167, n. 3.
23 *Ethical Writings*, ed. Ramsey, 159.
24 *Ethical Writings*, ed. Ramsey, 159.
25 *Ethical Writings*, ed. Ramsey, 159-160.
26 *Ethical Writings*, ed. Ramsey, 160-161.
27 *The Great Awakening*, ed. C. C. Goen (*The Works of Jonathan Edwards*, vol. 4; New Haven/London: Yale University Press, 1972), 281.
28 *Ethical Writings*, ed. Ramsey, 161-162.
29 Miscellany, no. 379 [*The 'Miscellanies'*, ed. Thomas A. Schafer (New Haven/London: Yale University Press, 1994), 449-450]. The description of the *Miscellanies* is that of Schafer (*'Miscellanies'*, ed. Schafer, 3).
30 *Ethical Writings*, ed. Ramsey, 162-163. Conscious that this text from Hebrews was 'an occasion of much stumbling and difficulty to many', Edwards launches into a lengthy digression of its meaning (*Ethical Writings*, ed. Ramsey, 163-166). For a discussion of Edwards' exegesis of this passage, see *Ethical Writings*, ed. Ramsey, 751-759.
31 *Ethical Writings*, ed. Ramsey, 166.
32 *Ethical Writings*, ed. Ramsey, 166-168.
33 *Great Awakening*, ed. Goen, 344.

34 A good illustration of this sort of thinking may be found in the early religious experience of Andrew Fuller (1754-1815), an English Baptist divine who was greatly influenced by the writings of Edwards. In a letter he wrote in 1798, Fuller recalls that during his teen years, 'I was at times the subject of such convictions and affections that I really thought myself converted and lived under that delusion for a long time. The ground on which I rested that opinion was as follows. One morning, I think about the year 1767, as I was walking alone, I began to think seriously what would become of my poor soul and was deeply affected in thinking of my condition. I felt myself the slave of sin and that it had such power over me that it was in vain for me to think of extricating myself from its thraldom. Till now, I did not know but that I could repent at any time; but now, I perceived that my heart was wicked and that it was not in me to turn to God or to break off my sins by righteousness. I saw that if God would forgive me all the past and offer me the kingdom of heaven on condition of giving up my wicked pursuits, I should not accept it. This conviction was accompanied with great depression of heart. I walked sorrowfully along, repeating these words: "Iniquity will be my ruin! Iniquity will be my ruin!" While poring over my unhappy case, those words of the Apostle suddenly occurred to my mind, "Sin shall not have dominion over you; for ye are not under the law, but under grace" [Rom. 6:14]. Now, the suggestion of a text of Scripture to the mind, especially if it came with power, was generally considered by the religious people with whom I occasionally associated as a promise coming immediately from God. I, therefore, so understood it, and thought that God had thus revealed to me that I was in a state of salvation, and that, therefore, iniquity should not, as I had feared, be my ruin. The effect was I was overcome with joy and transport. I shed, I suppose, thousands of tears as I walked along, and seemed to feel myself, as it were, in a new world. It appeared to me that I hated my sins and was resolved to forsake them. Thinking on my wicked courses, I remember using those words of Paul, "Shall I continue in sin, that grace may abound? God forbid!" [Rom. 6:1-2]. I felt, or seemed to feel, the strongest indignation at the thought. But, strange as it may appear, though my face was that morning, I believe, swollen with weeping, before night all was gone and forgotten, and I returned to my former vices with as eager a gust as ever. Nor do I remember that, for more than half a year afterwards, I had any serious thoughts about the salvation of my soul. I lived entirely without prayer and was wedded to my sins just the same as before, or, rather, was increasingly attached to them.' [John Ryland, *The Work of Faith, the Labour of Love, and the Patience of Hope, illustrated; in the Life and Death of the Rev. Andrew Fuller* (2nd. ed.; London: Button & Son, 1818), 13-14].

35 John E. Smith, 'Jonathan Edwards as Philosophical Theologian', *The Review of Metaphysics*, 30 (1976-1977), 309.

36 *Ethical Writings*, ed. Ramsey, 168-170.

37 *Religious Affections*, ed. Smith, 143-144. See also Miscellanies, no. 126 (*'Miscellanies'*, ed. Schafer, 289-291).

38 *Ethical Writings*, ed. Ramsey, 172-173.
39 See Chapter 2.
40 *Ethical Writings*, ed. Ramsey, 353-354.
41 *Ethical Writings*, ed. Ramsey, 354. In formulating this paragraph, I am indebted to Ramsey's discussion of this section of Sermon Fourteen, *Ethical Writings*, ed. Ramsey, 93-94.
42 *Ethical Writings*, ed. Ramsey, 355-356.
43 *Ethical Writings*, ed. Ramsey, 356-358. For further discussion of Edwards' thoughts on the cessation of the gifts, see Budgen, *Charismatics and the Word of God*, 170-176.
44 *Ethical Writings*, ed. Ramsey, 363.
45 *Ethical Writings*, ed. Ramsey, 70.
46 *Ethical Writings*, ed. Ramsey, 360.
47 *Ethical Writings*, ed. Ramsey, 361.
48 *A Glimpse of Sions Glory: or, The Churches Beautie specified* (London, 1641), 24. For Goodwin's authorship of this tract, see A. R. Dallison, 'The Authorship of the 'Glimpse of Sions Glory', in Peter Toon, ed., *Puritans, the Millennium and the Future of Israel: Puritan Eschatology 1600 to 1660* (Cambridge/London: James Clarke & Co. Ltd., 1970), 131-136.
49 Edwards' eschatological thinking is well explored by C. C. Goen, 'Jonathan Edwards: A New Departure in Eschatology', *Church History*, 28 (1959), 25-40 and John F. Wilson, 'History, Redemption, and the Millennium' in Nathan Hatch and Harry S. Stout, eds., *Jonathan Edwards and the American Experience* (New York/Oxford: Oxford University Press, 1988), 131-141. On Puritan postmillennialism, see Toon, ed., *Puritans, the Millennium and the Future of Israel*.
50 These remarks were made by the Unitarian William Ellery Channing (1780-1842). Cited by Joseph A. Conforti, *Samuel Hopkins and the New Divinity Movement: Calvinism, the Congregational Ministry, and Refom in New England Between the Great Awakenings* (Washington, D.C.: Christian University Press/Grand Rapids: 1981), 173. I am indebted to Gerald Robert McDermott, *One Holy and Happy Society: The Public Theology of Jonathan Edwards* (University Park, Pennsylvania: Pennsylvania State University Press, 1992), 44, for drawing my attention to these remarks as appropriate for Edwards.
51 *Ethical Writings*, ed. Ramsey, 361.
52 *Ethical Writings*, ed. Ramsey, 361-362.
53 *Ethical Writings*, ed. Ramsey, 363.
54 *Ethical Writings*, ed. Ramsey, 364-365.

CHAPTER 5

1 Letter to William McCulloch, 12 May 1743 [*Letters and Personal Writings*, ed. George S. Claghorn (*The Works of Jonathan Edwards*, vol. 16; New Haven/London: Yale University Press, 1998), 106].
2 *Gospel Mysteries Unveiled* (1701 ed.; repr. London: L. I. Higham, 1817), III,

310. For a full-length biography of Keach, see Austin Walker, *The Excellent Benjamin Keach* (Dundas, Ontario: Joshua Press, 2004).

3   See Chapter 3.

4   *The Great Awakening*, ed. C. C. Goen (*The Works of Jonathan Edwards*, vol. 4; New Haven/London: Yale University Press, 1972), 137.

5   For a recent overview of the revival in its transatlantic context, see Mark Noll, *The Rise of Evangelicalism: The Age of Edwards, Whitefield and the Wesleys* (*A History of Evangelicalism*, vol. 1; Downers Grove, Illinois: InterVarsity Press, 2003), 100-154.

6   Michael R. Watts, *The Dissenters. From the Reformation to the French Revolution* (Oxford: Clarendon Press, 1978), 397.

7   Cited R. Tudur Jones, 'The Evangelical Revival in Wales: A Study in Spirituality', in James P. Mackey, ed., *An Introduction to Celtic Christianity* (Edinburgh: T & T Clark, 1989), 249.

8   A. Skevington Wood, *The Inextinguishable Blaze: Spiritual Renewal and Advance in the Eighteenth Century* (Grand Rapids: Wm. B. Eerdmans Publishing Co., 1960), 117-118; R. E. Davies, *I Will Pour Out My Spirit: A History and Theology of Revivals and Evangelical Awakenings* (Tunbridge Wells, Kent: Monarch Publications, 1992), 87.

9   Michael J. Crawford, *Seasons of Grace. Colonial New England's Revival Tradition in Its British Context* (New York/Oxford: Oxford University Press, 1991), 160.

10   *Some Remarkable Passages in the Life of the Honourable Col. James Gardiner* [*The Works of The Rev. P. Doddridge, D.D.* (Leeds, 1803), IV, 88].

11   Cited Arnold A. Dallimore, *George Whitefield. The Life and Times of the Great Evangelist of the Eighteenth-Century Revival* (Westchester, Illinois: Cornerstone Books, 1980), 2:128. For further details and discussion of this revival, see especially Arthur Fawcett, *The Cambuslang Revival. The Scottish Evangelical Revival of the Eighteenth Century* (London: The Banner of Truth Trust, 1971); Crawford, *Seasons of Grace*, passim.

12   D. E. Meek, 'Revivals', *Dictionary of Scottish Church History & Theology*, eds. Nigel M. de S. Cameron et al. (Downers Grove, Illinois: InterVarsity Press, 1993), 713. Thus, the Congregationalist Joseph Williams could describe Whitefield as 'the Father' of the Methodists ['Charles Wesley in 1739 by Joseph Williams of Kidderminster', introd. Geoffrey F. Nuttall, *Proceedings of the Wesley Historical Society*, 42 (1979-1980), 182]. For the ministry and life of Whitefield, see especially the two-volume biography by Dallimore: *George Whitefield*.

13   *The Journal of the Rev. John Wesley, A.M.*, ed. Nehemiah Curnock (1911 ed.; repr. London: The Epworth Press, 1960), II, 256-257, n. 1.

14   C. C. Goen, *Revivalism and Separatism in New England, 1740-1800. Strict Congregationalists and Separate Baptists in the Great Awakening* (1962 ed.; repr. Middletown, Connecticut: Wesleyan University Press, 1987), 240.

15   Dallimore, *George Whitefield*, 1:263-264.

16 Arnold A. Dallimore, *George Whitefield: Evangelist of the 18th-Century Revival* (London: The Wakeman Trust, 1990), 221-222.

17 Cited Eifion Evans, *Daniel Rowland and the Great Evangelical Awakening in Wales* (Edinburgh: The Banner of Truth Trust, 1985), 243.

18 i.e. held in contempt or rejected.

19 *Letters and Personal Writings*, ed. George S. Claghorn (*The Works of Jonathan Edwards*, vol. 16; New Haven/London: Yale University Press, 1998), 80.

20 For somewhat contrasting accounts of his New England preaching tour, see Dallimore, *George Whitefield*, 1:527-544, and Harry S. Stout, *The Divine Dramatist: George Whitefield and the Rise of Modern Evangelicalism* (Grand Rapids: William B. Eerdmans Publishing Co., 1991), 113-132.

21 Cited *Great Awakening*, ed. Goen, 50.

22 *Great Awakening*, ed. Goen, 221-222.

23 For a full account of their time together, see George Marsden, *Jonathan Edwards: A Life* (New Haven/London: Yale University Press, 2003), 202-213.

24 *George Whitefield's Journals* ([London]: The Banner of Truth, 1960), 477; Jonathan Edwards, *The State of Religion at Northampton in the County of Hampshire, About a Hundred Miles Westward of Boston* (*Great Awakening*, ed. Goen, 544-545). The item by Edwards was actually a letter to Thomas Prince, which the latter printed in his *The Christian History*.

25 Iain H. Murray, *Jonathan Edwards – A New Biography* (Edinburgh: The Banner of Truth Trust, 1987), 175-176.

26 See Perry Miller, *Jonathan Edwards* (New York: William Sloane Associates, 1949), 143-144.

27 Henry D. Rack, *Reasonable Enthusiast. John Wesley and the Rise of Methodism* (London: Epworth Press, 1989), 276.

28 *Letters of John Ramsay of Ochtertyre, 1799-1812*, ed. Barbara L. H. Horn (Edinburgh: Scottish History Society, 1966), 15-16. Gibson had directed his attack on the evangelical revival against Whitefield. For Whitefield's response, see Dallimore, *George Whitefield*, 1:390-391.

29 For a discussion of Davenport's involvement in the revival, see Harry S. Stout and Peter Onuf, 'James Davenport and the Great Awakening in New London', *The Journal of American History*, 71 (1983-1984), 556-578; Murray, *Jonathan Edwards*, 223-229; Robert E. Cray Jr, 'More Light on a New Light: James Davenport's Religious Legacy, Eastern Long Island, 1740-1840', *New York History*, 73 (1992), 5-27.

30 *Great Awakening*, ed. Goen, 52; Christopher Grasso, *A Speaking Aristocracy: Transforming Public Discourse in Eighteenth-Century Connecticut* (Chapel Hill/London: University of North Carolina Press, for The Omohundro Institute of Early American History and Culture, Williamsburg, Virginia, 1999), 150.

31 John Turner Ames, *A Brief History of The First Presbyterian Church of East Hampton 1648-1998*, eds. Paul Vogel and David L. Filer ([East Hampton, New York]: n.p., 1998), [14-15] (this pamphlet has no pagination). Ames mistakenly calls Davenport 'John Davenport'. Ames's mistake goes back at least to Perry

Miller – Perry Miller, *Jonathan Edwards* (New York: William Sloane Associates, 1949), 203, 337 – though Miller rightly calls him 'James Davenport' on a couple of occasions (*Jonathan Edwards*, 145, 172).

32 Leigh Eric Schmidt, '"A Second and Glorious Reformation": The New Light Extremism of Andrew Croswell', *The William and Mary Quarterly*, 3rd series, 43 (1986), 214-244.

33 On visions in the Great Awakening and the problems that they caused, see Douglas L. Winiarksi, 'Souls Filled with Ravishing Transport: Heavenly Visions and the Radical Awakening in New England', *The William and Mary Quarterly*, 3rd series, 61 (2004), 3-46.

34 Clarke Garrett, *Spirit Possession and Popular Religion. From the Camisards to the Shakers* (Baltimore/London: The Johns Hopkins University Press, 1987), 115.

35 Garrett, *Spirit Possession*, 115.

36 Cited Thomas Templeton Taylor, 'The spirit of the awakening: The pneumatology of New England's Great Awakening in historical and theological context' (unpublished Ph.D. thesis, University of Illinois at Urbana-Champaign, 1988), 325.

37 For two firsthand accounts of the New London incident, see Charles Chauncy, *Seasonable Thoughts on the State of Religion in New-England* (1743 ed.; repr. Hicksville, New York; The Regina Press, 1975), 220-223, footnote; 'Religious Excess at New London: Boston Weekly Post-Boy, 1743', in Richard L. Bushman, ed., *The Great Awakening: Documents on the Revival of Religion, 1740-1745* (1970 ed.; repr. Chapel Hill/London: University of North Carolina Press for the Institute of Early American History and Culture, 1989), 51-53.

38 For the public recantation that he made, see *The Reverend Mr. James Davenport's Confession & Retractions* (Boston: S. Kneeland and T. Green, 1744). For an excerpt from eight-page tract, see Bushman, ed., *Great Awakening*, 53-55. In a sermon that Davenport preached in the final year of his life, 1757, he was surely thinking of his earlier errors when he stated that among the people of God ministers are subject to greater temptation than others, 'as officers in army are more aim'd at and pointed at by the Enemy than private soldiers' (cited Garrett, *Spirit Possession*, 126).

39 *A Letter from a Gentleman in Boston, to Mr. George Wishart, One of the Ministers of Edinburgh, Concerning the State of Religion in New-England* (Bushman, ed., *Great Awakening*, 121). Edwards himself was convinced that Davenport did more 'towards giving Satan and those opposers [of the revival] an advantage against the work than any other person' (Murray, *Jonathan Edwards*, 225).

40 Cited Taylor, 'Spirit of the awakening', 342-343.

41 Most of *Enthusiasm Described and Cautioned Against* may be conveniently found in Eugene E. White, *Puritan Rhetoric: The Issue of Emotion in Religion* (Carbondale and Edwardsville, Illinois: Southern Illinois University Press, 1972), 103-116. For a good discussion of Chauncy's theological position, see Conrad Cherry, *The Theology of Jonathan Edwards. A Reappraisal* (1966 ed.: repr. Bloomington/Indianapolis: Indiana University Press, 1990), 164-167; Taylor,

'Spirit of the Awakening', 335-370.
  42 White, *Puritan Rhetoric*, 106, 112-113.
  43 White, *Puritan Rhetoric*, 114-115. See also the discussion of this sermon by Taylor, 'Spirit of the awakening', 343-352.
  44 *Letter from a Gentleman in Boston* (Bushman, ed., *Great Awakening*, 120).
  45 *Seasonable Thoughts*, 327.

CHAPTER 6

  1 The title of this chapter is taken from a subtitle in Michael Jinkins, 'The "True Remedy": Jonathan Edwards' Soteriological Perspective as Observed in his Revival Treatises', *The Scottish Journal of Theology*, 48 (1995), 202.
  2 For the historical background, see George M. Marsden, *Jonathan Edwards: A Life* (New Haven/London: Yale University Press, 2003), 231-237.
  3 Thomas Templeton Taylor, 'The spirit of the awakening: The pneumatology of New England's Great Awakening in historical and theological context' (unpublished Ph.D. thesis, University of Illinois at Urbana-Champaign, 1988), 236. Pace John E. Smith, *Jonathan Edwards: Puritan, Preacher, Philosopher* (Notre Dame, Indiana: University of Notre Dame Press, 1992), 31.
  4 *Jonathan Edwards* (New York: William Sloane Associates, 1949), 301. See also Miller, *Jonathan Edwards*, 194: 'Puritanism is what Edwards is.'
  5 *The Great Awakening*, ed. C. C. Goen (*The Works of Jonathan Edwards*, vol. 4; New Haven/London: Yale University Press, 1972), 228.
  6 *Great Awakening*, ed. Goen, 227.
  7 *Great Awakening*, ed. Goen, 229. See also the remarks of Jinkins, 'Jonathan Edwards' Soteriological Perspective', 202-203.
  8 *Religious Affections*, ed. John E. Smith (*The Works of Jonathan Edwards*, vol. 2; New Haven: Yale University Press, 1959), 132.
  9 *Religious Affections*, ed. Smith, 133.
  10 *Religious Affections*, ed. Smith, 134.
  11 *Religious Affections*, ed. Smith, 134-135.
  12 *Great Awakening*, ed. Goen, 227.
  13 *Some Thoughts* (*Great Awakening*, ed. Goen, 300).
  14 *Great Awakening*, ed. Goen, 230-234.
  15 See Chapter 4.
  16 *Great Awakening*, ed. Goen, 268.
  17 *Great Awakening*, ed. Goen, 545-546.
  18 This account is taken from the diary of Stephen Williams (1693-1782), minister at Longmeadow, Massachusetts. It is cited by John D. Currid, foreword to Jonathan Edwards, *Sinners in the Hands of an Angry God* (Phillipsburg, New Jersey: P & R Publishing, 1992), 4.
  19 *Great Awakening*, ed. Goen, 234-235.
  20 *Great Awakening*, ed. Goen, 235-238.
  21 *Great Awakening*, ed. Goen, 238-241.

22 *Great Awakening*, ed. Goen, 241-243.
23 Jinkins, 'Jonathan Edwards' Soteriological Perspective', 203, n. 69.
24 *Great Awakening*, ed. Goen, 241.
25 *Great Awakening*, ed. Goen, 243-244.
26 *Great Awakening*, ed. Goen, 244-246.
27 *Great Awakening*, ed. Goen, 273.
28 J. I. Packer, 'Jonathan Edwards and Revival', in his *A Quest for Godliness. The Puritan Vision of the Christian Life* (Wheaton, Illinois: Crossway Books, 1990), 318.
29 *Great Awakening*, ed. Goen, 246-248.
30 Jinkins, 'Jonathan Edwards' Soteriological Perspective', 203.
31 *Great Awakening*, ed. Goen, 242.
32 *Great Awakening*, ed. Goen, 54.
33 *Great Awakening*, ed. Goen, 249-250, quotation from page 250.
34 *Keep In Step With the Spirit* (Old Tappan, New Jersey: Fleming H. Revell Co., 1984), 55, 65.
35 *Great Awakening*, ed. Goen, 250-253.
36 *Great Awakening*, ed. Goen, 253-254.
37 For example, see *Great Awakening*, ed. Goen, 234, 250. For a brief discussion of his critique of the Quakers, see Philip A. Craig, '"And prophecy shall cease": Jonathan Edwards on the Cessation of the Gift of Prophecy', *Westminster Theological Journal*, 63 (2002), 169-170.
38 *Jonathan Edwards on Revival*, 52.
39 'Spirit of the awakening', 242.
40 Cited Barry Reay, *The Quakers and the English Revolution* (New York: St. Martin's Press, 1985), 33.
41 *Letters of Isaac Penington* (2nd. ed.; repr. London: Holdsworth and Ball, 1829), 202-203. For access to these letters I am indebted to Heinz G. Dschankilic of Cambridge, Ontario.
42 See also the remarks by Richard Dale Land, 'Doctrinal Controversies of English Particular Baptists (1644-1691) as Illustrated by the Career and Writings of Thomas Collier' (unpublished D.Phil. thesis, Regent's Park College, Oxford University, 1979), 205-211. In the words of Richard Bauman [*Let Your Words Be Few: Symbolism of Speaking and Silence among Seventeenth-Century Quakers* (Cambridge: Cambridge University Press, 1983), 38]: 'The Quakers were intensely devoted to the Bible, not as a source of traditional authority, but as historical validation of the patterns and dynamics of their own charismatic prophetic mission.'
43 *Great Awakening*, ed. Goen, 254-255. See also the discussion by Stephen J. Nichols, *An Absolute Sort of Certainty: The Holy Spirit and the Apologetics of Jonathan Edwards* (Phillipsburg, New Jersey: P&R Publishing, 2003).
44 *Great Awakening*, ed. Goen, 255-259.
45 *Great Awakening*, ed. Goen, 258.
46 *Great Awakening*, ed. Goen, 263-264.
47 *Great Awakening*, ed. Goen, 266-267.

48 *Great Awakening*, ed. Goen, 270.

49 *Great Awakening*, ed. Goen, 270-275.

50 Iain H. Murray, *Jonathan Edwards – A New Biography* (Edinburgh: The Banner of Truth Trust, 1987), 236-237. Cf. Jinkins, 'Jonathan Edwards' Soteriological Perspective', 208.

51 *Great Awakening*, ed. Goen, 277.

52 *Great Awakening*, ed. Goen, 253.

53 *Great Awakening*, ed. Goen, 243-244.

54 *Great Awakening*, ed. Goen, 277.

55 Helpful in formulating the next few paragraphs has been Craig, 'Jonathan Edwards on the Cessation of the Gift of Prophecy', 163-184.

56 *Great Awakening*, ed. Goen, 281.

57 *Great Awakening*, ed. Goen, 282.

58 *Great Awakening*, ed. Goen, 282.

59 *Great Awakening*, ed. Goen, 253. In arguing thus, Edwards showed himself 'very much the son of Puritanism', for Puritanism was above all a Word-centred movement [Conrad Cherry, 'Imagery and Analysis: Jonathan Edwards on Revivals of Religion', in Charles Angoff, ed., *Jonathan Edwards: His Life and Influence* (Cranbury, New Jersey/London: Associated University Presses, 1975), 26].

60 *Sermons and Discourses 1720-1723*, ed. Wilson H. Kimnach (*The Works of Jonathan Edwards*, vol. 10; New Haven/London: Yale University Press, 1992), 3.

61 *Sermons and Discourses 1720-1723*, ed. Kimnach, 10-12.

62 *Sermons and Discourses 1720-1723*, ed. Kimnach, 15.

63 *Sermons and Discourses 1720-1723*, ed. Kimnach, 12.

64 *The Efficacy of the Fear of Hell to Restrain Men from Sin* (Boston, 1713), 5.

65 *Sermons and Discourses 1720-1723*, ed. Kimnach, 20.

66 Preface to *Discourses on Various Important Subjects* [*Sermons and Discourses 1734-1738*, ed. M. X. Lesser (*The Works of Jonathan Edwards*, vol. 19; New Haven/London: Yale University Press, 2001), 797].

67 *Great Awakening*, ed. Goen, 374.

68 Craig, 'Jonathan Edwards on the Cessation of the Gift of Prophecy', 184. See also the remarks of Doreen Moore about Edwards in this regard: 'The centrality of preaching stayed a conviction throughout his life' [*Good Christians, Good Husbands? Leaving a Legacy in Marriage & Ministry* (Fearn, Ross-Shire: Christian Focus Publications, 2004), 111]. Moore's comparison with contemporary perspectives on preaching is well worth pondering: *Good Christians, Good Husbands?*, 111-114.

CHAPTER 7

1 This quote is from Sarah Edwards' own account of her extraordinary experiences in early 1742 [cited Sereno E. Dwight, 'Memoirs of Jonathan Edwards, A.M.' in *The Works of Jonathan Edwards*, revised and corrected Edward Hickman (1834 ed.; repr. Edinburgh/Carlisle, Pennsylvania: The Banner of Truth Trust, 1974), 1:LXVII.

2   *The Great Awakening*, ed. C. C. Goen (*The Works of Jonathan Edwards*, vol. 4; New Haven/London: Yale University Press, 1972), 65, n. 9.

3   *Great Awakening*, ed. Goen, 499.

4   *Jonathan Edwards – A New Biography* (Edinburgh: The Banner of Truth Trust, 1987), 237-238.

5   *Great Awakening*, ed. Goen, 293-347.

6   *Great Awakening*, ed. Goen, 348-383. Quote is from page 348.

7   *Great Awakening*, ed. Goen, 384-408.

8   *Great Awakening*, ed. Goen, 409-495.

9   *Great Awakening*, ed. Goen, 496-530.

10 *Great Awakening*, ed. Goen, 411.

11 *Quenching the Spirit. Examining Centuries of Opposition to the Moving of the Holy Spirit* (Lake Mary, Florida: Creation House, 1992), 55. For the error of DeArteaga's position, see also George M. Marsden, *Jonathan Edwards: A Life* (New Haven/London: Yale University Press, 2003), 283-290, passim; Roger Ward, 'The Philosophical Structure of Jonathan Edwards's Religious Affections', *Christian Scholar's Review*, 29 (2000), 747: 'Edwards's main rhetorical task in *Religious Affections* is preventing the adulteration of conversion by enthusiasm, the uncontrolled emotional responses and special "convictions" that attended the Great Awakening.'

12 *Great Awakening*, ed. Goen, 331-341. For Sarah's own account that Jonathan drew upon for his rendition, see Dwight, 'Memoirs of Jonathan Edwards' (*Works of Jonathan Edwards*, 1:LXII-LXVIII).

13 *Feminine Spirituality in America: From Sarah Edwards to Martha Graham* (Philadelphia: Temple University Press, 1980), 49.

14 *Letters and Personal Writings*, ed. George S. Claghorn (*The Works of Jonathan Edwards*, vol. 16; New Haven/London: Yale University Press, 1998), 789-790. For a good study of Sarah's life, see Elisabeth D. Dodds, *Marriage To a Difficult Man. The Uncommon Union of Jonathan & Sarah Edwards* (1971 ed.; repr. Laurel, Mississippi: Audubon Press, 2004). For smaller studies, see Ethel Williams, 'A Colonial Parson's Wife: Sarah Pierrepont Edwards 1710-1758: "And a Very Eminent Christian"', *The Review and Expositor*, 47 (1950), 41-56; Ruth A. Tucker, *First Ladies of the Parish. Historical Portraits of Pastors' Wives* (Grand Rapids: Zondervan Publishing House, 1988), 73-81; Noël Piper, 'Sarah Edwards: Jonathan's Home and Haven' in John Piper and Justin Taylor, eds., *A God Entranced Vision of All Things: The Legacy of Jonathan Edwards* (Wheaton, Illinois: Crossway Books, 2004), 55-78. See also the references in Murray, *Jonathan Edwards* and Marsden, *Jonathan Edwards*. There is also the rare, but fascinating, study by A. E. Winship, *Jukes – Edwards: A Study in Education and Heredity* (Harrisburg, R.L. Myers & Co., 1900), in which the heritage of the Edwards family is compared with the heritage of a notorious criminal family, the Jukes.

15 Leonard I. Sweet notes that the word 'sweet' was 'incontestably Edwards's favorite word' ['The Laughter of One: Sweetness and Light in Franklin and Edwards', in Barbara B. Oberg and Harry S. Stout, eds., *Benjamin Franklin,*

Jonathan Edwards, and the Representation of American Culture (New York/Oxford: Oxford University Press, 1993), 126].

16 *Great Awakening*, ed. Goen, 334.

17 Samuel Hopkins observed that Jonathan 'took opportunities to converse' with each of his children 'in his study, singly and closely, about their souls' concerns; and to give them warning, exhortation, and direction, as he saw need'. Once, a week, each Saturday night, Jonathan instructed his children in the *Westminster Shorter Catechism*, 'not merely by taking care that they learned it by heart', Hopkins noted, 'but by leading them into an understanding of the doctrines therein taught, by asking them questions on each answer, and explaining it to them'. [*Memoirs of the Life, Experience and Character of the Late Rev. Jonathan Edwards, A.M.* in *The Works of President Edwards* (1817 London ed.; repr. New York: Burt Franklin, 1968), I, 46]. That their father's advice and counsel was something which the Edwards children cherished is borne out by a diary entry by Esther Edwards Burr. See Appendix 3. See also Marsden, *Jonathan Edwards*, 321, and the insightful paper by Ava Chamberlain, '"We Have Procured One Rattlesnake": Jonathan Edwards and American Social History' (unpublished paper presented to the American Society of Church History Conference, Seattle, January 2005).

18 *Great Awakening*, ed. Goen, 333.

19 Marsden, *Jonathan Edwards*, 239-240.

20 For Buell, see Deborah Gill Hilzinger, 'The Ministry of Samuel Buell' (unpublished M.A. thesis, Columbia University, 1989) and Douglas Dicarlo, 'The Religious Mind-Set of Samuel Buell, Clergyman of Eighteenth-Century Long Island' (unpublished M.A. thesis, Long Island University, 1994). Scott Bowman of Whitby, Ontario, is presently doing a Th.M. thesis on the spirituality of Buell for the American University of Biblical Studies, Atlanta, Georgia. It is hoped that this can be published, since there is nothing readily available regarding Buell.

21 Dwight, 'Memoirs of Jonathan Edwards' (*Works of Jonathan Edwards*, I:LXII).

22 Dodds, *Marriage To a Difficult Man*, 99. For some of the various analyses of Sarah's experiences, see James Wm McClendon Jr, *Ethics: Systematic Theology*, Vol. 1 (Nashville: Abingdon Press, 1986), 121-123. Also see the excellent recounting and analysis of Sarah's experiences by Marsden, *Jonathan Edwards*, 240-249.

23 See Piper, 'Sarah Edwards', 68-72.

24 *Great Awakening*, ed. Goen, 332. For the passage in Sarah's narrative that Edwards is drawing from, see Dwight, 'Memoirs of Jonathan Edwards' (*Works of Jonathan Edwards*, I:LXV, col.1).

25 *Great Awakening*, ed. Goen, 333.

26 *Great Awakening*, ed. Goen, 336.

27 *Great Awakening*, ed. Goen, 339.

28 Julie Ellison, 'The Sociology of "Holy Indifference: Sarah Edwards' Narrative', *American Literature*, 56 (1984), 489.

29 *Great Awakening*, ed. Goen, 332.

30 *Great Awakening*, ed. Goen, 336.
31 *Great Awakening*, ed. Goen, 336.
32 *Great Awakening*, ed. Goen, 337.
33 *Great Awakening*, ed. Goen, 332; also 333. Guy Chevreau [*Catch the Fire: The Toronto Blessing: An experience of renewal and revival* (London: HarperCollins, 1994), 83] wrongly maintains that on one of these occasions Sarah so lost bodily strength that 'she apparently fell face-first into her supper'. Neither Edwards' account in *Some Thoughts* nor Sarah's own narrative affirms any such thing.
34 *Great Awakening*, ed. Goen, 334-335. This point is noteworthy in view of the occurrence of uncontrollable laughing as part of the Toronto Blessing and the fact that this is viewed as physical evidence of the Spirit's anointing.
35 *Great Awakening*, ed. Goen, 341.
36 *Great Awakening*, ed. Goen, 335.
37 *Great Awakening*, ed. Goen, 253.
38 *Great Awakening*, ed. Goen, 255.
39 *Great Awakening*, ed. Goen, 335.
40 *Great Awakening*, ed. Goen, 339.
41 *Great Awakening*, ed. Goen, 340.
42 *Great Awakening*, ed. Goen, 340.
43 *Great Awakening*, ed. Goen, 341.
44 Porterfield, *Feminine Spirituality in America*, 44. For a male model of such revived spirituality, see Edwards' *An Account of the Life of the Late Reverend Mr. David Brainerd* (1749). In the words of George Marsden, *Jonathan Edwards*, 331: '*The Life of Brainerd*... is *Religious Affections* in the form of a spiritual biography.'
45 *Great Awakening*, ed. Goen, 338-339.
46 *Two Dissertations*, II. *The Nature of True Virtue* [*Ethical Writings*, ed. Paul Ramsey (*The Works of Jonathan Edwards*, vol. 8; New Haven/ London: Yale University Press, 1989), 542]. For a recent discussion of this treatise, see Philip L. Quinn, 'The Master Argument of The Nature of True Virtue', in Paul Helm and Oliver D. Crisp, eds., *Jonathan Edwards: Philosophical Theologian* (Aldershot, Hampshire: Ashgate Publishing Ltd./Burlington, Vermont: Ashgate Publishing Co., 2003), 79-97.
47 *Ethical Writings*, ed. Ramsey, 543.
48 *Systematic Theology*, 125. McClendon's whole discussion of this point has been extremely helpful in understanding this section of Edwards' *Some Thoughts*; see his *Systematic Theology*, 124-126.
49 Hopkins, 'Life and Character of the Late Reverend Mr. Jonathan Edwards', in Levin, ed., *Jonathan Edwards*, 80.
50 *Systematic Theology*, 127. See also Porterfield, *Feminine Spirituality in America*, 42-43.

CHAPTER 8

1 Diary, 3 February 1781, cited Andrew Gunton Fuller, 'Memoir' in *The Complete Works of the Rev. Andrew Fuller*, revised Joseph Belcher (1845 ed.; repr.

Harrisonburg, Virginia: Sprinkle Publications, 1988), I, 25. I owe this reference to Tom J. Nettles, 'Edwards and His Impact on Baptists', *The Founders Journal*, 53 (Summer 2003), 6.

2 Cited Martin Hood Wilkin, *Joseph Kinghorn, of Norwich: A Memoir* [1855 ed.; repr. in *The Life and Works of Joseph Kinghorn* (Springfield, Missouri: Particular Baptist Press, 1995), I, 183].

3 *Jonathan Edwards – A New Biography* (Edinburgh: The Banner of Truth Trust, 1987), 267.

4 See the summary of this scholarly perspective by Brad Walton, *Jonathan Edwards, Religious Affections and the Puritan Analysis of True Piety, Spiritual Sensation and Heart Religion* (Typescript ms., [2001]), 7-42.

5 Murray, *Jonathan Edwards*, 1. See also the similar arguments, from different vantage points, by Allen C. Guelzo, 'The Spiritual Structures of Jonathan Edwards', *Bulletin of the Congregational Library*, 44, No. 3 (Spring/Summer 1993), 45, No. 1 (Fall 1993), 4-5; Jan van Vliet, 'William Ames: Marrow of the Theology and Piety of the Reformed Tradition' (unpublished Ph.D. thesis, Westminster Theological Seminary, 2002), 387-404; Charles Hambrick-Stowe, 'The "Inward, Sweet Sense" of Christ in Jonathan Edwards', in D. G. Hart, Sean Michael Lucas and Stephen J. Nichols, eds., *The Legacy of Jonathan Edwards: American Religion and the Evangelical Tradition* (Grand Rapids: Baker Book House, 2003), 79-95.

6 See, for example, William Heller, *The Rise of Puritanism* (1938 ed.; repr. New York: Harper & Row, 1957), Chapter 2: 'The Spiritual Brotherhood'.

7 Murray, *Jonathan Edwards*, 231.

8 Cited *The Great Awakening*, ed. C. C. Goen (*The Works of Jonathan Edwards*, vol. 4; New Haven/London: Yale University Press, 1972), 64.

9 *Jonathan Edwards: Theologian of the Heart* (Grand Rapids: Wm. B. Eerdmans Publishing Co., 1974), 56.

10 *Religious Affections*, ed. John E. Smith (*The Works of Jonathan Edwards*, vol. 2; New Haven: Yale University Press, 1959), 84.

11 George M. Marsden, *Jonathan Edwards: A Life* (New Haven/London: Yale University Press, 2003), 284-290.

12 *Religious Affections*, ed. Smith, 96.

13 Scott Oliphint, 'Jonathan Edwards: Reformed Apologist', *The Westminster Theological Journal*, 57 (1995), 173. Oliphint's treatment of Edwards' theological anthropology has been very helpful; see 'Jonathan Edwards: Reformed Apologist', 170-175.

14 *Jonathan Edwards*, 281-282, 285.

15 John D. Hannah, 'Jonathan Edwards, the Toronto Blessing, and the Spiritual Gifts: Are the extraordinary ones actually the ordinary ones?', *Trinity Journal*, 17, New Series (1996), 175-176. Pace Stephen A. Marini, 'The Great Awakening', in Charles H. Lippy and Peter W. Williams, eds., *Encyclopedia of the American Religious Experience: Studies of Traditions and Movements* (New York: Charles Scribner's Sons, 1988), II, 793.

16 Helpful in framing this sentence has been Gerald R. McDermott, *Seeing God: Twelve Reliable Signs of True Spirituality* (Downers Grove, Illinois: InterVarsity Press, 1995), 31-32.

17 *Religious Affections*, ed. Smith, 14.

18 *Religious Affections*, ed. Smith, 95.

19 *Religious Affections*, ed. Smith, 102.

20 *Religious Affections*, ed. Smith, 100.

21 *The True Excellency of a Gospel Minister* [*The Works of Jonathan Edwards*, revised and corrected Edward Hickman (1834 ed.; repr. Edinburgh/Carlisle, Pennsylvania: The Banner of Truth Trust, 1974), 2:957]. For this sermon, see also Jonathan Edwards, *To All the Saints of God*, compiled and ed. Don Kistler (Morgan, Pennsylvania: Soli Deo Gloria Publications, 2003), 1-28.

22 *Religious Affections*, ed. Smith, 146. See also the discussion of Ava Chamberlain, 'Self-Deception as a Theological Problem in Jonathan Edwards's "Treatise Concerning Religious Affections"', *Church History*, 63 (1994), 541-556; Stephen J. Nichols, *An Absolute Sort of Certainty: The Holy Spirit and the Apologetics of Jonathan Edwards* (Phillipsburg, New Jersey: P&R Publishing, 2003), 116-121.

23 For some recent discussions of these twelve signs, see Iain D. Campbell, 'Jonathan Edwards' Religious Affections as a Paradigm for Evangelical Spirituality', *Scottish Bulletin of Evangelical Theology*, 21 (2003), 166-186; Mark R. Talbot, 'Godly Emotions (Religious Affections)' in John Piper and Justin Taylor, eds., *A God Entranced Vision of All Things: The Legacy of Jonathan Edwards* (Wheaton, Illinois: Crossway Books, 2004), 221-256; and Stephen R. Holmes, 'Religious Affections by Jonathan Edwards (1703-1758)', in Kelly M. Kapic and Randall C. Gleason, eds., *The Devoted Life: An Invitation to the Puritan Classics* (Downers Grove, Illinois: InterVarsity Press, 2004), 285-297. For Edwards' practical use of these twelve signs, see his 'Directions for Judging of Persons' Experiences' in Appendix 1.

24 *Religious Affections*, ed. Smith, 200.

25 *Religious Affections*, ed. Smith, 197-239. See John Hannah, 'Love as the Foundation of Theology: The Practical Implications of Jonathan Edwards' Doctrine of the Indwelling of the Spirit', in Peter A. Lillback, ed., *The Practical Calvinist: An Introduction to the Presbyterian & Reformed Heritage In Honor of Dr. D. Clair Davis* (Fearn, Ross-Shire: Christian Focus Publications, 2002), 271-274.

26 *Apocalyptic Writings*, ed. Stephen J. Stein (*The Works of Jonathan Edwards*, vol. 5; New Haven/London: Yale University Press, 1977), 341. See, in this regard, Hannah, 'The Practical Implications of Jonathan Edwards' Doctrine of the Indwelling of the Spirit', 271.

27 *Coherence in a Fragmented World: Jonathan Edwards' Theology of the Holy Spirit* (Washington, D.C.: University Press of America, Inc., 1978), 27.

28 *Religious Affections*, ed. Smith, 240-253.

29 *Religious Affections*, ed. Smith, 246.

30 *Religious Affections*, ed. Smith, 253-266.

31 *Religious Affections*, ed. Smith, 272.

32 *Religious Affections*, ed. Smith, 30.
33 *Religious Affections*, ed. Smith, 266.
34 *Religious Affections*, ed. Smith, 266-291.
35 'Imagery and Analysis: Jonathan Edwards on Revivals of Religion', in Charles Angoff, ed., *Jonathan Edwards: His Life and Influence* (Cranbury, New Jersey/London: Associated University Presses, 1975), 19-21.
36 *Religious Affections*, ed. Smith, 291-311. The quote is from page 291.
37 *Religious Affections*, ed. Smith, 292-293.
38 *Religious Affections*, ed. Smith, 311-340.
39 *Religious Affections*, ed. Smith, 311.
40 *Letters and Personal Writings*, ed. George S. Claghorn (*The Works of Jonathan Edwards*, vol. 16; New Haven/London: Yale University Press, 1998), 93. This letter has been recently reprinted in *Jonathan Edwards' Resolutions And Advice to Young Converts*, ed. Stephen J. Nichols (Phillipsburg, New Jersey: P&R Publishing, 2001).
41 *Religious Affections*, ed. Smith, 320-340. See also Marsden, *Jonathan Edwards*, 288.
42 *Religious Affections*, ed. Smith, 320.
43 *Religious Affections*, ed. Smith, 312-313.
44 *Personal Narrative* (*Letters and Personal Writings*, ed. Claghorn, 801-802).
45 *Religious Affections*, ed. Smith, 340-344.
46 *Religious Affections*, ed. Smith, 37.
47 *Religious Affections*, ed. Smith, 341-342.
48 *Religious Affections*, ed. Smith, 341.
49 *Religious Affections*, ed. Smith, 344-357. The quote is from page 344.
50 *Religious Affections*, ed. Smith, 352, 353.
51 *Religious Affections*, ed. Smith, 352.
52 *Religious Affections*, ed. Smith, 351.
53 *Religious Affections*, ed. Smith, 357-364.
54 *Religious Affections*, ed. Smith, 364.
55 *Religious Affections*, ed. Smith, 364.
56 *Religious Affections*, ed. Smith, 365-376.
57 *Religious Affections*, ed. Smith, 366.
58 *Religious Affections*, ed. Smith, 372.
59 *Religious Affections*, ed. Smith, 373.
60 *Religious Affections*, ed. Smith, 376-383.
61 *Religious Affections*, ed. Smith, 378.
62 *Religious Affections*, ed. Smith, 377.
63 *Religious Affections*, ed. Smith, 379.
64 *Religious Affections*, ed. Smith, 382.
65 *Religious Affections*, ed. Smith, 383-461. See also the comments of Marsden, *Jonathan Edwards*, 288.
66 *Religious Affections*, ed. Smith, 420, 424, 458.
67 *Religious Affections*, ed. Smith, 387.

68 *Religious Affections*, ed. Smith, 387.
69 *Religious Affections*, ed. Smith, 383-384.
70 *Religious Affections*, ed. Smith, 456-457. For an evangelical critique of Edwards' view of the place of works in the *ordo salutis*, see Robert Godfrey, 'Jonathan Edwards and Authentic Spiritual Experience', in *Knowing the Mind of God* ([London]: The Westminster Conference, 2003), 32-43, and George Hunsinger, 'Dispositional Soteriology: Jonathan Edwards on Justification by Faith Alone', *Westminster Theological Journal*, 66 (2004), 107-120. See, however, Jeffrey C. Waddington, 'Jonathan Edwards's "Ambiguous and Somewhat Precarious" Doctrine of Justification?', *Westminster Theological Journal*, 66 (2004), 357-372, where Waddington argues convincingly that Edwards stands squarely in the Reformed view of justification by faith alone.
71 'Religious Affections' in Kapic and Gleason, eds., *Devoted Life*, 296.

CHAPTER 9

1 Letter to a correspondent in Scotland, November 1745 [*Letters and Personal Writings*, ed. George S. Claghorn (*The Works of Jonathan Edwards*, vol. 16; New Haven/ London: Yale University Press, 1998), 183]. This appears to have been Edwards' first major discussion of the concept of the concert of prayer. See discussion by George M. Marsden, *Jonathan Edwards: A Life* (New Haven/London: Yale University Press, 2003), 311-313.

2 *A Loss of Mastery: Puritan Historians in Colonial America* (1966 ed.; repr. New York: Vintage Books, 1968), 111-113.

3 The words of the Calvinistic Baptist William Kiffin (1616-1701), writing about a fellow Puritan and Baptist, John Norcott (1621-1676), are typical of Puritanism in general: 'He steered his whole course by the compass of the word, making Scripture precept or example his constant rule in matters of religion. Other men's opinions or interpretations were not the standard by which he went; but, through the assistance of the Holy Spirit, he laboured to find out what the Lord himself had said in his word' [cited Joseph Ivimey, *A History of the English Baptists* (London: B. J. Holdsworth, 1823), III, 300].

4 John Geree, *The Character of an old English Puritan or Non-Conformist* (London, 1646) in Lawrence A. Sasek, *Images of English Puritanism. A Collection of Contemporary Sources 1589-1646* (Baton Rouge, Louisiana/Louisiana State University Press, 1989), 209.

5 *The Return of Prayers* [*The Works of Thomas Goodwin, D.D.* (Edinburgh: James Nichol, 1862), III, 362].

6 *Mr. John Bunyan's Dying Sayings* [*The Works of John Bunyan* (Philadelphia: John Ball, 1850), I, 47].

7 *Jonathan Edwards' Resolutions And Advice to Young Converts*, ed. Stephen J. Nichols (Phillipsburg, New Jersey: P&R Publishing, 2001), 26.

8 *Letters and Personal Writings*, ed. Claghorn , 758, n.5.

9 In what follows regarding this sermon, I am indebted to Stephen J. Nichols,

Jonathan Edwards: A Guided Tour of His Life and Thought (Phillipsburg, New Jersey: P&R Publishing, 2001), 205-218.

10 *The Most High A Prayer-Hearing God* [*The Works of Jonathan Edwards* (1834 ed.; repr. Edinburgh: The Banner of Truth Trust, 1974), 2:115].

11 *The Most High A Prayer-Hearing God* (*Works*, 2:115-116).

12 Robert O. Bakke, *The Power of Extraordinary Prayer* (Wheaton, Illinois: Crossway Books, 2000), 123.

13 *Jonathan Edwards*, 210.

14 *The Most High A Prayer-Hearing God* (*Works*, 2:116).

15 *The Most High A Prayer-Hearing God* (*Works*, 2:116).

16 Cited Richard F. Lovelace, *The American Pietism of Cotton Mather. Origins of American Evangelicalism* (Grand Rapids: Wm. B. Eerdmans Publ. Co., 1979), 244.

17 *Private Meetings Animated & Regulated* (Boston, 1706), 10-11, 19.

18 *Humble Attempt* [*Apocalyptic Writings*, ed. Stephen J. Stein (*The Works of Jonathan Edwards*, vol. 5; New Haven/London: Yale University Press, 1977), 320]. Recently the *Humble Attempt* has been published in two modern formats: as *A Call to United, Extraordinary Prayer…* (Fearn, Ross-shire: Christian Focus Publications, 2003) and as *Praying Together for True Revival*, ed. T. M. Moore (Phillipsburg, New Jersey: P&R Publishing, 2004).

19 See introduction above and Michael A. G. Haykin, *One heart and one soul: John Sutcliff of Olney, his friends and his times* (Darlington, Co. Durham: Evangelical Press, 1994), 153-171.

20 *Apocalyptic Writings*, ed. Stein, 321.

21 *Apocalyptic Writings*, ed. Stein, 317.

22 *Apocalyptic Writings*, ed. Stein, 341.

23 *Apocalyptic Writings*, ed. Stein, 344.

24 'If ye then, being evil, know how to give good gifts unto your children, how much more shall your heavenly Father give the Holy Spirit to them that ask him?' (KJV).

25 *Apocalyptic Writings*, ed. Stein, 347-348, 356.

26 *Apocalyptic Writings*, ed. Stein, 357-359.

27 *Apocalyptic Writings*, ed. Stein, 359.

28 *Apocalyptic Writings*, ed. Stein, 362.

29 See *Apocalyptic Writings*, ed. Stein, 289, n.3.

30 *Apocalyptic Writings*, ed. Stein, 363-364.

31 *Apocalyptic Writings*, ed. Stein, 364-365.

32 *Apocalyptic Writings*, ed. Stein, 366.

33 For a concise summary of Edwards' eschatology with regard to his advocacy of the concert of prayer, see Bakke, *Power of Extraordinary Prayer*, 56-62.

34 *Apocalyptic Writings*, ed. Stein, 428; Michael J. Crawford, *Seasons of Grace. Colonial New England's Revival Tradition in Its British Context* (New York: Oxford University Press, 1991), 41-42. See Crawford, *Seasons of Grace*, 229, for further examples.

35 *Jonathan Edwards: America's Evangelical* (New York: Hill and Wang, 2005), 143-144.

36 Alan Heimert, *Religion and the American Mind: From the Great Awakening to the Revolution* (Cambridge, Massachusetts: Harvard University Press, 1966), 336.
37 Bakke, *Power of Extraordinary Prayer*, 123.

CONCLUDING THOUGHTS

1 As Iain Murray comments, '[Jonathan Edwards] is being read today as he has not been read for over a century and in more countries than ever before. Such a recovery of truth has commonly been a forerunner of revival' [*Jonathan Edwards – A New Biography* (Edinburgh: The Banner of Truth Trust, 1987), 472]. See his documentation of this, *Jonathan Edwards*, 445-472.

2 See the introduction.

3 See, for example, the discussions by Douglas A. Sweeney, 'Taylorites, Tylerites, and the Dissolution of the New England Theology', in D. G. Hart, Sean Michael Lucas and Stephen J. Nichols, eds., *The Legacy of Jonathan Edwards: American Religion and the Evangelical Tradition* (Grand Rapids, Michigan: Baker, 2003), 181-199; Sean Michael Lucas, '"He Cuts Up Edwardism by the Roots": Robert Lewis Dabney and the Edwardsian Legacy in the Nineteenth-Century South', in Hart, Lucas and Nichols, eds., *Legacy of Jonathan Edwards*, 200-214; the essays in David W. Kling and Douglas A. Sweeney, eds., *Jonathan Edwards At Home and Abroad: Historical Memories, Cultural Movements, Global Horizons* (Columbia, South Carolina: University of South Carolina Press, 2003); and George M. Marsden, *Jonathan Edwards: A Life* (New Haven/London: Yale University Press, 2003), 498-502.

4 *Catch the Fire: The Toronto Blessing. An experience of renewal and revival* (London: Marshall Pickering, 1994), 142-144.

5 *Reckless Faith: When the Church Loses Its Will to Discern* (Wheaton, Illinois: Crossway Books, 1994), 163.

6 For studies in this debate, see John Legg, 'What would Jonathan Edwards say?', *Evangelical Times*, 28, no. 9 (September 1994), 12; Richard F. Lovelace, 'The Surprising Works of God', *Christianity Today*, 39, no. 10 (11 September 1995), 28-32; D. Bruce Hindmarsh, 'The "Toronto Blessing" and the Protestant Evangelical Awakening of the Eighteenth Century Compared', *Crux*, 31, no. 4 (December 1995), 3-13; James A. Beverley, *Holy Laughter and The Toronto Blessing. An Investigative Report* (Grand Rapids: Zondervan Publishing House, 1995), 76-82; John D. Hannah, 'Jonathan Edwards, the Toronto Blessing, and the Spiritual Gifts: Are the Extraordinary Ones Actually the Ordinary Ones?', *Trinity Journal*, 17 (1996), 167-189; Richard D. Easton, 'Jonathan Edwards on Revival: An Analysis of His Thought as Used by Proponents and Critics of the Toronto Blessing', *Reformation & Revival*, 8, no. 2 (Spring 1999), 23-40.

7 *Jonathan Edwards: The Man, his Experience and his Theology* (Richmond Hill, Ontario: Canadian Christian Publications, 1995), 296-305.

8 Cited Murray, *Jonathan Edwards*, 365.

9 Marsden, *Jonathan Edwards*, 505.

APPENDIX 1

1   See Arthur Sherbo, 'Grosart, Alexander Balloch (1827-1899)', in *Oxford Dictionary of National Biography*, ed. H. C. G. Matthew and Brian Harrison (Oxford: Oxford University Press, 2004).

2   George S. Claghorn, 'Transcribing a Difficult Hand: Collecting and Editing Edwards' Letters Over Thirty-Five Years', in D. G. Hart, Sean Michael Lucas and Stephen J. Nichols, eds., *The Legacy of Jonathan Edwards: American Religion and the Evangelical Tradition* (Grand Rapids: Baker, 2003), 223-224.

3   On Tryon Edwards, see Chapter 4.

4   *Writings on the Trinity, Grace, and Faith*, ed. Sang Hyun Lee (*The Works of Jonathan Edwards*, vol. 21; New Haven/London: Yale University Press, 2003), 520-521.

APPENDIX 2

1   This Appendix has appeared as 'Beauty as a Divine Attribute: Sources and Issues', *Churchman*, 116 (2002), 127-136. It is reprinted with a few slight changes with permission.

2   Jerome Stolnitz, 'Beauty' in Paul Edwards, ed., *The Encyclopedia of Philosophy* (New York: Macmillan Publishing Co., Inc./The Free Press/London: Collier Macmillan, 1967), 1:263-266.

3   Patrick Sherry, 'Beauty', in Philip L. Quinn and Charles Taliaferro, eds., *A Companion to Philosophy of Religion* (Oxford: Blackwell Publishers, 1997), 279-285; Norman Fiering, *Jonathan Edwards's Moral Thought and Its British Context* (Chapel Hill, North Carolina: University of North Carolina Press for the Institute of Early American History and Culture, 1981), 111, n. 14.

4   *Philebus* 51C [trans. Dorothea Frede in John M. Cooper and D. S. Hutchinson, eds., *Plato: Complete Works* (Indianapolis/Cambridge: Hackett Publishing Co., 1997), 441].

5   *Philebus* 50E-52B.

6   *Philebus* 51C-D (trans. Frede in Cooper and Hutchinson, eds., *Plato: Complete Works*, 441).

7   *Symposium* 211A-B (trans. Alexander Nehamas and Paul Woodruff in Cooper and Hutchinson, eds., *Plato: Complete Works*, 493).

8   *Symposium* 211C-D.

9   William A. Dyrness, 'Aesthetics in the Old Testament: Beauty in Context', *Journal of the Evangelical Theological Society*, 28 (1985), 425-426.

10   *Confessions* 10.27, trans. R. S. Pine-Coffin (Harmondsworth, Middlesex: Penguin Books, 1961), 231-232.

11   *Confessions* 11.4, trans. Pine-Coffin, 256-257.

12   *The Divine Names* 4.7 [trans. Colm Luibheid, *Pseudo-Dionysius: The Complete Works* (New York/Mahwah: Paulist Press, 1987), 76-77].

13   *Art and Beauty in the Middle Ages*, trans. Hugh Bredin (New Haven/London: Yale University Press, 1986), 18.

14 *Summa Theologiae* IA. 4.2.
15 Sherry, 'Beauty', 280-281; Umberto Eco, *The Aesthetics of Thomas Aquinas*, trans. Hugh Bredin (Cambridge, Mass.: Harvard University Press, 1988), 27-28.
16 Cited Thomas C. Oden, *The Living God* (San Francisco: Harper & Row, 1987), 170.
17 Stolnitz, 'Beauty', 264-265.
18 *Religious Affections*, ed. John E. Smith (*The Works of Jonathan Edwards*, vol. 2; New Haven: Yale University Press, 1959), 298.
19 Cited Roland André Delattre, *Beauty and Sensibility in the Thought of Jonathan Edwards. An Essay in Aesthetics and Theological Ethics* (New Haven/London: Yale University Press, 1968), 152; on beauty in Edwards also see Louis J. Mitchell, *Jonathan Edwards on the Experience of Beauty* (Princeton: Princeton Theological Seminary, 2003).
20 Michael J. McClymond, *Encounters with God. An Approach to the Theology of Jonathan Edwards* (New York/Oxford: Oxford University Press, 1998), 34-35.
21 *Personal Narrative* [*Letters and Personal Writings*, ed. George S. Claghorn (*The Works of Jonathan Edwards*, vol. 16; New Haven/ London: Yale University Press, 1998), 793-794].
22 *Encounters with God*, 25.
23 *Encounters with God*, 25-26.
24 *Encounters with God*, 112.
25 This section and the next one are indebted to Sherry, 'Beauty', 281-285.
26 *Summa Theologiae* IA.39.8.
27 'God's Grandeur', in *Poems and Prose of Gerard Manley Hopkins*, selected W. H. Gardner (Harmondsworth, Middlesex: Penguin Books, 1953), 27.
28 Covenant of Redemption: 'Excellency of Jesus Christ', in *Jonathan Edwards: Representative Selections*, selected by Clarence H. Faust and Thomas H. Johnson (Rev. ed.; New York: Hill and Wang, 1962), 373-374.
29 David C. Brand, *Profile of the Last Puritan: Jonathan Edwards, Self-Love, and the Dawn of the Beatific* (Atlanta, Georgia: Scholars Press, 1991), 145. I am grateful to Erroll Hulse of Leeds, England, for his allowing me to use his copy of this work.
30 Patricia Wilson-Kastner, *Coherence in a Fragmented World: Jonathan Edwards' Theology of the Holy Spirit* (Washington, D.C.: University Press of America, Inc., 1978), 57.

APPENDIX 3

1 Cited Carol F. Karlsen and Laurie Crumpacker, eds., *The Journal of Esther Edwards Burr 1754-1757* (New Haven/London: Yale University Press, 1984), 8. For a very brief biographical sketch of Esther, see Gerald R. McDermott, 'Burr, Esther Edwards', in Donald M. Lewis, *The Blackwell Dictionary of Evangelical Biography 1730-1860* (Oxford/Cambridge, Massachusetts: Blackwell, 1995), I, 175. See also the helpful chapter, 'Through Esther's Eyes', in Iain H. Murray, *Jonathan Edwards – A New Biography* (Edinburgh: The Banner of Truth Trust, 1987), 399-420. Also see

the various references in George M. Marsden, *Jonathan Edwards: A Life* (New Haven/London: Yale University Press, 2003), passim; Roxanne Hard, '"I don't like strangers on the Sabbath": Theology and Subjectivity in the Journal of Esther Edwards Burr', *Legacy*, 19, No. 1 (2002), 18-25.

2 Sereno E. Dwight ['Memoirs of Jonathan Edwards, A.M.' in *The Works of Jonathan Edwards* (1834 ed.; repr. Edinburgh: The Banner of Truth Trust, 1987), 1:CLXXIX] notes that Esther 'appeared to be the subject of divine impressions, when seven or eight years old'. Compare, for example, the impression made upon a six-year-old Bethan Lloyd-Jones, née Phillips, by the Welsh Revival of 1904-1905: Bethan Lloyd-Jones, 'Memories of the 1904-05 revival in Wales', *Evangelicals Now*, 20, No.1 (January 2005), 15-18.

3 Karlsen and Crumpacker, eds., *The Journal of Esther Edwards Burr*, 9.

4 Dwight, 'Memoirs' (*Works*, 1:CLXXIX); Karlsen and Crumpacker, eds., *Journal of Esther Edwards Burr*, 12.

5 On Burr, see Randall Blamer, 'Burr, Aaron', in Lewis, ed., *Blackwell Dictionary of Evangelical Biography*, I, 175.

6 Cited Marsden, *Jonathan Edwards*, 392.

7 Cited Herbert S. Parmet and Marie B. Hecht, *Aaron Burr: Portrait of an Ambitious Man* (New York: Macmillan Co./London: Collier-Macmillan, 1967), 1-2. Esther is wrongly called 'Sarah' in this book.

8 Karlsen and Crumpacker, eds., *Journal of Esther Edwards Burr*, 13.

9 Karlsen and Crumpacker, eds., *Journal of Esther Edwards Burr*, 92. The spelling in this entry and subsequent ones is Esther's.

10 Murray, *Jonathan Edwards*, 401.

11 Karlsen and Crumpacker, eds., *Journal of Esther Edwards Burr*, 14-15. See also Murray, *Jonathan Edwards*, 402.

12 For a study of their friendship, see Lucia Bergamasco, 'Amitié, amour et spiritualité dans la Nouvelle-Angleterre du XVIIe siècle: l'expérience d'Esther Burr et de Sarah Prince', *Annales ESC*, 41 (1986), 295-323. For a study of Sarah Prince, see Lucia Bergamasco, 'Female education and spiritual life: the case of ministers' daughters" in Arina Angerman et al., eds., *Current Issues in Women's History* (London/New York: Routledge, 1989), 39-60.

13 Karlsen and Crumpacker, eds., *Journal of Esther Edwards Burr*, 224. See also Ava Chamberlain, '"We Have Procured One Rattlesnake": Jonathan Edwards and American Social History' (unpublished paper presented to the American Society of Church History conference, Seattle, January 2005).

14 Karlsen and Crumpacker, eds., *Journal of Esther Edwards Burr*, 237, 243.

15 Karlsen and Crumpacker, eds., *Journal of Esther Edwards Burr*, 168, 245.

16 Karlsen and Crumpacker, eds., *Journal of Esther Edwards Burr*, 243.

17 Karlsen and Crumpacker, eds., *Journal of Esther Edwards Burr*, 124.

18 Karlsen and Crumpacker, eds., *Journal of Esther Edwards Burr*, 165.

19 Karlsen and Crumpacker, eds., *Journal of Esther Edwards Burr*, 142.

20 Karlsen and Crumpacker, eds., *Journal of Esther Edwards Burr*, 112. Compare

Karlsen and Crumpacker, eds., *Journal of Esther Edwards Burr*, 185: 'Nothing is more refreshing to the soul (except communication with God himself) then the company and society of a friend – One that has the spirit off, and relish for, true friendship – this is becoming [to] the rational soul – this is God-like.'
   21 Cited Edwards A. Park, 'Memoir of Nathanael Emmons' in Jacob Ide, ed., *The Works of Nathanael Emmons* (Boston: Congregational Board of Publication, 1861), I, 115.
   22 Karlsen and Crumpacker, eds., *Journal of Esther Edwards Burr*, 257.
   23 See also Marsden, *Jonathan Edwards*, 420.
   24 Karlsen and Crumpacker, eds., *Journal of Esther Edwards Burr*, 222.
   25 Karlsen and Crumpacker, eds., *Journal of Esther Edwards Burr*, 228-229.
   26 Cited Samuel Hopkins 'Appendix II. A brief Account of Mrs. Esther Burr, President Edwards's Daughter', in his *Memoirs of the Life, Experience and Character of the Late Rev. Jonathan Edwards, A.M.* in *The Works of President Edwards* (1817 London ed.; repr. New York: Burt Franklin, 1968), I, 99.
   27 Karlsen and Crumpacker, eds., *Journal of Esther Edwards Burr*, 222.
   28 Marsden, *Jonathan Edwards*, 427.
   29 Karlsen and Crumpacker, eds., *Journal of Esther Edwards Burr*, 243-244, 247.
   30 Karlsen and Crumpacker, eds., *Journal of Esther Edwards Burr*, 245.
   31 Karlsen and Crumpacker, eds., *Journal of Esther Edwards Burr*, 243, 245.
   32 Karlsen and Crumpacker, eds., *Journal of Esther Edwards Burr*, 245-246.
   33 Karlsen and Crumpacker, eds., *Journal of Esther Edwards Burr*, 245.
   34 Karlsen and Crumpacker, eds., *Journal of Esther Edwards Burr*, 247.
   35 Karlsen and Crumpacker, eds., *Journal of Esther Edwards Burr*, 247.
   36 Marsden, *Jonathan Edwards*, 427.

A CONCLUDING PRAYER

   1 'Edwards, Jonathan (1703-1758)', in Alister E. McGrath, ed., *The Blackwell Encyclopedia of Modern Christian Thought* (Cambridge, Massachusetts: Blackwell Publishers/Oxford: Blackwell, 1993), 145. This is not to exclude Edwards' portrayal of his wife also in such a light. See Chapter 7.
   2 *A Sermon Preached on the Day of the Funeral of the Rev. Mr. David Brainerd* [*The Life of David Brainerd*, ed. Norman Pettit (*The Works of Jonathan Edwards*, vol. 7; New Haven/London: Yale University Press, 1985), 548].
   3 *Life of David Brainerd*, ed. Pettit, 553-554.

SELECT BIBLIOGRAPHY

Robert O. Bakke, *The Power of Extraordinary Prayer* (Wheaton, Illinois: Crossway Books, 2000).

David Bebbington, *Evangelicalism in Modern Britain. A History from the 1730s to the 1980s* (1989 ed.; repr. Grand Rapids: Baker Book House, 1992).

Lucia Bergamasco, 'Amitié, amour et spiritualité dans la Nouvelle-Angleterre du XVIIe siècle: l'expérience d'Esther Burr et de Sarah Prince', *Annales ESC*, 41 (1986), 295-323.

John J. Bombaro, 'Dispositional Peculiarity, History, and Edwards's Evangelistic Appeal to Self-Love', *Westminster Theological Journal*, 66 (2004), 121-157.

David C. Brand, *Profile of the Last Puritan: Jonathan Edwards, Self-Love, and the Dawn of the Beatific* (Atlanta, Georgia: Scholars Press, 1991).

Richard L. Bushman, ed., *The Great Awakening: Documents on the Revival of Religion, 1740-1745* (1970 ed.; repr. Chapel Hill/London: University of North Carolina Press for the Institute of Early American History and Culture, 1989).

Diana Butler, 'God's Visible Glory: The Beauty of Nature in the Thought of John Calvin and Jonathan Edwards', *The Westminster Theological Journal*, 52 (1990), 13-26.

David B. Calhoun, 'David Brainerd: "A Constant Stream"', *Presbyterion*, 13 (1987), 44-50.

Ava Chamberlain, 'Self-Deception as a Theological Problem in Jonathan Edwards's "Treatise Concerning Religious Affections"', *Church History*, 63 (1994), 541-556.

Conrad Cherry, *The Theology of Jonathan Edwards. A Reappraisal* (1966 ed.; repr. Bloomington/Indianapolis, Indiana: Indiana University Press, 1990).

Joseph Conforti, 'Jonathan Edwards's Most Popular Work: "The Life of David Brainerd" and Nineteenth-Century Evangelical Culture', *Church History*, 54 (1985), 188-201.

Philip A. Craig, "And prophecy shall cease": Jonathan Edwards on the Cessation of the Gift of Prophecy', *Westminster Theological Journal*, 63 (2002), 163-184.

Michael J. Crawford, *Seasons of Grace. Colonial New England's Revival Tradition in Its British Context* (New York/Oxford: Oxford University Press, 1991).

Ronald E. Davies, 'Prepare Ye the Way of the Lord: The Missiological Thought and Practice of Jonathan Edwards (1703-1758)' (unpublished Ph.D. thesis, Fuller Theological Seminary, 1989).

Ronald E. Davies, *I Will Pour Out My Spirit: A History and Theology of Revivals and Evangelical Awakenings* (Tunbridge Wells, Kent: Monarch Publications, 1992).

Ronald E. Davies, 'Jonathan Edwards: Missionary Biographer, Theologian, Strategist, Administrator, Advocate – and Missionary', *International Bulletin of Missionary Research*, 21, no. 2 (April 1997), 60-67.

Ronald E. Davies, 'Jonathan Edwards, theologian of the missionary awakening' [EMA occasional paper, no. 3 (Spring 1999)] in *Evangel*, 17, No. 1 (Spring 1999).

Ronald E. Davies, *A Heart for Mission: Five Pioneer Thinkers* (Fearn, Tain, Ross-Shire: Christian Focus, 2002), 79-96.

Elisabeth D. Dodds, *Marriage To a Difficult Man. The Uncommon Union of Jonathan & Sarah Edwards* (1971 ed.; repr. Laurel, Mississippi: Audubon Press, 2004).

Norman Fiering, *Jonathan Edwards's Moral Thought and Its British Context* (Chapel Hill, North Carolina: University of North Carolina Press for the Institute of Early American History and Culture, 1981).

Clarke Garrett, *Spirit Possession and Popular Religion. From the Camisards to the Shakers* (Baltimore/London: The Johns Hopkins University Press, 1987).

John H. Gerstner, *Jonathan Edwards: A Mini-Theology* (Wheaton, Illinois: Tyndale House Publishers, Inc., 1987).

John H. Gerstner, *Heaven and Hell. Jonathan Edwards on the Afterlife* (1980 ed.; repr. Lake Mary, Florida: Ligonier Ministries/Grand Rapids: Baker Book House, 1991).

John H. Gerstner, *The Rational Biblical Theology of Jonathan Edwards* (Powhatan, Virginia: Berea Publications/Orlando, Florida: Ligonier Ministries, 1991, 1992, 1993), 3 vols.

Robert Godfrey, 'Jonathan Edwards and Authentic Spiritual Experience' in *Knowing the Mind of God* ([London]: The Westminster Conference, 2003), 25-45.

C. C. Goen, 'Jonathan Edwards: A New Departure in Eschatology', *Church History*, 28 (1959), 25-40.

Philip F. Gura, *Jonathan Edwards: America's Evangelical* (New York: Hill and Wang, 2005).

Roland A. Delattre, 'The Theological Ethics of Jonathan Edwards: An Homage to Paul Ramsey', *The Journal of Religious Ethics*, 19, No. 2 (Fall 1991), 71-102.

Allen C. Guelzo, 'Jonathan Edwards and the New Divinity: Change and Continuity in New England Calvinism, 1758-1858' in Charles G. Dennison and Richard C. Gamble, eds., *Pressing Toward the Mark. Essays Commemorating Fifty Years of the Orthodox Presbyterian Church* (Philadelphia: The Committee for the Historian of the Orthodox Presbyterian Church, 1986), 147-167.

Allen C. Guelzo, *Edwards on the Will. A Century of American Theological Debate* (Middletown, Connecticut: Wesleyan University Press, 1989).

John D. Hannah, 'Jonathan Edwards, the Toronto Blessing, and the Spiritual Gifts: Are the Extraordinary Ones Actually the Ordinary Ones?', *Trinity Journal*, 17 (1996), 167-189.

Joseph G. Haroutunian, 'Jonathan Edwards: Theologian of the Great Commandment', *Theology Today*, 1 (1944), 361-377.

D. G. Hart, Sean Michael Lucas and Stephen J. Nichols, eds., *The Legacy of Jonathan Edwards: American Religion and the Evangelical Tradition* (Grand Rapids, Michigan: Baker, 2003).

Nathan Hatch and Harry S. Stout, eds., *Jonathan Edwards and the American Experience* (New York/Oxford: Oxford University Press, 1988).

Michael A. G. Haykin, 'Jonathan Edwards (1703-1758) and his Legacy', *Evangel*, 9, no. 3 (Autumn 1991), 17-23.

Michael A. G. Haykin, 'Beauty as a Divine Attribute: Sources and Issues', *Churchman*, 116 (2002), 127-136.

Michael A. G. Haykin, 'Un profilo biografico di Jonathan Edwards', *Studi di teologia*, 29 (2003), 3-17.

Michael A. G. Haykin, 'Advancing the Kingdom of Christ: Jonathan Edwards, the Missionary Theologian', *The Banner of Truth*, 482 (November 2003), 2-10.

Paul Helm and Oliver D. Crisp, eds., *Jonathan Edwards: Philosophical Theologian* (Aldershot, Hampshire: Ashgate Publishing Ltd./Burlington, Vermont: Ashgate Publishing Co., 2003).

Samuel Hopkins, *Memoirs of the Life, Experience and Character of the Late Rev. Jonathan Edwards, A.M. in The Works of President Edwards* (1817 London ed.; repr. New York: Burt Franklin, 1968), I, 9-119.

George Hunsinger, 'Dispositional Soteriology: Jonathan Edwards on Justification by Faith Alone', *Westminster Theological Journal*, 66 (2004), 107-120.

Robert W. Jenson, *America's Theologian. A Recommendation of Jonathan Edwards* (New York/Oxford: Oxford University Press, 1988).

Michael Jinkins, *A Comparative Study in the Theology of Atonement in Jonathan Edwards and John McLeod Campbell: Atonement and the Character of God* (San Francisco: Mellen Research University Press, 1993).

Michael Jinkins, '"The Being of Beings": Jonathan Edwards' Understanding of God as Reflected in his Final Treatises', *Scottish Journal of Theology*, 46 (1993), 161-190.

Michael Jinkins, 'The "True Remedy": Jonathan Edwards' Soteriological Perspective as Observed in his Revival Treatises', *The Scottish Journal of Theology*, 48 (1995), 184-209.

Carol F. Karlsen and Laurie Crumpacker, eds., *The Journal of Esther Edwards Burr 1754-1757* (New Haven/London: Yale University Press, 1984).

Bruce Kuklick, *Churchmen and Philosophers. From Jonathan Edwards to John Dewey* (New Haven/London: Yale University Press, 1985).

Bruce Kuklick, *A History of Philosophy in America 1720-2000* (Oxford: Clarendon Press, 2001).

D. Martyn Lloyd-Jones, 'Jonathan Edwards and the Crucial Importance of Revival', in his *The Puritans: Their Origins and Successors* (Edinburgh: The Banner of Truth Trust, 1987), 348-371.

Samuel T. Logan Jr, 'The Hermeneutics of Jonathan Edwards', *The Westminster Theological Journal*, 43 (1980-1981), 79-96.

Samuel T. Logan Jr, 'Jonathan Edwards and the 1734-35 Northampton Revival' in *Preaching and Revival* (London: The Westminster Conference, 1984), 57-85.

Samuel T. Logan Jr, 'The Doctrine of Justification in the Theology of Jonathan Edwards', *The Westminster Theological Journal*, 46 (1984), 26-52.

Michael J. McClymond, *Encounters with God. An Approach to the Theology of Jonathan Edwards* (New York/Oxford: Oxford University Press, 1998).

Gerald Robert McDermott, *One Holy and Happy Society: The Public Theology of Jonathan Edwards* (University Park, Pennsylvania: Pennsylvania State University Press, 1992).

Gerald R. McDermott, *Seeing God: Twelve Reliable Signs of True Spirituality* (Downers Grove, Illinois: InterVarsity Press, 1995).

James Wm McClendon Jr, *Ethics: Systematic Theology*, Vol. 1 (Nashville: Abingdon Press, 1986).

Michael D. McMullen, ed., *The Glory and Honor of God. Volume 2 of the Previously Unpublished Sermons of Jonathan Edwards* (Nashville, Tennessee: Broadman & Holman, 2004).

George M. Marsden, 'Jonathan Edwards Speaks to our Technological Age', *Christian History*, 4, no. 4 (1985), 26-28.

George M. Marsden, *Jonathan Edwards: A Life* (New Haven/London: Yale University Press, 2003).

Perry Miller, *Jonathan Edwards* (1949 ed.; repr. New York: Dell Publishing, 1967).

Kenneth P. Minkema, 'Hannah and Her Sisters: Sisterhood, Courtship, and Marriage in the Edwards Family in the Early

Eighteenth Century', *The New England Historical and Genealogical Register*, 146 (January 1992), 35-56.

Doreen Moore, *Good Christians, Good Husbands? Leaving a Legacy in Marriage & Ministry* (Fearn, Ross-Shire: Christian Focus Publications, 2004).

Iain H. Murray, *Jonathan Edwards – A New Biography* (Edinburgh: The Banner of Truth Trust, 1987).

Tom J. Nettles, 'Edwards and His Impact on Baptists', *The Founders Journal*, 53 (Summer 2003), 1-18.

Stephen J. Nichols, *An Absolute Sort of Certainty: The Holy Spirit and the Apologetics of Jonathan Edwards* (Phillipsburg, New Jersey: P&R Publishing, 2003).

Mark Noll, *The Rise of Evangelicalism: The Age of Edwards, Whitefield and the Wesleys* (*A History of Evangelicalism*, vol. 1; Downers Grove, Illinois: InterVarsity Press, 2003).

Randall E. Otto, 'Justification and Justice: An Edwardsean Proposal', *The Evangelical Quarterly*, 65 (1993), 131-145.

William J. Petersen, 'Sarah and Jonathan Edwards: An Uncommon Union', *Partnership*, 4, no. 3 (May/June 1987), 41-45.

John Piper, *The Supremacy of God in Preaching* (Grand Rapids: Baker Book House, 1990).

John Piper, *God's Passion for His Glory: Living the Vision of Jonathan Edwards* (Wheaton, Illinois: Crossway Books, 1998).

John Piper and Justin Taylor, eds., *A God Entranced Vision of All Things: The Legacy of Jonathan Edwards* (Wheaton, Illinois: Crossway Books, 2004).

Amanda Porterfield, *Feminine Spirituality in America: From Sarah Edwards to Martha Graham* (Philadelphia: Temple University Press, 1980).

R. David Rightmire, 'The Sacramental Theology of Jonathan Edwards in the Context of Controversy', *Fides et Historia*, 21, No. 1

(January 1989), 50-60.

William J. Scheick, *The Writings of Jonathan Edwards: Theme, Motif, and Style* (College Station, Texas: Texas A&M University Press, 1975).

Leigh Eric Schmidt, '"A Second and Glorious Reformation": The New Light Extremism of Andrew Croswell', *The William and Mary Quarterly*, 3rd. Ser., 43 (1986), 214-244.

Harold P. Simonson, *Jonathan Edwards: Theologian of the Heart* (Grand Rapids: Wm. B. Eerdmans Publishing Co., 1974).

John E. Smith, *Jonathan Edwards: Puritan, Preacher, Philosopher* (Notre Dame: University of Notre Dame Press, 1992).

Stephen J. Stein, 'The Quest for the Spiritual Sense: The Biblical Hermeneutics of Jonathan Edwards', *The Harvard Theological Review*, 70 (1977), 99-113.

Bruce M. Stephens, *God's Last Metaphor. The Doctrine of the Trinity in New England Theology* (Chico, California: Scholars Press, 1981).

Leonard I. Sweet, 'The Laughter of One: Sweetness and Light in Franklin and Edwards' in Barbara B. Oberg and Harry S. Stout, eds., *Benjamin Franklin, Jonathan Edwards, and the Representation of American Culture* (New York/Oxford: Oxford University Press, 1993), 114-133.

Thomas Templeton Taylor, 'The spirit of the awakening: The pneumatology of New England's Great Awakening in historical and theological context' (unpublished Ph.D. thesis, University of Illinois at Urbana-Champaign, 1988).

Patricia J. Tracy, *Jonathan Edwards: Religion and Society in Eighteenth-Century Northampton* (New York: Hill and Wang, 1980).

Mark Valeri, 'The Economic Thought of Jonathan Edwards', *Church History*, 60 (1991), 37-54.

Jeffrey C. Waddington, 'Jonathan Edwards's "Ambiguous and Somewhat Precarious" Doctrine of Justification?', *Westminster Theological Journal*, 66 (2004), 357-372.

Patricia Wilson-Kastner, *Coherence in a Fragmented World: Jonathan Edwards' Theology of the Holy Spirit* (Washington, D.C.: University Press of America, Inc., 1978).

Helen Westra, *The Minister's Task and Calling in the Sermons of Jonathan Edwards* (Lewiston, New York/Queenston, Ontario: The Edwin Mellen Press, 1986).

OTHER TITLES BY
MICHAEL A. G. HAYKIN

DEFENCE OF THE TRUTH
CONTENDING FOR THE FAITH YESTERDAY AND TODAY

by Michael A. G. Haykin

THE NEED FOR CHRISTIANS to 'contend for the faith' against heresy and theological distortion is as great in our day as it was in the days of the early church. By studying the apologetics of such Church Fathers as Irenaeus of Lyons, Athanasius of Alexandria, Basil of Caesarea, Augustine, Patrick of Ireland, and others, we can glean valuable insight into how to argue effectively for the basic tenets of our faith in the midst of a pluralistic, post-modern culture. Ironically, it is often the theological battles *within* the church that are the most important in halting the erosion of truth and the invasion of worldly, distorted and unbiblical thinking.

In each chapter of *Defence of the truth*, Michael Haykin considers an incident in which an ancient Christian leader engaged in apologetics. As these early defenders of Christianity interacted with those who were opposed to the truth or propounding aberrant theology, they rooted their rebuttals in Scripture, employed rational argument, utilized creedal statements and, above all, they did not neglect to pray for those they were seeking to convince. These men recognized that ultimately God is the one who illuminates hearts and minds and that the need to pray for those who are embracing error is profound.

From the unknown author of the *Letter to Diognetus* to the well-known Augustine, *Defence of the truth* provides a brief look at these pivotal figures as they confronted errors such as Gnosticism, Arianism, and modalism, as well as denial of the trinity, confusion about the nature of Christ, uncertainty because of the 'newness' of Christianity, unbiblical views of Christ's reign in history and opposition to evangelizing and missions. Many extant texts are referenced to illustrate both the nature of the controversies and the biblical defences employed. It is an instructive overview of key heresies and of those who faithfully defended the truths of Scripture, often at great personal cost.

ISBN 0 85234 554 2
Published by Evangelical Press

DEFENCE OF THE TRUTH

CONTENDING FOR THE FAITH YESTERDAY AND TODAY

MICHAEL HAYKIN

ONE HEART AND ONE SOUL
JOHN SUTCLIFF OF OLNEY, HIS FRIENDS AND HIS TIMES

by Michael A. G. Haykin

THE STORY OF WILLIAM CAREY and his ministry in the Indian sub-continent in the late eighteenth and early nineteenth centuries has been told and retold many times. It captured the imagination of untold numbers of evangelicals in his own day, sparked the formation of a host of missionary societies and generally initiated what has been termed the modern missionary movement.

What is often forgotten, however, is that Carey did not set out alone, nor would his ministry or that of his colleagues in India have been possible without the faithful support over many years of a circle of friends back at home. As one of these men later recalled, when they contemplated the possibility of a mission to India they thought of it in terms of a gold-mine. Carey said that he was prepared to 'venture to go down' the mine to explore its possibilities but, he told his close friends, Andrew Fuller, John Sutcliff and John Ryland, they 'must hold the ropes'.

This book is a tribute to that circle of loyal friends, who saw themselves as being so closely bound together that they were all 'of one heart and one soul', and in particular to one of them, John Sutcliff, the pastor of the church at Olney which originally set apart Carey for the ministry. As well as remaining a lifelong friend of Carey, he was one of the founders of the Baptist Missionary Society, one of the joint authors of the Prayer Call which initially led to the interest in overseas missions and a faithful pastor and teacher in whose home many candidates for the ministry, both at home or abroad, received valuable training for the work to which they were called.

ISBN 0 85234 326 4
Published by Evangelical Press

ONE HEART
and ONE SOUL

John Sutcliff of Olney, his friends and his times

MICHAEL A. G. HAYKIN

──── A WELWYN BIOGRAPHY ────

A wide range of excellent books on spiritual subjects is
available from Evangelical Press. Please write to us for
your free catalogue or contact us by e-mail.

Evangelical Press
Faverdale North, Darlington, Co. Durham, DL3 0PH, England
email: sales@evangelicalpress.org

Evangelical Press USA
P. O. Box 825, Webster, NY 14580, USA
email: usa.sales@evangelicalpress.org

www.evangelicalpress.org